K

Aspects of Teaching Secondary Design and Technology

The Open University *Flexible* Postgraduate Certificate of Education

The readers and the companion volumes in the *flexible* PGCE series are:

All of these subjects are part of the Open University's initial teacher education course, the *flexible* PGCE, and constitute part of an integrated course designed to develop critical understanding. The set books, reflecting a wide range of perspectives, and discussing the complex issues that surround teaching and learning in the twenty-first century, will appeal to both beginning and experienced teachers, to mentors, tutors, advisers and other teacher educators.

If you would like to receive a *flexible* PGCE prospectus please write to the Course Reservations Centre at The Call Centre, The Open University, Milton Keynes MK7 6ZS. Other information about programmes of professional development in education is available from the same address.

Aspects of Teaching Secondary Design and Technology

Perspectives on practice

Edited by Gwyneth Owen-Jackson

London and New York

First published 2002
by RoutledgeFalmer
11 New Fetter Lane, London EC4P 4EE

Simultaneously published in the USA and Canada
by RoutledgeFalmer
29 West 35th Street, New York, NY 10001

RoutledgeFalmer is an imprint of the Taylor & Francis Group

Typeset in Bembo by Bookcraft Ltd, Stroud, Gloucestershire
Printed and bound in Great Britain by Bell & Bain Ltd, Glasgow

British Library Cataloguing in Publication Data
A catalogue record for this book is available from the British Library

Library of Congress Cataloging in Publication Data
Aspects of teaching secondary design and technology: perspectives on
practice/edited by Gwyneth Owen-Jackson.
    p. cm.
  Includes bibliographical references and index.
  1. Technology–Study and teaching (Secondary)
  2. Design–Study and teaching (Secondary)
  I. Owen-Jackson, Gwyneth, 1956–

607.1'2–dc21   2001031751

ISBN 0–415–26083–3

Contents

SECTION 1 Design and Technology in the curriculum

SECTION 2 Design and Technology in the classroom

SECTION 3 Design and Technology and wider school issues

SECTION 4 Design and Technology and the community

Figures

Tables

Abbreviations

ACCAC   Qualifications Curriculum and Assessment Authority for Wales
AQA   Assessment and Qualifications Alliance
AVCE   Advanced Vocational Certificate in Education
BTEC   Business and Technology Education Council
CGLI   City of Guilds of London Institute
DENI   Department of Education Northern Ireland
DfEE   Department for Education and Employment (now Department for
         Education and Skills, DfE)
GCE   General Certificate of Education
GCSE   General Certificate of Secondary Education
GNVQ   General National Vocational Qualification
NCVQ   National Council for Vocational Qualifications
NVQ   National Vocational Qualification
OCR   Oxford, Cambridge and RSA Examinations
QCA   Qualifications and Curriculum Authority
RSA   Royal Society of Arts
VET   Vocational Education and Training

Note
In the chapters which have previously been published elsewhere an ellipsis denotes
omitted material, while an ellipsis in square brackets […] indicates that a paragraph
or more has been omitted.

Sources

Where a chapter in this book is based on or is a reprint or revision of material previously published elsewhere, details are given below, with grateful acknowledgements to the original publishers. In some cases titles have been changed from the original; in such cases the original chapter or article title is given below.

Chapter 3 This is an edited version of an article originally published as 'Examining GCSE design and technology – insights from the Nuffield Project', in the *Journal of Design and Technology Education* 3(3), Design and Technology Association, Wellesbourne (1998).

Chapter 8 This is an edited version of a chapter originally published in Owen-Jackson, G. (ed.) (2000) *Learning to Teach Design and Technology in the Secondary School*, RoutledgeFalmer, London.

Chapter 10 This is an edited version of a chapter originally published as 'ICT in design and technology', in Owen-Jackson, G. (ed.) (2000) *Learning to Teach Design and Technology in the Secondary School*, RoutledgeFalmer, London.

Chapter 11 This is an edited version of an article originally published as 'Taking risks as a feature of creativity' in the *Journal of Design and Technology Education* 4(2), Design and Technology Association, Wellesbourne (1999).

Chapter 12 This is an edited version of an article originally published as 'Managing problem-solving in the context of design and make activities: Reflections on classroom practice' in the *Journal of Design and Technology Education* 5(2), Design and Technology Association, Wellesbourne (2000).

Chapter 13 This is an edited version of Chapter 5.3 in Cowie, H. and Rudduck, J. (1993) *Teaching and Learning Technology*, Addison Wesley, Harlow.

Chapter 14 This is an edited version of a chapter originally published in Banks, F. (ed.) (1994) *Teaching Technology*, Routledge, London.

Chapter 15 This is an edited version of a chapter originally published in Banks, F. (ed.) (1994) *Teaching Technology*, Routledge, London.

Chapter 16 This is an edited version of an article originally published as 'Developing capability in technology through collaborative approaches with mathematics and science', in the *Journal of Design and Technology Education* 1(1), Design and Technology Association, Wellesbourne (1996).

Chapter 17 This is an edited version of a chapter originally published in Banks, F. (ed.) (1994) *Teaching Technology*, Routledge, London.

Chapter 19 Davies, L. This is an edited version of an article originally published as 'Design and technology's contribution to the development of the use of language, numeracy, ICT, key skills, creativity and innovation and thinking skills', in the *Journal of Design and Technology Education* 5(2), Design and Technology Association, Wellesbourne (2000).

Chapter 20 This is an edited version of an article originally published as 'Design evaluation: Beyond likes and dislikes', in the *Journal of Design and Technology Education* 4(3), Design and Technology Association, Wellesbourne (1999).

Chapter 21 This is an edited version of a chapter originally published as 'Design and technology', in Bigger, S. and Brown, E. (eds) (1998) *Social, Moral, Spiritual and Cultural Education*, David Fulton, London.

Chapter 22 This is an edited version of an article originally published as 'Sustainability and design and technology in schools', in the *Journal of Design and Technology Education* 3(2), Design and Technology Association, Wellesbourne (1998).

Chapter 23 This is an edited version of an article originally published as 'Design and technology and the challenge of refugee children', in the *Journal of Design and Technology Education* 5(2), Design and Technology Association, Wellesbourne (2000).

Chapter 24 This is based upon edited versions of two articles originally published as 'Modelling industrial production methods in lower secondary school design and technology projects', in the *Journal of Design and Technology Education* 4(1); and 'Industrial practices, systems and control at key stage 4', in the *Journal of Design and Technology Education* 4(3), Design and Technology Association, Wellesbourne (1999).

Foreword

The nature and form of initial teacher education and training are issues that lie at the heart of the teaching profession. They are inextricably linked to the standing and identity that society attributes to teachers and are seen as being one of the main planks in the push to raise standards in schools and to improve the quality of education in them. The initial teacher education curriculum therefore requires careful definition. How can it best contribute to the development of the range of skills, knowledge and understanding that makes up the complex, multi-faceted, multi-skilled and people-centred process of teaching?

There are, of course, external, government-defined requirements for initial teacher training courses. These specify, amongst other things, the length of time a student spends in school, the subject knowledge requirements beginning teachers are expected to demonstrate or the ICT skills that are needed. These requirements, however, do not in themselves constitute the initial training curriculum. They are only one of the many, if sometimes competing, components that make up the broad spectrum of a teacher's professional knowledge that underpin initial teacher education courses.

Certainly today's teachers need to be highly skilled in literacy, numeracy and ICT, in classroom methods and management. In addition, however, they also need to be well grounded in the critical dialogue of teaching. They need to be encouraged to be creative and innovative and to appreciate that teaching is a complex and problematic activity. This is a view of teaching that is shared with partner schools within the Open University Training Schools Network. As such it has informed the planning and development of the Open University's initial teacher training programme and the *flexible* PGCE.

All of the *flexible* PGCE courses have a series of connected and complementary readers. The *Teaching in Secondary Schools* series pulls together a range of new thinking about teaching and learning in particular subjects. Key debates and differing perspectives are presented, and evidence from research and practice is explored, inviting the reader to question the accepted orthodoxy, suggesting ways of enriching the present curriculum and offering new thoughts on classroom learning. These readers are accompanied by the series *Perspectives on practice*. Here, the focus is on the application of these developments to educational/subject policy and the classroom, and on the illustration of teaching skills, knowledge and understanding in a variety of school contexts. Both series include newly commissioned work.

This series from RoutledgeFalmer, in supporting the Open University's *flexible* PGCE, also includes two key texts that explore the wider educational background. These companion publications, *Teaching and Learning and the Curriculum in Secondary Schools: A reader* and *Aspects of Teaching and Learning in Secondary Schools: Perspectives on practice*, explore a contemporary view of developments in secondary education with the aim of providing analysis and insights for those participating in initial teacher training education courses.

Hilary Bourdillon – Director ITT Strategy
Steven Hutchinson – Director ITT Secondary
The Open University
September 2001

Introduction

This book is aimed at students in initial teacher training, but may be of use to newly-qualified teachers or those returning to teaching. It may also prove useful to practising teachers who are mentoring students or inducting newly-qualified teachers, as it addresses issues covered in initial teacher training.

Design and Technology is an innovative subject, and one that will continue to change to take account of developments in science, industry and society. What is unlikely to change, however, are the principles on which the subject is built and the unique role that it plays in pupils' development. Not only does it develop their knowledge about materials and processes, it also helps them to develop valuable skills. Design and Technology integrates theoretical and practical knowledge, and draws on a wide knowledge base. It presents endless possibilities for teachers and pupils, and this is what makes it exciting and interesting.

The book begins with a section which attempts to describe what Design and Technology is in the school context. The first chapter outlines the current national curriculum for Design and Technology. Chapters 2 to 4 then look in more detail at the subject in primary school, at GCSE level and post-16. There is an increasing interest in the role of vocational qualifications in school, and Chapter 5 looks at these in relation to Design and Technology. The final chapter in this section considers how Design and Technology departments structure and organize themselves.

The second section is concerned with various aspects of Design and Technology in the classroom, an important area for new teachers, given the complex nature of the subject. Chapters 7 and 8 consider the importance of planning lessons, managing resources and selecting appropriate teaching strategies to help secure effective learning. Chapter 9 looks in detail at the 'design' aspect of the subject, and issues involved in the teaching and learning of design.

Design and Technology aims to reflect industrial practices, and the next five chapters look at some aspects of these which can be found in classrooms. Information and communications technology (ICT) is growing rapidly in schools, but more so in industry. Chapter 10 gives some insights into how ICT can be utilized effectively in the teaching and learning of Design and Technology. Industrial and business practices often involve taking risks, problem-solving, working in teams and working on projects. Chapters 11 to 14 cover these areas in relation to Design and Technology in schools. Chapter 15 looks at ways in which teachers can plan work to meet the needs of all pupils, including those with special educational needs. Designing and making relies on knowledge from across the curriculum, and

Chapter 16 considers ways in which teachers of Design and Technology, Mathematics and Science could collaborate to provide a more beneficial learning experience for pupils.

The final two chapters in this section address important aspects of teaching and learning, how pupils develop and progress in the subject and how their learning can be assessed.

Design and Technology doesn't just draw on knowledge from other areas, however: through its content and ways of working it also contributes to pupils' learning across the curriculum. Chapter 19 assesses the contribution the subject makes to the development of a range of skills, including literacy and numeracy. Chapters 20 and 21 consider personal and social values, which are an integral part of Design and Technology, and how these can be made explicit in teaching and learning.

The final section in the book considers Design and Technology's relationship with the community outside school. Chapter 22 looks at the role that the subject can play in making pupils aware of environmental issues. Chapter 23 considers how Design and Technology can help refugee pupils to settle in to schools. Chapter twenty-four looks at ways of introducing and developing industrial practices in the classroom, whilst Chapter 25 suggests ways that the community can be used to benefit the teaching of Design and Technology.

It is hoped that this book will help new teachers and those working with them to understand the nature and purpose of Design and Technology, and its role in the school curriculum. It aims to provide guidance on and an understanding of classroom practice, and to encourage students and teachers to think about what they do and why, to enable further development of effective classroom practice.

1 Design and Technology in the curriculum

1 National Curriculum Design and Technology

Gwyneth Owen-Jackson

This chapter introduces Design and Technology by describing, briefly, what is required to be taught by the National Curriculum documents of England, Wales and Northern Ireland.

Introduction

Design and Technology has been in the National Curriculum for ten years and has now become established as an important foundation subject. This has not been an easy process, however, as 'Design and Technology' was a new subject in 1990 and there was much discussion and debate about its purpose and its content. Early debates centred on the balance between the theoretical and practical aspects of the subject, and on its vocational or general educational purposes. There were also concerns that teachers from the various contributing subjects[1] did not have the experience to teach 'Design and Technology', especially in primary schools.

These concerns have now, to some extent, been resolved and Design and Technology is a popular subject with pupils. The 2000 National Curriculum for England contains the following statement to describe the importance of Design and Technology to the curriculum:

> … [it] prepares pupils to participate in tomorrow's rapidly changing technologies. They learn to think and intervene creatively to improve quality of life. The subject calls for pupils to become autonomous and creative problem solvers, as individuals and members of a team. They must look for needs, wants and opportunities and respond to them by developing a range of ideas and making products and systems. They combine practical skills with an understanding of aesthetics, social and environmental issues, function and industrial practices. As they do so, they reflect on and evaluate present and past design and technology, its uses and effects. Through design and technology, all pupils can become discriminating and informed users of products and become innovators.
>
> (DfEE/QCA 1999b: 134)

The study of Design and Technology includes working with resistant materials such as wood and metal; compliant materials such as plastics and textiles; electronics; and food. Graphic skills should be taught through all these areas, and are offered separately as an examination subject (Graphics Products). Most schools offer opportunities for pupils to work with all these materials, but some omit experiences in food and/or textiles. In the National Curriculum 2000 the government states that it:

> … believes that schools should be encouraged to look for opportunities to teach both food and textiles as part of the range of contrasting materials that pupils should use …
>
> (DfEE/QCA 1999b: 17)

Design and Technology is a subject which brings together intellectual skills – knowing something – and practical skills – doing something. It emphasizes the importance of the ability to *apply* knowledge and skills, and provides opportunities for pupils to develop their abilities to innovate, to make decisions and to create new solutions. Through the 'design' strand of the work it encourages pupils to evaluate objects, and become critical users and consumers. The subject plays a unique role in helping pupils to develop personal qualities and competences through these ways of working.

Design and Technology can also contribute to helping pupils develop an awareness of business and industrial practices, and the ways in which technological developments can change the workplace and influence lifestyles, through its requirement for computer-aided design and manufacture (CAD/CAM) as an integral part of learning. Provision for CAD/CAM will, initially, be uneven as schools need time to build up the resources and expertise required for teaching and learning in this way. Pupils will also be developing an awareness of the influences of society on technological developments, with the need to consider aesthetics, social issues and environmental issues in their designing and making, and in looking at technology from different historical and cultural perspectives.

Programmes of Study

The Programme of Study is the section of the National Curriculum that sets out what pupils should be taught. In Design and Technology it requires that pupils acquire knowledge and understanding of materials and components, systems and control, and structures, which they can apply when developing ideas, planning and making products and when evaluating products. They are also expected to draw on knowledge and understanding from other areas of the curriculum, where relevant.

The knowledge and understanding required at Key Stage 1 includes that pupils be taught:

a   about the working characteristics of materials *(for example, folding paper to make it stiffer)*
b   how mechanisms can be used in different ways *(for example, wheels and axles).*

(DfEE/QCA 1999a: 92)

At Key Stage 3 this becomes more complex: for example, in relation to materials and components pupils should be taught:

a   to consider physical and chemical properties and working characteristics of a range of common and modern materials

b   that materials and components can be classified according to their properties and working characteristics

c   that materials and components can be combined, processed and finished to create more useful properties and particular aesthetic effects

d   how multiple copies can be made of the same product.

(DfEE/QCA 1999b: 137)

Throughout the Key Stages there is a requirement that pupils be taught the knowledge, skills and understanding outlined in the Programme of Study through:

a   product analysis (this refers to evaluation of existing products)

b   focused practical tasks that develop a range of techniques, skills, processes and knowledge

c   design-and-make assignments, which in Key Stage 1 should use a range of materials, including food, items that can be put together and textiles. In Key Stage 3 assignments should be set in different contexts, and in Key Stage 4 they should include activities related to industrial practices.

There is also a general requirement that pupils be taught about health and safety issues and risk assessment when working with tools, equipment and materials in practical environments.

Attainment Targets

The Attainment Targets in the National Curriculum describe what pupils should achieve as a result of following the Programmes of Study. In the previous National Curriculum, Design and Technology had two Attainment Targets – related to 'Designing' and 'Making' – but there is now only one – 'Design and Technology'. The Attainment Target has eight levels, which cover pupils from Key Stage 1 to Key Stage 3, and one additional level of 'exceptional performance'. At Key Stage 4 attainment is covered by examination requirements.

The new Attainment Target includes aspects of both designing and making. To achieve level 2, for example, in their work:

Pupils generate ideas and plan what to do next, based on their experience of working with materials and components. They use models, pictures and words to describe their designs. They select appropriate tools, techniques and materials, explaining their choices. They use tools and assemble, join and combine materials and components in a variety of ways. They recognize what they have done well as their work progresses and suggest things they could do better in the future.

(DfEE/QCA 1999b Attainment Targets: 24)

At the higher level, level 5, they should:

… draw on and use various sources of information. They clarify their ideas through discussion, drawing and modelling. They use their understanding of the characteristics of familiar products when developing and communicating their own ideas. They work from their own detailed plans, modifying them where appropriate. They work with a range of tools, materials, equipment, components and processes with some precision. They check their work as it develops and modify their approach in the light of progress. They test and evaluate their products, showing that they understand the situations in which their designs will have to function and are aware of resources as a constraint. They evaluate their products and their use of information sources.

(ibid.: 25)

Exemptions from Design and Technology

Design and Technology is a foundation subject in the National Curriculum, and as such should be studied by all pupils aged 5–16. However, there are now regulations in place which allow schools to 'disapply' the National Curriculum requirements for certain pupils. Individual pupils may be exempted from studying Design and Technology if a school wishes to:

- provide wider opportunities for work-related learning than are possible alongside the full statutory requirement …
- allow pupils making significantly less progress than their peers to study fewer national curriculum subjects in order to consolidate their learning across the curriculum
- respond to pupils' individual strengths and talents by allowing them to emphasize a particular curriculum area by exchanging a statutory subject for a further course in that curriculum area.

(DfEE/QCA 1999b: 17)

These regulations are intended to apply to only a few individual pupils and should not cause large numbers to omit Design and Technology from their studies.

Design and Technology: Wales

In Wales, study of Design and Technology is compulsory at Key Stages 1, 2 and 3, and optional at Key Stage 4.

In the Programme of Study, each Key Stage begins with a Focus Statement: these summarize the learning and teaching for each Key Stage and state that pupils' Design and Technology capability should be developed through:

… combining Designing and Making skills with Knowledge and Understanding in order to design and make products.

(ACCAC 2000: 6, 8, 10)

At Key Stages 1 and 2, what pupils should be taught is described under the headings of Knowledge and Understanding; Designing skills and Making skills. At Key

Stage 3, the headings are Systems and Control; Structures; Materials; Designing skills; and Making skills. At Key Stage 3 they are required to include the use of CAD/CAM in their designing and making.

The Programme of Study states that pupils should be taught through investigation and evaluation of familiar products, focused practical tasks and design-and-make activities. They are required to work with a range of materials, including wood, metal, plastics, textiles and food, and with control systems and structures.

There are a number of common requirements in the Welsh National Curriculum, which are:

- Curriculum Cymreig, knowledge and understanding of the cultural, economic, environmental, historical and linguistic characteristics of Wales
- Communication skills
- Mathematical skills
- Information technology skills
- Problem-solving skills
- Creative skills
- Personal and social education.

Where there are opportunities within the Design and Technology curriculum for one of these areas to be addressed this is indicated symbolically in the Programme of Study.

There is one Attainment Target, Design and Technology, which has eight levels and one level for exceptional performance.

Technology and Design: Northern Ireland

The curriculum for Technology and Design in Northern Ireland is, in some ways, significantly different from that of England, but there are similarities. In the introduction to the Programme of Study, designing is identified as a key activity and is said to require pupils:

> To bring together and apply knowledge, understanding and skills relating to materials and components, energy and control, and manufacturing. Within the design activities there should be opportunities to analyse, investigate and generate ideas, and to evaluate those ideas.
>
> (DENI 1996: 3)

Areas covered by the Programme of Study are:

- Communicating, including oral, written and graphic communication
- Planning, where pupils plan their own work in a logical and organized manner
- Appraising, where pupils review and refine their design work and skills in relation to manufacturing
- Materials and components

- Energy and control, which is considered to be central to technology and design activities; this includes electronic and mechanical control systems
- Electronic systems and control
- Mechanical systems and control
- Computer control.

The main difference between the Northern Ireland and English curriculum is that Technology and Design requires pupils to work only with wood, metals and plastics (textiles may be used as an additional material) and there is a stronger emphasis on control systems. Food work is carried out in Home Economics, which is a separate subject.

Technology and Design is also required to contribute to a number of cross-curricular themes: education for mutual understanding/cultural heritage; health education; information technology; economic awareness and careers education; and the national curriculum illustrates how these may be covered.

There is one Attainment Target, Technology and Design capability, which has eight levels, and states that:

Pupils should develop, in parallel, their ability to:

- apply knowledge and understanding;
- communicate effectively;
- manipulate a range of materials and components to make products;
- use energy to drive and control products they design.

(DENI 1996: 10)

In Key Stage 4, attainment is governed by examination criteria.

Despite the differences in some areas of content, the underlying rationale for Design and Technology and the emphasis on process is the same across the three countries. Pupils' experiences will differ mainly in the materials that they work with, but the abilities and capabilities that they develop will be broadly the same.

Note

1   Under the umbrella of 'Technology', the first National Curriculum brought together the previously separate subjects of Art; Business Studies; Craft, Design and Technology; Home Economics (including Textiles) and Information Technology. In later revisions, and in practice, 'Design and Technology' became a joint venture between Craft, Design and Technology and Home Economics (including Textiles).

References

ACCAC (2000) *The School Curriculum in Wales*, Cardiff: ACCAC.

DENI (1996) *Circular 1996/21*, Belfast: DENI.

DfEE/QCA (1999a) *The National Curriculum Handbook for primary teachers in England*, London: HMSO.

DfEE/QCA (1999b) *The National Curriculum Handbook for secondary teachers in England*, London: HMSO.

2 Design and Technology in the primary school

Rob Bowen

It is important when teaching to know something about pupils' previous experiences. This chapter, therefore, describes Design and Technology in the primary school.

Introduction

Design and technology is not a new concept in the education of young children, though it is often portrayed as such. Comment on its educational value can be found as early as the 1750s when Rousseau, describing the education of Emile, said:

> If instead of keeping a child at his books I keep him busy in a workshop, his hands labour to the benefit of his mind.
>
> (Rousseau 1762, translated by Boyd 1956: 79)

This notion of mind and hand interaction was further developed through the work of the Assessment of Performance Unit (Kimbell *et al.* 1991). They proposed that it be on this premise that the subject should be justified:

> It is our contention that this inter-relationship between modelling ideas in the mind, and modelling ideas in reality is the cornerstone of capability in design and technology. It is best described as 'thought in action'.
>
> (Kimbell *et al.* 1991: 21)

Further, it can be seen that the roots of design and technology are in each individual and are an essential part of being human:

> [Design and] Technology is the critical variable with respect to the human condition, a variable which becomes more complex with the creation of each new tool, material, machine, process, or technical system. This variable must be understood if human beings are to comprehend their past and create a more humane future.
>
> (DeVore 1980: 7)

Design and Technology in the primary school, as in the secondary, aims to foster the development of these fundamental human characteristics.

The development of Design and Technology in the primary school

The subject began its development into what we now recognize as National Curriculum Design and Technology in the early 1980s. At this time the effects of Plowden (DES 1967) were still to the fore. There was little formal constraint over the curriculum and teachers, having recognized the potential of the subject, began to teach it.

A little known but interesting work by Evans, *A Case of Primary School Technology* (1983), explored the applicability of the 'Project Technology'[1] approach to primary schools. His concern was with children designing and making devices that solved practical problems. The focus of his activity was the function of the product and children measuring the performance of their product against functional criteria:

> Paintings, patterns, drawings, puppets and pottery work which form much of the mass of things which children make, are not open to objective evaluation. Their quality, like their beauty, lies in the eyes of their beholders, preferably favourably prejudiced parents on open evenings. Functional devices, on the other hand, are inescapably open to objective evaluation; the functional question being does the device perform the intended function? The device is capable of doing what it is intended to do, or it is not, and whatever the answer to the question the child and other children know it just as certainly as the teacher. Plaintive questions like 'Have I done enough?' and 'Will this do?' and 'Is this alright?' do not arise. More refined forms of assessment involve the application of mathematical skills to obtain statistical evidence of device performance. … the child must attempt to describe explain and record the whole or certain aspects of his or her technological enterprise in spoken of written English and through other forms of communication …
>
> (Evans 1983: 2)

Here, then, is the key characteristic that differentiates Design and Technology from other creative and practical activities in the primary curriculum. Children are making apparent the quality of their thinking and their value judgements, through modelling – conceptually and physically – objects and systems that meet human needs.

All curriculum subjects require children to display their thinking and much of this thinking will involve making value judgements. In English, for example, children produce their thinking in the form of stories; in physical education, in the form of body movements; in art, through drawings or sculpture. These are concrete examples of children's thinking. The uniqueness of technology education lies in the means of validating that thinking. To participate in technology requires the production of a particular kind of product – one that meets the practical day to day needs and wants of the human species. These products have a testable set of functions, and assessing the quality of value judgements against functional criteria provides a unique test of thinking.

The process of designing is meta-cognitive. It is axiomatic that we have no direct access to the process as it takes place within the mind. However, that technology does require children to synthesize procedural and subject knowledge is evidenced by the ideas children express through their discussion, writing, drawing and making. Nevertheless, designing is not restricted to technology education, neither is making. The unique educational attribute of technology is in the combining of designing with making to produce physical products that meet human needs. It is impossible for the teacher to perceive the sum knowledge of any individual child in the class. We have not had their life experience; consequently, the breadth of knowledge that any one individual brings to a design situation is, potentially, all human knowledge. It is unlikely that a young child would understand particularly advanced knowledge in an obscure field but, as communications technologies advance, the opportunities grow for children to gain knowledge outside that taught directly in school. This 'uncertainty factor' is one that makes the subject live for both children and teachers.

Children are, therefore, validating the quality of their decision-making in a way that is not possible in other subjects. Through this process children learn to appreciate that technology is not magic, though to the uninitiated it may seem so. For the teacher, it is challenging to recognize that, potentially, all human knowledge has relevance to any given designing and making activity. Nevertheless, being aware of this can provide teachers with a personal ideological position from which to make judgements about the nature of Design and Technology activities they offer and the overall form of the curriculum they provide.

Evans also notes the relationship that Design and Technology has with other key facets of the primary child's learning. The power of Design and Technology to integrate worthwhile learning from across the breadth of the primary curriculum can be seen as one of the key features that initially attracted many primary teachers to teach it when there was no compulsion to do so.

The inclusion of Design and Technology in the National Curriculum (1988) for all children from 5 to 16 was heralded with fervour by many; however, this has provided many problems in the primary sector. The rationale that had been developed for including Design and Technology in the curriculum, i.e. that it helped children to:

- develop thinking skills
- understand the made world
- integrate knowledge

was not part of the National Curriculum documentation in general circulation. There was much uncertainty about the nature and purpose of the subject in the minds of primary teachers. The clarity of purpose that had been part of its genesis was lost in the welter of Programmes of Study and Statements of Attainment (DES 1988). Many debates over its purpose and role within the curriculum (both primary and secondary) took place in the late 1980s and early 1990s. The constant review of the subject eventually resulted in a new Order, which was published in January 1995. This was much simpler and more functional than the previous one. It came with a promise that it would not be changed for five years – a promise which lasted three years. The Qualifications and Curriculum Authority published *Maintaining Breadth and Balance at Key Stages 1 and 2* for implementation in September 1998. This stated that:

> … schools will no longer be required to teach the full programmes of study in (the) six national curriculum foundation subjects.
>
> (QCA 1998: 3)

Schools were, in theory, required to maintain 'a broad and balanced curriculum; including the ten national curriculum subjects and religious education' (QCA 1998: 3). However, many schools reduced Design and Technology teaching to a bare minimum or even abandoned it completely.

Given the above, it could be seen as surprising that the subject has survived as part of the primary curriculum. Perhaps it is a key facet of the subject that has yet to be mentioned that has been crucial – Design and Technology is an exciting activity; children like it! This justification for a subject is one that is currently out of fashion, standards and testing being much more to the fore. However, Design and Technology is in the advantageous position that it not only has a clear philosophical rationale, but also allows children to have fun! The National Curriculum has, after many years of navel-gazing, begun to acknowledge this fact. The version of the National Curriculum implemented in September 2000 states as part of its rationale:

> Design and technology is about making things that people want and that work well. Creating these things is hugely exciting: it is an inventive, fun activity.
>
> (James Dyson, in DfEE/QCA 1999a: 14)

The influence of government strategy

Since the Education Reform Act of 1988 government has been to the fore in controlling the purpose, content and direction education has taken. This has remained the case regardless of the political party in power. The education of young children has been the focus for much of this attention. The fact that Design and Technology was included in the National Curriculum for primary children was a triumph for its advocates, but the struggle to clarify its purposes damaged its progress during the 1990s. Its clarion re-emergence in National Curriculum 2000 following the decline engendered by *Maintaining Breadth and Balance at Key Stages 1 and 2* (1998) – a misnomer if there ever was one – is nothing short of amazing, given the number of initiatives that have been imposed. For example, most recently, the Literacy and Numeracy Strategies (1998 and 1999 respectively) have been highly influential in changing the structure of the school day and in allocating curriculum time. Design and Technology in the primary school has had to live within these constraints and accommodate them. However, given the pressures on primary teachers to 'deliver' ever-increasing standards of performance in the core subjects, it is unlikely that the subject would have survived without its continued presence within the documentation. Hence, government strategy has been both tormentor and saviour.

The Foundation Stage

The emerging direction from government is encouraging. Guidance for early years (3–5 years old) practitioners, *Curriculum Guidance for the Foundation Stage* (2000), has been greeted with enthusiasm by many and its suggestions will encourage those teaching Design and Technology in the primary sector. The areas of learning identified, and the suggested methods of teaching, provide the ideal platform for encouraging Design and Technology-related understanding. The document suggests planning a curriculum for:

- personal, social and emotional development
- communication, language and literacy
- mathematical development
- knowledge and understanding of the world
- physical development
- creative development.

(QCA 2000: 5)

Further, it suggests an integrated approach to the development of these attributes. Clearly, the kind of activity that is required in Design and Technology can encompass these. For example, the majority of activities within Design and Technology would provide effective learning in which children:

… share their experiences with peers and practitioners …
… think about and practise ways of solving problems …

(personal and social development: 29)

… learn necessary skills in this area by using a range of tools …
… learn by doing …
… work with a range of materials …
… design … using a range of a variety of joining methods and materials …

(knowledge and understanding of the world: 82–83)

… develop skills in cutting and sticking … designing and making models …

(physical development: 102)

… learn to respond, explore, express, communicate their ideas and use their imagination …

(creative development: 117)

Importantly, in the area of 'knowledge and understanding of the world', the document notes that this area of learning will provide a foundation for later work in Design and Technology.

The 'early learning goals', which describe the learning outcomes of the Foundation Stage, link directly to the National Curriculum and provide children with knowledge and understanding which is 'broadly equivalent to level 1 of the national curriculum' (DfEE/QCA 2000: 23). Hence, we now have the beginnings of a coherent approach to education 3–16 in which Design and Technology can play a central part.

The National Curriculum

After a decade of trauma the National Curriculum for Design and Technology has matured. We have in the 2000 documentation a degree of clarity about the purpose of the subject, and a structure that gives primary teachers the support they need whilst allowing them to be adventurous. The national Schemes of Work (QCA 1998) provide an interpretation of the document through examples that can be made to work in the majority of contexts. The 'importance of design and technology' statement does much to capture its essence and importance in our rapidly developing technological society:

> Design and technology prepares pupils to participate in tomorrow's rapidly changing technologies. They learn to think and intervene creatively to improve quality of life. The subject calls for pupils to become autonomous and creative problem solvers, as individuals and members of a team. They must look for needs, wants and opportunities and respond to them by developing a range of ideas and making products and systems. They combine practical skills with an understanding of aesthetics, social and environmental issues, function and in-dustrial practices. As they do so, they reflect on and evaluate present and past design and technology, its uses and effects. Through design and technology, all pupils can become discriminating and informed users of products, and become innovators.
>
> (QCA/DfEE 1999a: 90)

Primary teachers will be pleased to see, even if they have to look in the subject booklet (DfEE/QCA 1999b) rather than the primary handbook (QCA/DfEE 1999a) to find it, that there is at last in formal government documentation the recognition of Design and Technology's contribution to other aspects of the curriculum. For example:

> *social development*, through helping others recognize the need to consider the views of others when discussing design ideas …
>
> *application of number*, through measuring assembling materials and components, evaluating processes and products and recording data and presenting findings …
>
> *communication*, through exchanging designing and making ideas with their teachers and peers …
>
> *working with others*, through drawing on other people's experiences to generate ideas … both in group projects and when seeking support for individual work, and through researching the needs and values of intended users of their products.

thinking skills, through pupils … developing criteria for designs to guide their thinking.

education for sustainable development, through developing knowledge and understanding of the principles of sustainable design and production systems, developing skills in creative problem solving and evaluation, and exploring values and ethics in relation to the application of design and technology.

(DfEE/QCA 1999b: 8–9)

Many of these statements relate to the 'framework for personal, social and health education and citizenship at Key Stages 1 and 2', guidance from the DfEE/QCA (DfEE/QCA 1999a: 136). Here, there is a recognition that the education of young children consists of more than engagement with subject content. It is acknowledged that schools have a role in engaging with the emerging value systems of young children. The connections with Design and Technology are easy to make. The guidance for Key Stage 1 suggests:

pupils learn about themselves as developing individuals and as members of their communities, building on their own experiences and the early learning goals for personal and social development. They learn the basic rules for keeping themselves healthy and safe and for behaving well. They have opportunities to show that they can take some responsibility for themselves and their environment. They begin to learn about their own and other people's feelings and become aware of the views, needs and rights of other children and older people. As members of a class, school and community, they learn social skills such as how to share, take turns, play, help others, resolve simple arguments and resist bullying. They begin to take an active part in the life of their school and its neighbourhood.

(137)

Primary teachers, at last, have the governmental support for the clear rationale that evolved in the early 1980s. Within the context of the English National Curriculum the subject can become recognizably 'primary' again.

An interesting way of tracking the changing emphasis of the National Curriculum through Key Stages is to examine introductory statements from each Key Stage. Within the primary phase the following apply:

Key Stage 1
During key stage 1 pupils learn how to think imaginatively and talk about what they like and dislike when designing and making. They build on their early childhood experiences of investigating objects around them. They explore how familiar things work and talk about, draw and model their ideas. They learn how to design and make safely and could start to use ICT as part of their designing and making.

(DfEE/QCA 1999b: 16)

Key Stage 2

During key stage 2 pupils work on their own and as part of a team on a range of designing and making activities. They think about what products are used for and the needs of the people who use them. They plan what has to be done and identify what works well and what could be improved in their own and other people's designs. They draw on knowledge and understanding from other areas of the curriculum and use computers in a range of ways.

(DfEE/QCA 1999b: 18)

Progression from Key Stage 1 to Key Stage 2 can be seen in the movement

- from personal likes and dislikes to teamwork as well as working individually
- from building from previous experience to thinking about the needs of others
- from working from the personally familiar to a more conscious use of cross-curricular links
- from talking about, drawing and modelling their ideas to more formal planning and evaluation.

Development in these areas is linked to progression in the Programmes of Study. Children in each Key Stage should improve in:

- developing, planning and communicating ideas
- working with tools, equipment, materials and components to make quality products
- evaluating processes and products
- knowledge and understanding of materials and components

(DfEE/QCA 1999b: 6)

They should do this through the 'investigation and evaluation of products, product analysis, focused practical tasks and design and make assignments' (DfEE/QCA 1999b: 6).

Now that there is a clear mandate, this commonality of approach to content and task will enable the improvement that has been so sadly lacking whilst the subject has been in such turmoil.

Design and Technology in the primary classroom

Much of what is described below is taken from a research project undertaken over five years. This project was classroom-focused and involved hands-on teaching. Teaching is a messy business. It relies on decision-making in the complex, intimate, interactive society of the classroom (see, for example, Ackoff 1979 for an exploration of the messy world of professional decision-makers). Clark and Yinger (1987) discuss the skills required:

The skills called for in these [messy interactions of the classroom] are not the systematic application of predetermined models or standardised techniques.

These situations require from the practitioner the artful use of skills such as problem discovery, and formulation, design invention, and flexible adaptation.

(97)

It was within the very 'messy' context of the classroom that the ideas about Design and Technology described above had to be given life.

To explore the reality of the theoretical ideas, illustrations are drawn from the research project. These 'vignettes' are extracted from taped conversations between the author and classroom teachers. To further help in contextualizing points made and to 'ground' the vignettes, below is an extract from one of the research school's policy statements:

Design and Technology should:

1 Develop creative problem solving abilities through the interaction of hand and mind.
2 Develop motor skills through performance with tools.
3 Cultivate personal qualities – e.g. persistence, determination, respect for others and their views, a personal value system.
4 Respect the values of craftsmanship.
5 Accept responsibility for the consequences of decisions.
6 Acquire appropriate conceptual knowledge.
7 Value knowledge as a tool for the realization of a design rather than an end in itself.
8 Recognize that the possession of procedural knowledge is crucial.
9 Establish designing as a life skill.
10 Develop a set of skills and appropriate knowledge that enable the maturing of views on the advantages and disadvantages of technological developments.

This is by no means an exhaustive set of learning intentions, but it does illustrate how one school has begun to interpret a rationale into practical learning intentions. Further, it provides a link from the philosophical justifications for the subject as discussed above to the more focused discussion about intentions and outcomes detailed below.

Modelling human needs and wants

Our world surrounds us with products. These are the results of design and technology. The concept of design and technology is, consequently, familiar to the youngest child and it is a short step to use these products as a vehicle for teaching. The early learning goals and the National Curriculum recognize this in their discussion of product investigation. Using existing products is a common way of introducing a Design and Technology activity in the primary classroom. This approach is also used in other curriculum areas, for example History and Art and Design, and so is familiar to teachers and pupils. From this starting point, children need to know two things in order to progress. They have to have some idea about what to do next – procedural knowledge – and they have to understand something about materials, components, and the equipment and processes used to work them – subject knowledge. It is in the synthesis of procedural knowledge and subject knowledge that conceptual modelling takes place. It is impossible to access directly children's conceptual modelling, as it is a mental process. Indirect evidence of the process can be found in the products children make, their design sheets and in conversations about the ideas they have. The vignettes below illustrate this:

(RB)   Design and technology requires you get a picture in your head, what I would call modelling conceptually, then to get that idea outside of your head using materials, physically model it, to meet your needs.

Class teacher Yes, well definitely. I was thinking about Child E and her bus and the stairs and putting them in, then thinking the stairs need to be inside the bus. I could see that (conceptual modelling) going on quite a lot. These children with the rabbits, they knew what they wanted them to look like and kept (coming) back and trying, from just having a ball of cotton wool, to making the shape, to modelling it so it looked more like it, to the one who gave it a carrot. They'd pictured it and knew they wanted it to be like that.

Here the physical model is providing the vehicle for the expression of the conceptual model. To develop a physical model requires skilled performance with tools and equipment. This ability is central to technology and children spend considerable amounts of time developing their products using tools and, therefore, developing motor skills. However, the purpose of using tools is not simply to become more skilled and be able to make higher quality products as in the craft tradition. The purpose of developing skilled use of tools is to achieve design ends and to develop physical models that evidence the conceptual model. For example:

There was the thought and the skills together. I really did see that. It was something that struck me very much. … The thought processes were definitely there and building on the skills and the things that they knew, or trying to find out … wanting … to have more knowledge to go on to do it. The stimulation was there, the wanting to 'crack the problem' was there and the wanting to use the thought processes was there.

(RB)

There is, however, a problem for us as adults in looking at children's modelling in primary schools. Children's ability to model conceptually frequently outstrips their ability to model physically. This sometimes leads to a degree of frustration, particularly amongst younger children, in that they wish to make highly complex models, focusing on their initial ideas, without thinking through the reality of their situation. However, Design and Technology brings with it the restrictions of 'the reality of the possible'. It is only possible to design and make within the resources of personal skills, knowledge, materials and tools available. This is a positive feature of the subject as it makes children aware of the realities of the technological world in which we live – technology is not magic. The implication for teaching is that, whilst the thrust is to achieve the ideas from within the possible, there should be a spark in the work that generates creative responses from the children. Children need to be in situations where they are attempting to realize their more exotic ideas. However, a key skill in teaching is the ability to recognize where the critical threshold of frustration is being reached, where there is not going to be a creative response, and to intervene appropriately to enable progression. This might be some teaching input on procedural or subject knowledge, a re-direction of the child's effort in a more meaningful (to the teacher) direction or simply a 'teacher solution'. All of these forms of teacher intervention impose the teacher's view of progress and influence the ultimate product. The reality of teaching Design and Technology is that decisions of this kind have to be made; quality teaching comes from making them appropriately.

Children's work often leads to products that, through adult eyes, seem unfinished or even unrecognizable! That this is the case does not detract from their educational value. One of the problems with our concept of 'quality' in artefacts made by children is that we are surrounded by the output of our highly sophisticated, industrialized society. Our allusions to quality in children's work are biased by viewing these products as the benchmark upon which to base our judgements. This is wrong. The products must have a 'child flavour'. Adult conceptions must not be allowed to cloud our vision of children's products. We need to recognize the qualities of children's design and technological work in the same way that we recognize children's art work, as a category that is unique to children. It has a quality that is contextualized by the child and not by society's external standards. The product is likely to reflect the age and ability of the child who made it; it does not have the 'high gloss' of the commercial product. This does not mean that the product is not of high quality, but that the product reflects the real expectations of a young child. There is an issue here that relates to child art, which is recognized as having its own special merit and is not compared in a direct way to adult art.[2] We must establish a culture of 'child design and technology' and recognize the outputs of Design and Technology activity within this context and not compare them in a direct way to adult technology.

Children exploring their personal value systems and developing interpersonal skills

Helping children to mature and explore their personal value systems is central to primary schooling. The National Curriculum recognizes this:

> **Aim 2: The school curriculum should aim to promote pupils' spiritual, moral, social and cultural development and prepare all pupils for the opportunities, responsibilities and experiences of life.**
> The school curriculum should promote pupils' spiritual, moral, social and cultural development and, in particular, develop principles for distinguishing between right and wrong. It should develop their knowledge, understanding and appreciation of their own and different beliefs and cultures, and how these influence individuals and societies. The school curriculum should pass on enduring values, develop pupils' integrity and autonomy and help them to be responsible and caring citizens capable of contributing to the development of a just society. It should promote equal opportunities and enable pupils to

challenge discrimination and stereotyping. It should develop their awareness and understanding of, and respect for, the environments in which they live, and secure their commitment to sustainable development at a personal, local, national and global level. It should also equip pupils as consumers to make informed judgements and independent decisions and to understand their responsibilities and rights.

The school curriculum should promote pupils' self-esteem and emotional well-being and help them to form and maintain worthwhile and satisfying relationships, based on respect for themselves and for others, at home, school, work and in the community. It should develop their ability to relate to others and work for the common good. It should enable pupils to respond positively to opportunities, challenges and responsibilities, to manage risk and to cope with change and adversity. It should prepare pupils for the next steps in their education, training and employment and equip them to make informed choices at school and throughout their lives, enabling them to appreciate the relevance of their achievements to life and society outside school, including leisure, community engagement and employment.

(DfEE/QCA 1999a: 11)

The nature of Design and Technology, as expressed within the primary school, is particularly good at addressing this intention. Young children need to establish social skills and the ability to function in different kinds of relationships. Design and Technology in the primary classroom is frequently a social activity, often involving groups of individuals contributing from their individuality to a common aim. To achieve a functioning product requires the ability to communicate effectively, to relate to others whilst working in pairs or groups, to share or behave in a manner appropriate to the context – some of which could involve danger to themselves or others. Young children are establishing their position in the world relative to others and the process of communication with peers involves more than the transmission of information. There is the maturing of the ability to relate to others and explore their own value systems by reference to the value systems of others. It is one of the strengths of Design and Technology that it can enable this kind of human interaction and provide a context in which this maturation can take place. Further, the practical outcomes of Design and Technology provide evidence of the quality of communication. It is sometimes very evident, particularly in group-based work, that there has not been good communication. Often, for young children, it is relationship issues that have caused the poor communication, and the power of Design and Technology to enhance interpersonal skills is great. For teachers of very young children it is one of its major strengths:

Plenty of constructive interaction. Pupils who had made models previously (were) keen to help … but mostly non-intrusive. Children watched each other and advised each other in a helpful way.

(Class Teacher)

> Making decisions was quite important, particularly when you said they had to start off by making their own (design) in their pairs then put these ideas together. That was quite a hard decision for lots of them. To say well, we'll do yours … they were 'arguing' about it, it took them quite a long time to come to a decision.
>
> (Class Teacher)

However, working together is difficult and common teacher input does not guarantee a common pupil response, as this comment by a class teacher illustrates:

> Straight away you'd got one group working fantastically and it was a child with special needs and a child, shall we say in the middle, it was a nice little partnership, it was working well … what was so noticeable was that three tables were talking constantly about the work they were doing, and now and again if a child was involved in sawing, then someone from another group said 'no you are not holding it right, hold it this way' so you got a nice interaction. But there was one table which was very passive. Not once during the whole of the morning did they interact with each other.
>
> (Class Teacher)

The development of these kinds of interpersonal skills is not specific to Design and Technology but the nature of the subject provides an excellent vehicle for their development.

Developing independence

As well as interdependence, Design and Technology can be seen as developing independence. Often, young children need to be taught how to work independently, as shown by the comment below:

> One of the big learning features was that the children were learning to work independently of the teacher. I was impressed with the way quite a few of the children who I know have a need for teacher to be there all the time, were working quite well and independently and going to do things and get things without asking. I thought this was really good. They were learning to help each other in a sensible and creative way … the use of appropriate language … learning about sequence … I've noted the key learning of staying on task and succeeding, this is really important … This gives them the confidence, which is something that they need.
>
> (Class Teacher)

Decision-making based on personal values

Technology education is fundamentally about decision-making. Often these decisions are made in the context of a personal value system. One dimension of the system – interpersonal interactions – is explored above. There are others which are associated with the product itself and respond to the effects of those decisions on other people and the world around us. A vignette constructed from a 'food'-focused activity will further illustrate this point:

> The activity was initiated by exploring both commercially and naturally produced food products. The analysis was carried out graphically by exploring packaging and producing a poster. This enabled children to gain some insight into information about food products related to their activity and was an example of an 'Investigating and Disassembly Activity' (DfE 1995). The children utilized and developed their ICT skills by using a spreadsheet, again looking at packaging information. All of this work was recorded by the children and contributed to their background understanding of the designing and making activity. The children moved on to design and make 'transportable food' – a sandwich.
>
> Throughout the activity, the children made clear judgements about personal preferences for foods. The class teacher was surprised at the power of this activity to engage children in debate about the importance of food in their lives. Exploring the packaging gave children insights into the range of ingredients in foods and how foods are 'sold'. The need for packaging and its effects on the environment, both in terms of the resources used to make it and its disposal, were discussed.
>
> The concept of the aesthetic element of foods, both visually and in terms of taste, was addressed. Children made decisions to taste food that they had not tasted before and, as there were a number of children from different cultural and ethnic backgrounds, this enlightened children about cultural preferences or religious objections to particular foods.
>
> The notion was that the work was all their own, that it was not the teacher deciding what the children should do, how they should do it or the ingredients they should use. It was the children that were to the fore. This aspect of the work developed as the sessions progressed.
>
> The summative evaluation involved children in tasting each other's products. This required judgements about the consequences of decisions made about their comments on other children's work.

The impact of design decisions

There is also the need to consider how children address the impact of their decision making on themselves and on others. All design decisions have consequences. In the world outside school these can be large scale, for example, environmental – products that are not consciously designed to be biodegradable or recycled. They can be societal – products that make our lives easier, e.g. the washing machine, and release people to take on other roles. Within the classroom children also make decisions which impact on themselves, others and the products that they make. Even very young children can discuss their likes and dislikes about the products they have made, and the products of others, given an appropriate framework through which to focus their thinking. There is also a link here to the concept of 'quality' in children's work within Design and Technology. Quality cannot be simply explored in terms of product or process or even consideration of both together. A quality design and technology activity will also engage children's personal value systems. This is difficult, if not impossible, to quantify in terms of 'attainment targets' but is, nevertheless, a key feature of the subject.

The organization of the primary classroom for Design and Technology

Most Design and Technology is taught in primary classrooms that have no specialist facilities. They may well have specialist equipment, that is, specialist in terms of the primary classroom, e.g. a junior hacksaw to cut small section wood, but they rarely have any specialist facilities. This environment fundamentally affects the nature of the subject. Often, primary classrooms operate on an organizational pattern of rotating groups. This, laid alongside the requirement to establish a balance across all subjects so the National Curriculum is delivered effectively, obligates teachers to carry out very elaborate juggling acts in the use of their personal time and effort in a complex teaching/learning situation. Introducing Design and Technology into this setting is problematic, and to achieve success the crucial factor is the planning of activities. Primary teachers make professional decisions about the amount of teacher input required to introduce and sustain all the activities planned and where the focus of their teaching effort should be at any particular point in the progression of the session. To progress, the learning must be able, at times, to be independent of direct teacher action. To do this effectively in Design and Technology is often dependent on the resources – both the nature of the physical resources the children are designing and making with and the learning resources provided to facilitate children's procedural progression. The determinant of class organization should be the learning intentions set for the particular activity.

Investigating products, Focused Practical Tasks and Assignments

It is noted above that the common structure of the National Curriculum will be beneficial in improving the quality of the teaching of the subject, in particular the commonality in the kinds of activity that are to be undertaken. However, there is a danger of being divided by a common language if the concepts of these activities are not unpicked.

Focused Practical Tasks (FPTs) and Designing and Making Assignments (DMAs) are described in the 2000 National Curriculum (as they were in the 1995 version) as if they are different from each other. However, their concept in the primary school is often not one of difference but of continuity. The two activities are the extreme poles of a continuum: at one end FPTs – highly teacher controlled; at the other end DMAs – in which children have complete control over the procedural aspects of the work. Figure 2.1 illustrates this point.

Any design and technology activity can be placed on this scale. Most activities would not be at one single point but would cover a span because, except for the simplest of tasks, there will be some degree of pupil decision about how to proceed bal-

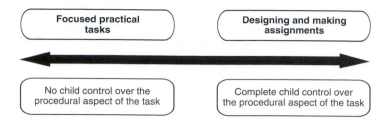

Figure 2.1 A continuum of design and technology activities

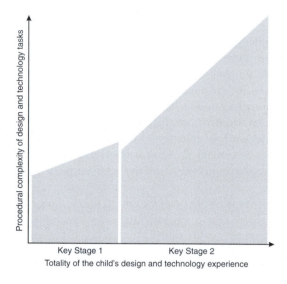

Figure 2.2 The increasing procedural complexity of Design and Technology tasks

anced against teacher control. Activities may start out as an FPT, moving to be more DMA in nature even when clearly planned as an FPT. Further, within each Key Stage of the primary sector there is an advance in the degree of control that children have over procedural matters. Figure 2.2 captures this idea.

As can be seen, the amount of procedural control that children have over their work increases with the age of the children. It would be interesting to explore the amount of control children have over the procedural aspects of their work as they enter Key Stage 3. This variation in the concept of FPTs and DMAs questions the notion of the DMA as being consistent from Key Stage to Key Stage: a DMA at Key Stage 1 – an activity placed towards the centre on the continuum in Figure 2.2 – could be seen as a FPT within Key Stage 2. The contention here is that the notion of a DMA and FPT must be Key Stage related, with the range of work expanding from Key Stage to Key Stage. Figure 2.3 illustrates this.

In consequence, to establish continuity to Key Stage 3, teacher colleagues need to share their understandings about the nature of the activities that are being undertaken at each Key Stage.

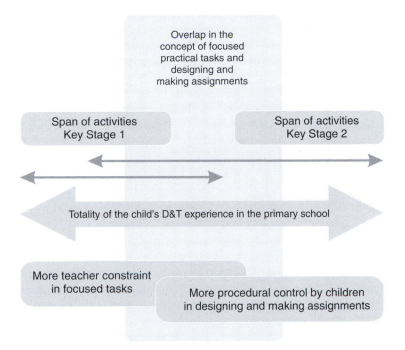

Figure 2.3 *The progressive relationship between focused tasks and design-and-make assignments*

Moving forward

Communication, a key skill developed by Design and Technology, will be one determinant of improvement in the teaching and learning of the subject. Specifically, communication is vital between colleagues in different Key Stages. As the Foundation Stage curriculum becomes more embedded, early years practitioners will be contributing more to the development of children's Design and Technology related abilities and Key Stage 1 teachers should be accounting for this. Likewise, those teaching in Key Stage 2 will need to be fully apprised of foundations laid down in Key Stage 1. Once the 2000 National Curriculum has become established in primary schools, secondary teachers can anticipate receiving children who have a range of skills and abilities in Design and Technology. The depth of understanding, as in any other subject, will vary but by the end of their primary schooling children should:

- understand the process of designing and how to approach a design problem
- have a good understanding about how to work together and communicate effectively on a design-and-make activity
- have experience of the three kinds of activity required by the National Curriculum
- be familiar with a range of materials (including wood, card, textiles and food), processes and components

- be able to make judgements about the quality of their own work and that of others
- have some insight into how the made world functions, the impact of technology on themselves and others and be able to discuss their views.

From the child's perspective, Design and Technology enables them to gain understanding about the human-made world around them. It develops their decision-making and problem-solving abilities. It allows them to explore their personal value systems and enhances their interpersonal skills.

From the primary teachers' perspective the above are also important, but there are a number of additional advantages. Design and Technology integrates knowledge, adds interest to the curriculum and can be used to motivate children to learn by providing a context within which other elements of the curriculum can be made relevant.

Notes

1 A curriculum development project established by the Schools Council in 1966, seeking to explore technology education in secondary schools (Porter 1967).
2 For further discussion on the nature of child art see Woof (1976).

References

Ackoff, R. (1979) In Schon, D. (1983) *The Reflective Practitioner: How professionals think in action*, London: Temple Smith.

Clark, C.M. and Yinger, R.J. (1987) 'Teacher planning', in J. Calderhead (ed.) *Exploring Teachers' Thinking*, London: Cassell Education.

De Vore, P. (1980) *Technology: An Introduction*, Worcester, MA: Davies Publications.

DES. (1988) *Education Reform Act 1988*, London: HMSO.

DfE (1995) *Design and Technology in the National Curriculum (The New Order)*, London: HMSO.

DfEE/QCA (1999a) *The National Curriculum Handbook for Primary Teachers*, London: DfEE/QCA.

DfEE/QCA (1999b) *Design and Technology: The National Curriculum for England*, London: DfEE/QCA.

Evans, P. (1983) *A Case of Primary School Technology*, Nottingham: NCSR.

Kimbell, R., Stables, K., Wheeler, A.D., Wozniak, A.V., and Kelly, A.V. (1991) *The Assessment of Performance in Design and Technology*, London: Schools Examinations and Assessment Council.

Porter, D. (1967) *A Schools Council Approach to Technology: Curriculum Bulletin No. 2*, London: HMSO.

QCA (1998) *Maintaining Breadth and Balance*, London: QCA.

QCA (2000) *Curriculum Guidance for the Foundation Stage*, London: QCA.

Rousseau, J.-J. (Trans. Boyd) (1956) *Emile for Today: The Emile of Jean-Jacques Rousseau*, London: Heinemann.

Woof, T. (1976) *Developments in Art Teaching*, London: Open Books.

3 Examining GCSE Design and Technology
Insights from the Nuffield Design and Technology Project
David Barlex

GCSE examination syllabus content is largely based on the requirements of the National Curriculum. Examination Boards vary in some of the details, and in the organization and structure of the examinations, they offer. Schools generally use the syllabus which best suits their resources and expertise. So, rather than simply describe what is on offer at GCSE level, this chapter offers a critique of GCSE examinations in Design and Technology. It questions what is examined, and how, and asks if this is the best way to test design and technology capability.

Introduction

This article looks critically at the ways in which Design and Technology is currently examined at GCSE level. It identifies two key elements, designer-maker capability and technology for citizenship, and explores how these might be assessed. It discusses the issue of group work in examined projects and questions the place of written examinations in assessing designer-maker capability. It presents a preliminary analysis of 1998 higher tier examination papers in terms of eight question types discussed in the Nuffield Design and Technology Key Stage 3 Teachers' Guides. Finally the article makes a plea for an assessment scheme that matches the requirements of teaching designer-maker capability and technology for citizenship.

Some background considerations

Design and Technology is a relatively new subject, although one with a long and intriguing history, with influences from a variety of traditions – craft, home economics, art and design, technical and vocational education and technology education. The professional association for teachers of Design and Technology, DATA, is itself only nine years old and the current form of their journal is only three years old. The work of those who designed the first set of design and technology National Curriculum Orders provided a robust rationale for its inclusion in the curriculum. In the Parkes Report, the unique reason for teaching it to children and young people is given as follows:

What is it that pupils can learn from design and technological activities which can be learnt in no other way? In its most general form, the answer to this question is in terms of capability to operate effectively and creatively in the made world. The goal is competence in the indeterminate zones of practice.

(Parkes 1988)

Initially this was almost incomprehensible to many teachers and over six years a range of revisions has led to a much more pragmatic (some would say limited) definition:

Pupils should be taught to develop their design and technology capability through combining their Designing and Making skills with Knowledge and Understanding in order to design and make products.

(SCAA 1995)

It is worth reviewing that initial rationale in the light of politicians' and industrialists' comments on the requirements for our nation to compete in global markets, comments such as:

The new workplace is characterised by ambiguity and unpredictability. In order to cope, staff need skills such as resilience, judgement and the ability to think in a much more creative way.

(Amin Rajan, Chief Executive, Create, in Design Council 1998a)

I believe it is time to show a fresh face to the world and reshape Britain as one of the 21st century's most forward thinking and modern nations. I challenge companies to demonstrate that the UK can lead the world by creating products and services that exemplify our strengths in innovation, creativity and design.

(Rt Hon Tony Blair, Prime Minister, in Design Council 1998b)

We are now in a position to regard Design and Technology as a coherent subject in its own right concerned with developing designer-maker capability in the young, whatever the materials and components used for the designing and making.

It is important to be clear on both what and how we choose to assess: on what we assess because we want to be sure we are assessing what we think is important in Design and Technology – the assessment must be valid: and on how we assess because we want our assessment methods to be understood by teachers and candidates as well as being reliable and consistent. And, of course, we want it to be easily manageable.

Assessing students' designing and making

There is general agreement that students' ability in designing and making should be assessed – the 'what' of assessment is not contested. It is in considering the 'how' that interesting issues arise. It is well known that the physical artefact produced by a student tells only a partial story. The struggle of bringing ideas in the mind to the reality of the product remains hidden to the untutored eye and is almost inevitably mysterious to those who have not worked with the young person doing the designing and making. It is here that the argument for a design folder is at its strongest – to provide evidence of that struggle, evidence of the intellectual and practical endeavours that turn ideas into products that can be used and evaluated.

What would I want to see in a student's work? Here is my wish list:

- the individual signature of the child should be clear – designing is a personal activity
- an intelligent use of strategies for designing should be obvious – there are different ways of designing for different purposes and these should be obvious
- an appropriate use of communication techniques should be apparent – different techniques for different purposes
- an intelligent use of researched information should be clearly visible
- a rational use of technical information should be in evidence.

Overall, I want the student to tell a clear, internally consistent and coherent story of the decisions they made in designing and making the product. I want evidence of designerly behaviour. I want to see a balanced combination of:

- technical and aesthetic creativity
- sensitivity to user needs
- appreciation of market forces
- understanding of, and skill in, manufacturing.

During 1997 and 1998 several of the Nuffield Area Field Officers wrote reports with comments about the uniformity, anonymity and 'safeness' of much GCSE coursework. The students had been well taught, and followed the requirements of the assessment scheme to the letter. The better candidates got the better grades but the work generally lacked flair, and personal signatures were not much in evidence at any level of achievement. There is evidence that teachers give Key Stage 3 students more autonomy in designing and making assignments than they give to Key Stage 4 students, and some have argued that this is due to examination coursework assessment requirements.[1]

In the context of these comments, and to discover how Examination Boards coursework requirements compared with my wish list, I asked them to provide the following information:

- 1998 full course lower tier examination paper for all focus areas, plus marking scheme
- 1998 full course higher tier examination paper for all focus areas, plus marking scheme
- the 1998 syllabuses that refer to these examinations
- instructions and mark schemes for full GCSE coursework submissions for 1998.

Northern Examinations and Assessment Board (NEAB), Midland Examining Group (MEG) and London Examinations (EdExcel) supplied all this information. Southern Examining Group (SEG) supplied only the syllabus. NEAB provided, in addition, coursework guidance for pupils' materials.

All the Examination Boards give guidance about design portfolios and made outcomes to be submitted for GCSE coursework. The main features of coursework requirements as included in the syllabus for each Board are summarized in Table 3.1.

Invariably the assessment criteria are linked to a seemingly linear set of stages in a designing and making process, although there is usually a caveat about flexibility; for example:

> These are not necessarily consecutive stages of designing, although in much design work they do follow logically from one another. Design requires a flexible approach which allows all aspects to be considered and reconsidered whenever it is appropriate.
>
> (NEAB)

> It is appreciated that for assessment purposes, the criteria have been written in a linear form. It may be that within focus areas of design and technology some stages may interrelate and be cyclical in approach.
>
> (MEG)

Even with these caveats it is easy to see how this can become a series of ritualistic hoops to be jumped through – where the activity has lost dynamic purpose as far as the student is concerned and has become reduced to 'what I must put in my folder'. From the teachers' viewpoint, structuring the folder according to the assessment criteria makes the assessment much easier to manage.

Nick Givens, Nuffield Area Field Officer for the South West, writes passionately about this:

> Our problem always has been, and remains, that of finding efficient painless ways of generating EVIDENCE that doesn't stifle the creativity. So the ritualisation of designing, the conversion of the design folio into a product and the inflexible narrow interpretation of what constitutes design, represent a major problem. There needs to be scope for pupils to model and record their thinking in a variety of ways AND orders. We can't carry on letting a narrow view of what constitutes EVIDENCE-of-design dictate the nature of design.
>
> (In Nuffield 1998)

Only if there is the possibility of diverse response will students be able to respond from within themselves and reveal their personal designing signatures. Is it too much to ask for a broad sweep approach to 'telling the story of your designing and making' with general guidelines indicating the areas of consideration – the balanced combination of features referred to above? The production of such portfolios would then cease to be a chore; they would be working documents and lay the foundation of skills for life.

Table 3.1 Coursework requirements for full course GCSE Design and Technology syllabuses

Focus areas (same for all Boards)	Northern Examination and Assessment Board	Southern Examining Group	Midland Examining Group	London Examinations (Edexcel)

resistant materials
food
textiles
graphic products
electronic products
systems and control
	COMMON ACROSS ALL FOCUS AREAS
	■ design-and-make activity
	■ design folio
	■ product
	■ evidence of:
	  – description of problem
	  – research analysis
	  – specification
	  – generation of ideas
	  – development of solution
	  – planning and production of outcome
	  – evaluation
	■ plus series of questions dealing with key issues and pointers towards overarching issues
	■ spelling, punctuation and grammar criteria
	
	DIFFERENCES BETWEEN FOCUS AREAS
	Time requirements for coursework supervised time:
	■ resistant materials technology, textiles technology and electronic products – 40–50 hours
	■ graphic products – 40 hours
	■ food technology – 25 hours
	■ systems and control: minor project – 15 hours; major project 40–50 hours
		COMMON ACROSS ALL FOCUS AREAS
		■ design and make a product
		■ 40 hours curriculum time
		■ marking criteria:
		  – formulation of the design brief and specification
		  – research and investigation
		  – generation of ideas
		  – selection and development
		  – planning and organization
		  – production/outcome
		  – evaluation
		  – communication skills
		■ spelling, punctuation and grammar criteria
			COMMON ACROSS ALL FOCUS AREAS
			■ design-and-make activity
			■ 40–50 hours curriculum time
			■ design folder
			■ quality product
			■ related to industrial/ commercial practices
			■ including appropriate applications of systems and control
			■ assessment objectives:
			  – identification of a need or opportunity leading to a brief
			  – research into a design brief resulting in a specification
			  – generation of ideas
			  – product development
			  – product planning and realization
			  – evaluation and testing
			■ spelling, punctuation and grammar criteria
				COMMON ACROSS ALL FOCUS AREAS
				■ design-and-make a product
				■ not less than 30 hours curriculum time
				■ design folder
				■ practical outcome
				■ investigation of a product, not less than 10 hours
				■ illustrated report
				■ assessment objectives:
				  – developing ideas
				  – communication
				  – evaluation
				  – materials, tools and equipment
				  – industrial practices
				■ spelling, punctuation and grammar criteria

What about group work in examined projects?

I know that many examiners feel strongly that the candidates are individuals and should be assessed as such, but I believe that one of the most important qualities of an individual is his or her ability to work as part of a group or team. The Nuffield Project has promoted opportunities for this in all the focus areas, identifying those parts of a designing and making assignment where students working on the same line of interest[2] can cooperate – on research activity, brainstorming, reviewing progress, evaluating. But for those who see the design and technology endeavour as naturally a team-based activity – this includes *all* the senior designers from a range of highly successful design consultancies who made presentations to the examiners at a recent QCA meeting[3] – this falls short of the mark.

So I wonder if it is possible to have lines of interest where group work is the natural way of working and to give some students this option, with the inducement that their certificate will indicate their ability to work well in a group. I believe industry and commerce would welcome this. Interestingly the acquisition of much-vaunted 'key skills', seen as essential to national prosperity, can be shown to occur quite naturally within group-based working within design and technology[4] – yet another reason why industrial and commercial support should be forthcoming.

Here are two examples, from commercial graphic products, which would be suitable for group-based projects. First, the Star Trek *These are the Voyages* pop-up book, which consists of four double pages. Each double-page spread is a master work of cardboard engineering and would constitute a major project in itself. Designing and making such a book as a whole represents a real challenge for a group of four students, with opportunities for both conventional and ICT-based designing and making. Second, the *Marvel Comics Super Heroes GIANT Board Game Book* – six different games, each with its own rules in an A2 format card book complete with electronic dice. Even without the electronic dice (and it has to be admitted that this feature is extremely irritating), the production of such a giant book is a delightful challenge for a small group of 16-year-olds. Clearly we don't want copies of these products but they do represent interesting product types suitable for group designing and making.

It is not a big curriculum development exercise to identify a range of product types for each focus area suitable for group or team work, and then develop them into full-blown designing and making assignments. The Nuffield Design and Technology Project has already developed a 14-point framework for describing capability tasks – the designing and making assignments of the National Curriculum (Barlex 1996a, 1996b). Identifying a set of features that are important for group work, and that could form the basis for assessment, is not a difficult exercise. The literature already contains well developed examples (Barlex 1988; Denton 1989), and I think that this is an endeavour that could attract industrial sponsorship.

What about a written examination?

First, I must ask, 'Do we really need one?' Is it important to examine across the entire Programme of Study or examination syllabus? Or should we be interested in what students do with what they have been taught? It is obvious that students are unlikely to use all the syllabus in a single capability task – but does that matter?

Second, I ask, 'Does it have to be like this?' If we decide that it is important to test students' subject knowledge in a context outside their own designing and making then it is important that this is done efficiently and effectively – not, I suggest, as a design on paper exercise. The Key Stage 4 Teacher's Guides in the Nuffield Design and Technology Project materials identify a range of question types that can be used for a written examination (see Table 3.2). If we really do need such a written paper – and I'm not convinced that we do – then I would like to see these question types taken into account.

One way of starting a discussion about this issue is to examine the current GCSE higher tier full course examination papers for two different focus areas, from different examination boards, for the presence of these different questions types. In one sense this is an unfair analysis as the question papers were not necessarily designed to meet the criterion of including a spread of different question types, but the analysis will reveal the question types currently prevalent in GCSE written papers.[5]

Inspection of these results show there is only minimal comparability between the question type profile of the different focus areas within a single examination board (with the exception of electronic products and systems and control). It also shows that there is some similarity in the question type profile between the examination papers from different examination boards for the same focus area. The limited presence and absence of question types is noteworthy. Type 1 questions, dealing with knowledge but without requiring detailed recall, are almost completely absent. Type 4 questions, about speculating, are almost completely absent. Type 6 questions, about strategies, are scarce. Type 7 questions, about presenting and interpreting information, are almost completely absent. Type 8 questions, requiring the interpretation of case studies, are completely absent.

Examining technology for citizenship

Now I ask, 'What about a written examination that tests 'technology for citizenship', as a counterpoint to designer-maker ability tested through project work?' This would be a very interesting exercise. The questions need *not*, and I stress this, be answered by essays. They could involve reading about technology in action and answering questions exploring value judgements of differing complexity. Candidates could be required to use a range of evaluation strategies as part of this. Some questions could involve interpreting images by annotating. Of course there will need to be precautions taken here. At a recent Nuffield Area Field Officer meeting Torben Steeg voiced a concern: 'It's important that expertise in this area is as the result of teaching, not simply a casual read of the *Guardian*.' The challenge here is to both syllabus and examination question designers. However, it will be important not to be over-conventional in designing either the questions or the teaching materials, as indicated by a recent Design Council discussion paper:

Many of today's young people prefer to receive their messages about life in visual form. They have the ability to decipher messages quickly from visual imagery. This has huge implications for education and training. To be more

Table 3.2 Types of written answer questions discussed in Key Stage 4
Teachers' Guides

Question type 1 about knowledge definitions (what?)

The candidate is expected to show understanding of key terms, principles and concepts. The question will be written in a form which requires candidates to recognize or give an example which illustrates the meaning, but does not expect candidates to be able to recall and state a definition.

Question type 2 about knowledge of purpose (why?)

The candidate is expected to show understanding of:

- why things are done in a particular way (why do it in that way?)
- why actions or decisions are significant or important (why would you do 'x'? or why is it like that?)
- why decisions are appropriate or have been made (why has it been made from 'x'?).

The question will be written in a form which asks the student to explain or justify.

Question type 3 about knowledge of method (how?)

The candidate is expected to describe or explain showing understanding of:

- processes, materials and techniques (how could I make this design from particular materials?)
- the application of technological principles (show how you would do 'x' or make 'x' happen)
- the application of design strategies (how would you research, analyse, review, make decisions, plan, test, evaluate, etc.).

The question will be written in a form which asks students to describe using a suitable mode of response, such as notes and diagrams, grid/matrix or flow chart, etc.

Question type 4 about speculating about change (what if?)

The candidate will be asked to predict the results of given changes in circumstances or variables, including:

- the direct consequences of things (what would happen if you did 'x'?)
- the effect on connected things (if you changed 'x' then what effect would this have on 'y'?).

The question will be written in a form which asks the student to suggest what would happen if …

Question type 5 about creative problem-solving

The candidate will be asked to develop a personal response to a short technical design problem.

The question will be written in a form which requires the student to suggest possible solutions, compare alternatives, select and justify a recommended solution.

Question type 6 about design strategies

The candidate will be asked to use design strategies on a short design scenario.

The question will be written in a form which requires the student to use a given strategy to carry out design analysis, development or evaluation.

Strategies could include:

- clarifying briefs – turning an open-ended brief into a more specific form
- writing specifications – turning a headline specification into a more detailed form
- attribute analysis – analysing possible product characteristics
- brainstorming – completing a started brainstorm or organizing a random list from a brainstorm to show categories and links
- impact of Design and Technology – interrogating a completed winners' and losers' chart
- user trip – interpreting user views and opinions.

Question type 7 about presenting and interpreting information

The candidate will be asked to make sense of Design and Technology research data.

The question will be written in a form which requires the student to:

- present the information clearly
- interpret the data and reach conclusions.

Question type 8 about interpreting a short Case Study

The candidate will be asked to use comprehension skills, design strategies and knowledge to demonstrate their understanding about Design and Technology activity from the world outside school.

The question will be written in a form which requires the student to:

- find a piece of information from the text
- explain something that is described in the text
- make judgements about the quality and effects of the design and technology described.

effective, teaching may need to be more visually based; literacy may need to be more visual than written.

(Design Council 1998c)

Concluding remarks

If we are interested in an education that values and promotes designer-maker ability and technology for citizenship then we should use appropriate assessment techniques – project work for the former, structured questioning for the latter. Design and Technology teachers know how to teach and assess project work; it is one of their strengths and, with established moderation procedures, we know that their professional judgement can be trusted.

Teaching technology for citizenship is less certain territory which is why a robust examination, supported by appropriate training and good curriculum materials, will be needed. This is not beyond current resources; the good curriculum materials already exist – Nuffield case studies. There is also a large and growing body of expertise in this area of the curriculum,[6] and examination boards have an established track record in providing in-service training. So I believe we are in a strong position to match the examination techniques we use to our educational aims and intentions, and there is evidence that the new GCSE specifications (for examination in 2003) are beginning to engage with these issues. As I said at the start, however, the effectiveness of these specifications for GCSE Design and Technology will only be apparent in time, through the practice of teachers and the work of pupils.

Notes

This article was written in 1998 in response to concerns about the quality of GCSE coursework. Since then new GCSE specifications have been introduced by the Qualifications and Curriculum Authority (QCA) in an attempt to engage with some of the issues raised in the article. The response of the examination boards to these specifications varies but it will be to the changed practice of teachers, and the coursework the candidates produce, that the profession must look for evidence of the effectiveness of the new specifications.

1 Preliminary findings of Nuffield Design and Technology National Survey 1998 – unpublished results.
2 The capability tasks are organized into lines of interest where each line of interest represents a product type. These have been chosen to include both familiar and unfamiliar product types. In work with resistant materials the lines of interest are body adornment; seating; storage; lighting; automata; toys and games; testing equipment. In textiles the lines of interest are items for protection; for the theatre; fashion accessories; to reflect street style; for interiors; bags and carriers; tents and kites.
3 GCSE Design and Technology Focus Area Forum meetings organized by QCA: meeting 1–24 November 1997 at Cambridge Consultants; meeting 2–13 March 1998 at Pankhurst Design Developments.

4 See, for example, the Summer 1998 issue of *Update – the Nuffield Design and Technology newsletter* which took key skills as its theme.

5 The results of this analysis plus comments are available from the Nina Towndrow at Nuffield Design and Technology, 28 Bedford Square, London WC1B 3EG.

6 See, for example, *Validate News*, the newsletter of Values In Design And Technology Education available from Validate, c/o Mike Martin. To contact the VALIDATE network email Mike Martin at mike.martin@uce.ac.uk.

References

Barlex, D. (1996a) *Nuffield Design and Technology Product Design Teacher's Guide*, London: Addison Wesley Longman.

Barlex, D. (1996b) *Nuffield Design and Technology Textiles Teacher's Guide*, London: Addison Wesley Longman.

Barlex, D. (1988) *Project Work, Unit 5, Open University Advanced Diploma in Technology in Schools*, Buckingham: Open University Press.

Denton, H.G. (1989) *Group task management: a key element in technology across the curriculum*, DATER. pp. 46–51.

Design Council (1998a) *Design and Key Skills*, London: Design Council.

Design Council (1998b) *Millennium Products*, London: Design Council.

Design Council (1998c) *Leading the way, What can future generations learn from the start of the new Millennium?* London: Design Council.

Nuffield (1998) *Nuffield Design and Technology Project response to the National Advisory Committee on Creative and Cultural Education*, London: Nuffield Foundation.

Parkes, Lady M. (1988) *National Curriculum Design and Technology Working Group Interim Report*, Department for Education and Science and the Welsh Office. London: HMSO.

SCAA (1995) *Design and Technology in the National Curriculum*, London: School Curriculum and Assessment Authority.

4 Design and Technology at post-16
Gwyneth Owen-Jackson

As the examination system at post-16 level has recently changed (September 2000), this chapter describes the new examinations available, and their impact on Design and Technology.

Introduction

There was a major overhaul of post-16 education in September 2000, so even if you are only relatively recently out of school it is likely that you will be unfamiliar with the range of options available to pupils at this age.

The changes resulted from a review of qualifications for 16–19-year-olds by Lord Dearing, which were published in a report of the same name (Dearing 1996). The rationale offered for these changes included:

- to ensure that all qualifications are valued and equally worthwhile
- to encourage the study of a broader curriculum
- to raise and widen levels of participation and achievement.

A National Qualifications Framework was introduced to try to ensure parity of esteem between the different types of qualifications (see Table 4.1). The framework puts qualifications into three categories: general qualifications; vocationally-related qualifications and occupational qualifications. These are then ordered into five levels, from level 1 – which is equivalent to grades D–G at GCSE – through to level 5 which is higher level study. Most post-16 qualifications would be level 3.

General qualifications – changes to A levels

To encourage breadth of study, and to raise and widen levels of participation, traditional A level courses have been revised. Where previously they were a two-year course of study with a final examination, they are now a series of units. The first three units of a course can be studied for the award of an Advanced Subsidiary certificate (AS), or six units can be studied for a GCE A level certificate. Each unit is assessed separately: some are internally assessed by the school (with moderation by the examination board) and some are externally assessed through written examinations or coursework. Examinations for most units are currently offered twice a year, in January and June, and students can choose to re-sit a unit once if they wish, the better mark of the two then being recorded. The six-unit A level courses include

Table 4.1 The National Qualifications Framework

Levels of attainment	General qualifications	Vocationally-related qualifications	Occupational qualifications
Higher level/5			eg NVQ level 5
Higher level/4			eg NVQ level 4
Advanced level/3	eg Advanced Subsidiary and Advanced GCE	eg Advanced GNVQ Vocational A level Vocational Advanced Subsidiary	eg NVQ level 3
Intermediate level/2	eg GCSE grades A*–C	eg Intermediate GNVQ	eg NVQ level 2
Foundation level/1	eg GCSE grades D–G	eg Foundation GNVQ	eg NVQ level 1
Entry level	Entry level qualifications can provide a basis for progression to qualifications across the framework at Foundation level		

synoptic assessment in the final units of assessment, as at this level students are required to show that they are able to integrate knowledge and understanding from the various units which make up the course.

Vocationally-related courses – changes to GNVQ

Vocational courses have also been revised and renamed. There are now three-unit, six-unit and twelve-unit vocational courses available, named respectively: Advanced Subsidiary Vocational Certificate of Education (or vocational AS); Advanced Vocational Certificate of Education (or vocational A level) and Advanced Vocational Certificate of Education – Double Award.

The specifications for these courses are set out differently from traditional examination syllabuses. Each unit has a section describing what the unit is about, what students need to learn or do to cover the required content and what evidence they must produce to show 'achievement' of the unit. The evidence is assessed against the 'grade criteria' specified in the unit in order for a grade to be awarded. Grades are A–E, as for AS/A levels. Each unit has its own set of grade criteria: these are not generic. An example of grade criteria is shown in Figure 4.1: this is from the OCR vocational A level in Manufacturing, Unit 4 – Manufacturing products.

The evidence required varies from unit to unit: it could be a report, a presentation, a practical task, a case study; examples are numerous. Each unit is assessed separately; external assessment makes up one-third of total assessment, and two-thirds are assessed internally (but moderated by the examination boards).

Assessment Evidence

You need to produce a batch of products manufactured as part of a team according to a production plan. The products should involve a number of components, and different materials, and must be supported by:

- a record of observation of your participation in the production activity;
- preparatory work showing how the production plan and schedule were used, and how the production system was set up;
- process flow charts and diagrams;
- a written risk assessment for the production activity;
- records of team meetings, showing how tasks were allocated, how progress was monitored, how problems were dealt with and how improvements were made.

To achieve a grade E you must show you can:	To achieve a grade C you must also show you can:	To achieve a grade A you must also show you can:
E1 actively participate in team planning meetings E2 use information from the production plan to structure production and maintain output to meet the production schedule E3 complete a full and useful risk assessment, identifying and evaluating hazards, and suggesting appropriate precautions E4 work effectively and safely in a production team to manufacture products to specification E5 operate tools and machinery safely and use safety equipment and health and safety procedures and systems correctly E6 apply a good understanding of quality assurance to the whole production process so the product consistently meets the specification E7 apply appropriate quality control techniques at appropriate stages of production, and keep accurate records E8 take part in regular review meetings to consider production and quality issues.	C1 prepare detailed process charts and diagrams, based on good use of the information contained in the production plan and schedule and using specialist language appropriately C2 manufacture products that are capable of functioning as intended, completing procedures competently and confidently C3 demonstrate self-organisation and motivation as a co-operative and proactive member of the production team.	A1 take a leading role in planning effectively, comparing plans and schedules with the original product specification and suggesting adjustments where necessary to achieve its objectives A2 evaluate the production activity as a simulation of industrial practice, making comparisons and identifying constraints.

Figure 4.1 *An example of grade criteria in vocational A levels*

Each specification also contains a section, 'Essential information for teachers'. This provides the teacher with information about the depth and breadth of knowledge required by students and suggests teaching strategies and resources which could be used. It also gives guidance on assessment. The example in Figure 4.2 is from the Edexcel vocational A level in Engineering, Unit 3 – Engineering materials.

General and vocationally-related courses

The National Qualifications Framework grid (shown in Table 4.1) shows how the general and vocational courses relate to each other, in terms of parity.

One intention of the revisions was that, by making the two types of courses more similar (each with three-unit or six-unit options), students would be encouraged to 'mix and match' their study of academic and vocational courses. UCAS has offered some models of how this might work in practice (see Figure 4.3).

However, what students will be able to choose to study will depend on what is offered by the school. This will, in turn, depend upon the resources the school has available, the organization of the timetable and their philosophy and beliefs about the value of general and vocational qualifications.

Key skills

A further change to encourage breadth of study was the introduction of Key Skills qualifications. The key skills are defined as:

- Communication
- Application of number
- Information technology
- Improving one's own performance and learning
- Working with others
- Problem-solving.

These are not obtained through undertaking specific 'key skills' courses of study, but through the development of a portfolio of evidence, which demonstrates the student's competence against the specified criteria, plus a test. The evidence can be gathered from work carried out in other courses – AS/A/vocational A level courses. The specification for each subject course, such as AS/A level Design and Technology or AVCE Manufacturing, indicates where it presents opportunities for key skills evidence to be gathered. Where a key skill is deemed to be 'integral' to a subject it will be assessed through that subject and again this will be clearly indicated in the specification. However, evidence can also come from extra-curricular activities, voluntary work, leisure activities or part-time work. Nor does evidence have to be written: it could be an observation of the student giving a presentation, the completion of a piece of work using number, or ICT. None of the key skills is compulsory, but the government wishes to encourage their study. One encouragement to students to obtain key skills certificates is that they have UCAS points attached to them, which may help some students in their applications to higher education institutions. (The use of UCAS points by universities is not obligatory but they are encouraged to use

ESSENTIAL INFORMATION FOR TEACHERS

Teaching strategies

This unit is intended to be treated in a practical way with the emphasis on developing the student's ability to:

- recognise a wide range of engineering materials by applying simple evaluations
- perform measurement tests on some materials
- use secondary material with test data
- interpret the results and values of test data
- make links between processing effects and properties and structure of materials
- identify and select alternative materials for engineered products.

The type or types of product used for the assessment may be electrical, mechanical or electro-mechanical. It may be a complex or even fairly simple object. However, it should be noted that students need to consider at least one material from all four types. Possible examples range from subassemblies for cars to items of electronic equipment such as PCs. The product students look at may not cover all the properties listed in 'What you need to learn', and indeed they are not expected to cover all the aspects of each of those properties.

This unit could benefit from having a major project as an integral part of the course. Projects such as building a hovercraft, electric car and wind generator have been proposed and been used. A focus of this kind enables the various subjects to be actually applied in practice, as well as motivating the students. It will also help the students to see the relevance of choosing the correct materials for specific applications.

Some practical experience of testing will be essential, even if this consists only of comparative tests of materials involving improvised testing methods. Formal testing can be used to confirm the identity of the materials, while secondary source data can be used for comparison purposes. Industry-standard testing equipment is not essential for practical activities. Testing equipment is available from various educational firms and some improvised procedures might also be used to produce comparative values. Students working around the grade E boundary may need some help with using test equipment, in selecting data and in interpreting data.

The use of real sources for data about properties of materials is valuable but it should be remembered that the values, formats and units may at first be difficult for the student to understand.

Assessment strategies

When grading student evidence you should consider the following general qualities that distinguish between the three grades:

- increasing depth and breadth of understanding
- increasing coherence, evaluation and analysis
- increasing independence and originality
- increasing objectivity and critical understanding.

This unit is externally assessed. Copies of assessment materials such as test specifications and supporting resources can be obtained from your awarding body.

Resources

Useful sources of information include:

- textbooks in GNVQ series, and similar texts
- testing equipment: available from various educational firms
- some improvised testing procedures might also be used to produce comparative values
- engineering data handbooks and manufacturers' specifications
- tables of physical properties of materials from science data books, or sections of textbooks
- some BS/ISO specifications which may be useful for reference purposes include BS278, BSEN10002, BSEN10045, BSEN233878, BS240, BS4175, BS7663, BS5714.

Figure 4.2 *An example of 'Essential information for teachers' in vocational A level specifications*

them; some universities use them, but with qualification as to the number of points which must come from specific subjects.)

Design and Technology courses post-16

These changes have had some impact on Design and Technology, in that the new specifications have led to major changes in the traditional A level courses. Not only have the structure and assessment of the courses changed, but much of the content has too, in order to present a natural progression from Design and Technology pre-16 courses.

The general qualifications AS/A level courses now available in Design and Technology are:

- Product design, with an option to focus on graphics products, resistant materials and/or textiles
- Systems and control technology
- Food technology.

These courses are offered by all the examination boards in England and Wales. The regulatory bodies in each country[1] have set out the 'subject criteria' for Design and Technology general qualifications at AS and A level, and the specifications from each examination board must comply with these. The subject criteria are designed to ensure consistency and comparability across the examination boards, and between the AS and A level. There is, however, still some variation between the specifications from the boards and it is worth looking at a number of these. Again, schools will select the one most appropriate to their resources, including the knowledge and expertise of the teaching staff.

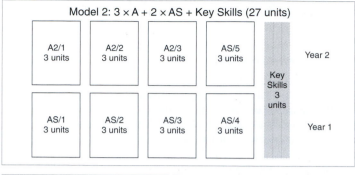

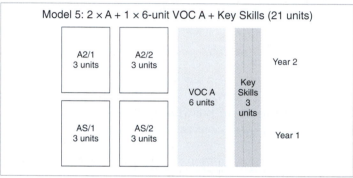

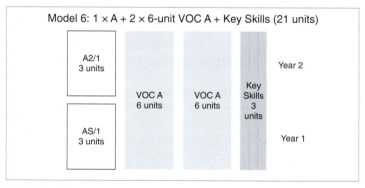

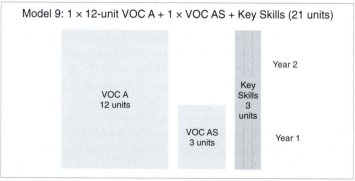

Figure 4.3 UCAS models of students' possible study choices

All the AS/A levels, in whatever focus area, include the study of:

- materials, components and their uses
- industrial and commercial practice
- product development.

In addition, for A level, study includes:

- in-depth study in the selected focus area
- designing and making activity
- one other area, which is determined by each examination board independently.

The skills to be covered by students in their studies include:

- designing, to include   clarifying tasks
  generating and developing ideas
  developing proposals
  detail designing
  communication of ideas and information
- planning, of production, with reference made to industrial methods and volume production
- evaluation, throughout the process, not just at the end
- making, which includes   using ICT
  working with materials, components and appropriate technologies
  planning and evaluating (in production).

The areas of knowledge and understanding identified for study include:

- materials and components
- industrial and commercial practices
- quality
- health and safety, of designers, makers, users and the public
- systems and control (all candidates will be expected to have some knowledge of systems and control; this could range from a manufacturing production system, a quality assurance system to a security system. Those specializing in this area will, of course, be expected to have a more detailed knowledge)
- products and applications.

Each of these headings, in skills and knowledge, is amplified in the subject criteria from the regulatory bodies and in the specifications from the examination boards. In addition, the knowledge and understanding are amplified for each of the optional focus areas.

Although different from previous Design and Technology A level courses, these new general A levels build on students' National Curriculum studies and GCSE courses.

Vocational courses relevant to Design and Technology have also been revised. At vocational AS level, only four courses in total are available (as at September 2000) and two of these are relevant to Design and Technology: Engineering, and Health and Social Care. At vocational A level there are currently 15 courses available: those relevant to Design and Technology are:

- Engineering
- Health and Social Care
- Hospitality and Catering
- Manufacturing
- (possibly) Construction and the Built Environment.

As described above, each of these vocational courses has its own specification covering what students will need to learn and do, the evidence they must generate and the criteria for assessment. These courses are a development from General National Vocational Qualifications (GNVQs) and, where staff have previously taught these, they are a welcome improvement.

It is possible that some vocational courses will be co-taught by staff from different departments: for example, Engineering could involve staff from Design and Technology, Science and Mathematics; Health and Social Care courses could be taught by staff from Design and Technology, Science, Physical Education and Personal and Social Education. It will be important, therefore, for Design and Technology departments to be aware of developments in the post-16 curriculum in the school, to look for opportunities and to be prepared to work with staff from other departments. (Vocational courses are discussed further in Chapter 5).

The post-16 courses offered in schools will vary according to the number of students, the resources available (such as availability of staff, their areas of expertise) and timetabling arrangements. At the time of writing it is difficult to assess the impact that these changes will have on Design and Technology, although there are some indications that numbers may rise. Design and Technology departments should be encouraged by this and should plan and prepare teachers and students to expect post-16 courses; in this way they will help to ensure the continued development of new and exciting initiatives which will raise the profile and perceptions of the subject and contribute to its continuing success.

Note

1   In England this is the Qualifications and Curriculum Authority (QCA), in Wales the Qualifications, Curriculum and Assessment Authority (ACCAC) and in Northern Ireland the Council for Curriculum, Examinations and Assessment (CCEA).

References

Dearing, R. (1996) *A Review of Qualifications for 16–19-year-olds*, London: HMSO.
UCAS (2000) *Changes to Post-16 Qualifications*, Cheltenham: UCAS.

5 Design and Technology and vocational qualifications

David Yeomans

Preceding chapters have examined Design and Technology in the context of the National Curriculum, primary schooling, GCSE and post-16 education. This chapter extends this contextual exploration to an examination of the place of Design and Technology within vocational qualifications.

Introduction

There are many thousands of vocational qualifications and, within the scope of this chapter, it is not possible to examine the place of design and technology across all these qualifications. The chapter will therefore focus upon the main full-time vocational qualifications taken in schools and colleges, thus excluding the many qualifications pursued mainly within workplaces.

The chapter has five main sections. The first outlines the rationale for the introduction of the main full-time vocational qualifications. This is followed by a short account of the complex and tangled story of their recent development. The remaining three sections explore in more detail the relationship between Design and Technology and vocational qualifications, first through outlining the courses which are available, then by exploration of the knowledge and skills embedded in the courses and the ways these are assessed, and finally through consideration of aspects of teaching and learning in vocational courses.

As I illustrate below, the take-up of those vocational courses which focus mainly on aspects of Design and Technology has been small, particularly in schools. However, some consideration of Design and Technology-related vocational courses is justified in this book because these courses emerged, in curricular terms, from vocational traditions and practices and, institutionally, from the National Council for Vocational Qualifications and the Department of Employment. They have thus embodied somewhat different aims and assumptions and had rather different content, structure and assessment patterns compared with GCSE and GCE A level courses. Therefore some knowledge of Design and Technology in vocational courses is useful because it enables us to get outside the dominant assumptions which have shaped the subject within the school tradition and thus engage more critically with those assumptions. In addition, the reform of advanced level qualifications in September 2000 was designed to make it easier for students to mix academic and vocational studies and it is possible that the take-up of vocational qualifications courses will increase, thus involving more Design and Technology teachers, although this is uncertain at the time of writing.

The background and rationale for recent developments in vocational qualifications

This section will outline briefly some of the background and rationale for recent developments in full-time vocational qualifications taken mainly in schools and colleges. Vocational qualifications need to be understood in the context of the enduring academic–vocational divide in the curriculum in England and Wales, particularly at post-16 level. While the academic side of this divide, embodied by GCSE and GCE A levels, has been widely understood by parents, pupils and employers, the vocational side of the divide has been highly fragmented and fractured, having grown in a piecemeal and sometimes highly localized fashion. The academic–vocational split is important because it signifies not only different approaches to curriculum content, pedagogy and assessment but is also marked by great status differences between the two routes. GCE A level has often been seen as the 'gold standard' of the post-16 curriculum, a standard against which other forms of curriculum are judged. For those developing and teaching vocational curriculums this poses a cruel dilemma . They can seek to ape academic courses in an attempt to raise the status of vocational courses and risk losing the *raison d'être* of these courses as alternative forms of practically and vocationally based knowledge and skill. Alternatively, they may resist this process of academic drift and be forced to accept second-class status for the courses in the eyes of students, parents, higher education tutors and even the employers at whose behest vocational courses are ostensibly provided. As I shall show, this dilemma has been very much evident in the recent evolution of vocational courses.

In the 1980s the Conservative government attempted to rationalize the jungle of vocational provision through its Review of Vocational Qualifications and the subsequent establishment of the National Council for Vocational Qualifications (NCVQ). The intention was to establish a system of National Vocational Qualifications (NVQs) into which existing and new qualifications would be slotted. The review, the NCVQ and the new framework were also intended to raise the quality of vocational education and training and ensure that the vocational education and training (VET) system played a more effective role in promoting economic development.

NVQs were developed as occupationally specific qualifications: they were modular and designed to attest to the competence of candidates within narrowly drawn vocational areas. NVQs attracted a lot of criticism, among which was that they were too narrow and were not equipping candidates with the broader, more transferable skills which it was claimed were needed in the modern workplace. It was partly as a result of such criticisms that the government decided that a third track was needed, between the occupationalism of NVQs and the academicism of GCE A levels. It was out of this diagnosis that GNVQs were born (Raggatt and Williams 1999).

General National Vocational Qualifications were first publicly mooted in the British government's 1991 White Paper *Education and Training for the 21st Century* and the first pilot courses began in 1992. The White Paper stated that:

General NVQs should cover broad occupational areas, and offer opportunities to develop the relevant knowledge and understanding, and to gain an appreciation of how to apply them at work. General NVQs should also:

- offer a broad preparation for employment as well as an accepted route to higher level qualifications, including higher education;
- require the demonstration of a range of skills and the application of knowledge and understanding relevant to the related occupations;
- be of equal standing with academic qualifications at the same level;
- be clearly related to the occupationally specific NVQs, so that young people can progress quickly and effectively from one to the other;
- be sufficiently distinctive from occupationally specific NVQs to ensure that there is no confusion between the two;
- be suitable for use by full-time students in colleges and, if appropriate, in schools, who have limited opportunities to demonstrate competence in the workplace.

(DES/DOE/Welsh Office 1991: 19)

Responsibility for developing GNVQs was given to NCVQ and the vocational awarding bodies of BTEC, RSA and CGLI. Thus, while GNVQs were intended to constitute a middle route through the post-16 curriculum, they were also clearly on the vocational side of the academic–vocational divide. Many of the tensions involved in GNVQs, as reflected in their rather tortured history, can be traced back to their original formulation as offering this 'middle route', preparing candidates for work *and* higher education and establishing what came to be called parity of esteem with academic qualifications (Edwards *et al.* 1997; Gleeson and Hodkinson 1995). Despite these tensions, however, GNVQs proved popular and became the main form of full-time vocational provision in schools and colleges during the 1990s.

The recent development of vocational qualifications

Few, if any, qualifications can have changed so often in such a short period of time as GNVQs. In September 2000 the third major version in eight years was introduced. With the introduction of Curriculum 2000 in September 2000, Advanced GNVQs were renamed Advanced Vocational Certificates of Education. The name GNVQ was retained for Part One, Foundation and Intermediate level courses. Both names are used appropriately through this text, so AVCE refers to post-16 Advanced level courses and GNVQ to pre-16, Foundation and Intermediate level courses, and to all vocational qualifications prior to 2000.

The changes over the period 1992–2000 were complex and technical, but several major trends can be identified. In their initial formulation, GNVQs clearly reflected their origins in NCVQ and their sibling-like relationship with NVQs. Like NVQs, the qualifications were modularised, with each module or unit broken down further into elements (sub-units) and performance criteria (what had to be achieved), which were to be demonstrated through evidence indicators (what had to be presented for assessment). GNVQs were therefore strongly outcome-based. Thus, rather than sampling among potential outcomes, as was typically done in academic courses, they required *all* the specified outcomes to be achieved in order to gain the qualification. They were coursework-based, with assessment taking place through a portfolio of evidence gathered by candidates.

The GNVQ mastery learning internal assessment system, in which candidates either achieved pre-specified outcomes or did not, came under pressure even during the design of the qualification. This led to a limited element of external assessment, involving multiple choice questions, and a grading system with merit and distinction grades being brought in, although these developments in some ways contradicted the original philosophy of the qualification as derived from the NVQ model (Raggatt and Williams 1999; Sharp 1998). The subsequent changes to GNVQs, which are described below, can be seen as a further drift away from the original model, as it came under criticism for both lack of 'rigour' and an overly bureaucratic and unmanageable assessment regime (Smithers 1998).

GNVQs were initially attacked by some critics as having no syllabuses (Smithers 1993). This was based upon a particular view of what constitutes a syllabus, since there *were* detailed specifications which laid out in considerable detail the outcomes which had to be achieved. However, these specifications took a rather different form from GCSE and A level syllabuses and it was necessary for teachers to become accustomed to the form and structure of the specifications, and the GNVQ jargon.

The specifications introduced for the September 2000 version of GNVQs were quite different. The performance criteria, range statements and evidence indicators were removed and the unit specifications divided into the following main sections:

- About this unit
- What you need to learn
- Assessment evidence.

The language was simplified and the specifications were much closer in style to conventional syllabuses. Assessment was simplified and was to be conducted at unit, rather than element, level. A much stronger element of external assessment was introduced. Overall, there was a shift away from atomized assessment (Kimbell 1997) towards a more holistic approach, although with one-third of the course assessed through externally set assignments.

This transformation of GNVQs can be interpreted as the failure of an alternative assessment-led curriculum model which emphasized outcomes and, in theory at least, left it to teachers to decide what content and pedagogy they employed to reach the pre-specified ends. Politically and educationally, this model failed to pass muster and through a process of academic drift was translated into something closer to the conventional academic model. Curriculum history (Goodson 1987) suggests that a process of academic drift was always likely to occur once vocational qualifications were explicitly claimed to enjoy parity of esteem with A levels. The changes also paralleled in some respects those made to the National Curriculum from the mid-1990s: in both there was a retreat from an extreme version of criterion-referenced assessment which atomized assessment and brought in its wake distortion and assessment overload, for teachers and pupils alike.

Design and Technology and vocational qualifications

Having set out some of the general features of vocational qualifications and the ways in which these have changed, I now turn to the place of Design and Technology within the qualifications. Vocational qualifications are mainly post-16 qualifications (see Chapter 4 for details of these).

GNVQ Part One courses are available at Foundation and Intermediate levels as part of the Key Stage 4 curriculum for 14–16-year-olds, where they provide an alternative to GCSE. These Part One courses have a similar structure to those offered at post-16 and are offered in seven vocational areas including Manufacturing and Engineering. The government has announced that Part One GNVQs will be replaced by Vocational GCSEs in 2002. These will be available in subjects including Manufacturing, Information Technology, Health Care and Engineering. The government sees these new courses as providing a 'further rung in the coherent ladder of vocational learning, rooted in school and moving through Foundation and Modern Apprenticeships into Foundation degrees and work-based qualifications'. Thus, despite its commitment to a more flexible curriculum framework at 16+, the government continues to perceive progression, at least partly, in terms of clearly differentiated academic and vocational routes (or ladders). An additional comment in the DfEE press release announcing the new courses – that Vocational GCSEs will also 'help to tackle truancy among disaffected young people' – is also hardly likely to raise the status of vocational qualifications (DfEE 2000).

GNVQs were originally introduced in five vocational areas – Business, Health and Social Care, Leisure and Tourism, Art and Design and Manufacturing – and ten further subject areas were subsequently introduced. The first four areas have remained the most popular. For the year ending July 1999, 78 per cent of all Advanced level awards were in those four areas, with the Business GNVQ accounting for almost half of those. The areas most closely related to Design and Technology saw very small numbers of awards: Engineering – 3 per cent of the total; Construction and the Built Environment – 1.7 per cent; Land and Environment – 0.06 per cent; Manufacturing 0.2 per cent; in total only 2,370 awards were made in England and Wales in those four areas in 1999. Data are not available but it is likely that most of these awards were from colleges rather than schools. Similar patterns were also evident at Intermediate and Foundation levels (across all GNVQ courses, Intermediate and Advanced levels accounted for over 90 per cent of all awards).

It is clear that the take-up of the main GNVQ courses involving aspects of design and technology has been small. Elements of design and technology can, however, also be found within GNVQ courses in Information Technology; Health and Social Care; Art and Design; Hospitality and Catering, and Design and Technology teachers in schools are more likely to experience GNVQ as members of course teams in these more popular courses rather than through courses in Engineering, Construction and the Built Environment, Land and Environment or Manufacturing.

Knowledge, skills and assessment in vocational qualifications

Despite the small numbers of awards, however, GNVQ courses are of interest to students of design and technology because the specialist courses – Engineering, Manufacturing, Construction and the Built Environment, Land and Environment, Health and Social Care, Hospitality and Catering – illustrate ways in which it is possible to develop different curricular emphases, compared to those which are familiar from GCSE and GCE A level Design and Technology courses.

In exploring the knowledge and skills included in the courses I shall focus particularly upon the Advanced Vocational Certificate of Education in Manufacturing introduced in September 2000. Manufacturing is the longest established of the courses in the design and technology area and is more likely to be offered in schools than the other specialist areas, since it is probably the closest of the specialist vocational courses, in terms of subject matter, to Design and Technology as practised in schools. However, the general orientation towards knowledge, skills and assessment in the Manufacturing course is broadly similar to that found in the Engineering, Construction and the Built Environment and Land and Environment courses and, therefore, exemplifies a general vocational approach to curriculum and assessment design[1].

Under the heading 'Aims', the Manufacturing course is said to encourage students to:

- design and manufacture products
- acquire knowledge and understanding of the characteristics of the manufacturing sector as a whole and specialist knowledge and understanding of the specific manufacturing areas of food, drink, textiles, print, biological and chemical manufacturing
- acquire knowledge and understanding of the physical and economic factors that influence the work of the sector
- acquire knowledge and understanding of the processes involved in the sector, and apply the knowledge and understanding through practical work
- acquire and apply the skills and techniques needed to work effectively in the sector
- develop an appreciation of the world of manufacturing, including an awareness of the commercial opportunities available.

While 'design' and 'manufacture' appear in the first of these aims the acquisition of 'knowledge and understanding' has considerable prominence among the aims as a whole, together with developing 'appreciation' of the world of manufacturing. Thus, the aims raise questions about the balance between investigational work aimed at promoting understanding of manufacturing processes, the characteristics of manufacturing and its role within the economy and practical work in which students undertake their own manufacturing.

One of the criticisms of earlier versions of GNVQ Manufacturing was that the courses implicitly, and sometimes explicitly, assumed that there were sets of generic skills which were applicable across a broad and ill-defined sector (Yeomans 1998). The

September 2000 course moved away from this position somewhat by giving greater attention to specific manufacturing areas as outlined in its second aim. This more specific focus is also reflected in the optional units which include: Chemical manufacturing; Biological manufacturing; Textile manufacturing; Print manufacturing; and Food manufacturing. This development makes it possible for colleges and schools, or students, to develop more specialized knowledge in particular areas of manufacturing.

The nature of the knowledge and skills involved in the course is further revealed through the identification of the 'key manufacturing processes' of:

- identifying customer needs
- design
- presentation
- production planning
- manufacture and quality control.

While the first two of these processes are likely to be familiar to teachers of Design and Technology the last three will be less so, and this serves to distinguish vocational courses from GCSE and GCE courses. In particular, it is the focus upon production planning and quality control which best exemplifies the character of the manufacturing course.

The orientation of the course is also evident from the titles of the six compulsory units:

1 The world of manufacturing
2 Health and safety and environmental impact
3 Production planning and costing
4 Manufacturing products
5 Quality assurance and control
6 Production creation and development.

Units 1 and 2 are designed to provide students with a knowledge base drawn from studies of a local manufacturing organization and the manufacturing process. Unit 1 is described as introducing students to 'the breadth of manufacturing, covering as it does shipbuilding to soft drinks, clothing to manufacturing'. Unit 2, despite its title, focuses on various aspects of the manufacturing process.

The assessment evidence required also indicates the orientation of the course. Students must produce the following for assessment in each unit:

Unit 1   Case study of a local manufacturing organization
Unit 2   A study of a manufacturing process
Unit 3   Application of skills in production planning using a given product specification
Unit 4   A batch of products manufactured as part of a team according to a production plan
Unit 5   Application of understanding of how different manufacturing organizations approach the achievement and maintenance of quality standards

Unit 6   A design portfolio developed from a given customer brief.

(Units 3 and 5 are externally assessed)

From the above list the assessment evidence for Unit 6 is of a type likely to be most familiar to teachers of Design and Technology in schools. However, the more detailed guidance given in the unit makes clear that the design portfolio must give considerable attention to market research and even more attention to the design of a production system for the designed item. It is this latter emphasis which most clearly distinguishes the Manufacturing course from GCSE and GCE Design and Technology courses. The one-off, individually designed and made, hand-crafted artefacts which have been the typical products of Design and Technology courses (Donnelly and Jenkins 1992; Kimbell *et al.* 1996; Medway and Yeomans 1988) are largely disallowed in the Manufacturing course. Thus, Unit 4 requires the production of a batch of products. The unit focus is upon 'production and teamwork' and requires students to work in a team. It is stated that 'Although it may involve hands-on practical work the emphasis is not on demonstrating a high level of individual craft skills but on showing that you can cooperate with others to manufacture relatively simple items consistently to agreed quality standards.' A teacher described how he responded to very similar guidelines in an earlier version of the course:

> I came up with an expression – 'Simple artefacts replicated to agreed quality standards'. How about that? Something that's simple, most of the kids can do it even though they're not skilled, but with tolerances tight enough that they've got to be careful to get them right. You know, there's enough stages in it so they've got to be coordinated but not so many stages that it defeats them.

The AVCE Manufacturing guidance suggested that products for manufacture might include: candlesticks, simple mechanical toys, hats, key rings, mouse mats, or packaged cakes. This points to another important difference between vocational and GCSE/GCE Design and Technology, in that design within the manufacturing course is much more strongly focused upon the design of production processes rather than the design of individual products. This comes out strongly in Unit 3, in which students are told they will 'use what you know about product design to turn a product specification into a realistic and comprehensive production plan. You will also develop a production schedule and detailed costing.' The list of what students need to learn for this unit includes: production resource requirements, materials order points, lead time elements, direct and indirect production costs and selling price. The importance of costing is emphasized throughout and the unit opens with the statement that 'To make a profit, manufacturing businesses must make products efficiently, according to specification and within budget. The importance of careful planning and of correctly calculating costs cannot be underestimated.' Thus, while the products themselves may draw upon relatively simple design skills, it is the design of a process through which they can be manufactured in sufficient quantities, at an acceptable level of quality, such that a profit can be made, which is central to the concept of design in this course.

The list of assessment evidence above also shows that for five of the compulsory modules the main assessable outcomes will be written work. Only for Unit 4 will students be required to produce, and be assessed upon, a designed and made *batch* of products. The guidance for teachers stresses that the unit 'should be mostly practical and the production of long reports should be avoided', although the assessment evidence calls for a variety of observational and documentary evidence on the processes of the production of the artefacts – a GNVQ/AVCE equivalent of the GCSE/GCE design folder. Units 3 and 5 are assessed through an externally set written assignment and Units 1, 2 and 6 through evidence in students' portfolios.

This emphasis upon assessment through written work makes it clear that the course is principally about acquiring knowledge of manufacturing industry. In comparison with GCSE/GCE Design and Technology courses there is a greater emphasis upon propositional knowledge, which is firmly grounded in industrial contexts. The course draws upon some elements of scientific and engineering knowledge, e.g. on the properties of particular materials, but has as its chief focus knowledge of operational procedures in manufacturing industry. There is very little emphasis upon the broadly conceived, individualized, creative design process which has been at the heart of Design and Technology courses in schools.

This raises important questions about the Design and Technology curriculum. These questions include: Is 'design' as operationalized in GCSE/GCE Design and Technology courses over-emphasized? Do those courses project an image of the solo, inspirational, generic design technologist which has few counterparts in the 'real' world of specific technologies, driven principally by the realities of modern industrial practice and the need to turn a profit? Even if this is true, if Design and Technology in schools is primarily part of a broad, liberal education rather than a preparation for specific work, does it matter? Does the Manufacturing course embody the broad, vocational requirements of the sector or have these been mediated by the course designers in ways which have distanced them from manufacturing processes? Is a course which emphasizes knowledge acquisition and written work really what is needed from a vocational course? Despite the increased focus on specific technologies, does the Manufacturing course represent a misguided attempt to derive generic knowledge and skills from a field of activity which is too highly differentiated to make this meaningful?

Teaching and learning in vocational qualifications

The previous section has been largely based upon a textual analysis of the intended vocational qualifications curriculum, particularly as expressed through the specifications for the AVCE in Manufacturing. This section is both more speculative, in that at the time of writing no evidence is yet available about the ways in which the new courses are being taught, and more evidence-based, in drawing upon some of the limited research on the ways in which vocational courses based upon the previous specifications were taught.

Research across a wide range of curricular contexts has shown that, despite increasing central prescription, teachers remain crucial mediators and interpreters of curriculum (Bowe *et al.* 1992; Helsby and McCulloch 1997; Pollard 1994). The original GNVQ with its plethora of performance criteria, evidence indicators and range statements was particularly tightly prescribed, but still provided evidence of teacher mediation, although researchers have differed somewhat in their estimations of the extent of this mediation (Bates 1998; Knight *et al.* 1998; Yeomans 1999).

One of the very few studies of the implementation of GNVQ Manufacturing revealed wide differences between three courses which were studied in depth (Yeomans 1998). One course, based in a college of technology, emphasized engineering knowledge and technical skills in using tools, equipment and materials. A second course, based in a sixth-form college, was taught by science teachers and focused on propositional and theoretical knowledge of materials and processes. There was limited designing and making in this course. In both colleges the units were taught separately, often by different teachers, with little or no integration between them. The third course studied was in a school and was based in the Design and Technology department. Here design remained the dominant concept around which the course was built. The students completed three major design projects during the course and these acted as integrating mechanisms around which were gathered the atomized assessment items. In each case the experience and values of the teachers were crucial in determining the character of the course. Each of the course teams took the GNVQ and moulded it to their prior experience and current values. The material resources available were also important in shaping the courses. The college of technology had large workshops used for the engineering courses which had once been the mainstay of its provision; in the sixth-form college the course was taught in the science laboratories, while in the school it was taught in workshops primarily designed to cater for National Curriculum and GCSE Design and Technology. Thus, the versions of GNVQ Manufacturing which emerged, and hence student experiences, were quite different across the three courses. The GNVQ moderation procedures involving internal and external verification made little or no difference to the highly diverse practices across the courses. If anything, they tended to confirm the teachers in their particular approaches.

Thus, the GNVQ, far from imposing a dull uniformity, accommodated a variety of teaching and learning practice. This variety was greater in Manufacturing than in other vocational areas (Higham *et al.* 1997). GNVQ Manufacturing was peculiarly open to adaptation by teachers because it had been specially invented for GNVQ and so lacked any unified tradition of practice. The low take-up of the course also meant that centres tended to be isolated from each other with limited opportunities to share experiences. There was little in the way of support from LEAs or other agencies and there were few textbooks or other guidance materials. Teachers, to a large extent, were thrown back on their own resources in the interpretation and implementation of this GNVQ.

Further research will be needed on the impact on teaching and learning of the September 2000 revision of vocational qualifications and courses. The move from atomistic to more holistic assessment may increase the opportunities for teachers and students to bring into play their particular perspectives and interests. On the other hand, the provision of externally set assignments may bring a greater degree of uniformity in teaching and learning within the courses. It may be that there will be marked differences between externally and internally assessed units, although this will depend upon the nature of the externally set assignments.

Two further features of teaching and learning in vocational courses are the importance of industrial links and the promotion of independent learning. Vocational courses require strong industrial links. In the case of manufacturing, students require access to industrial sites for researching organizations and industrial processes and, given the absence of textbooks and the general paucity of support material, much of the knowledge required for the course must be derived directly from manufacturing companies. At a more fundamental level, a key aim of the course can be seen as the socialization of students into the norms, assumptions and practices of manufacturing industry: this cannot be achieved solely within schools, which inevitably lack the facilities to provide realistic manufacturing simulations and where few teachers will have recent experience in manufacturing industry.

Independent learning has often been a key feature of vocational courses throughout their history. Its importance in the original GNVQ was enshrined in the grading criteria for the achievement of merit and distinction grades. In the September 2000 version, the grading criteria were extensively modified and the importance of independent learning made less explicit. However, the descriptors of grade A work include 'critical evaluation', 'fluent description', 'reasoned suggestions' and 'thorough understanding', all of which arguably require students to show evidence of independent learning. The required assessment evidence with its emphasis on case studies also suggests that independent learning will continue to be important within the courses. Certainly vocational qualifications have been sold to students in many schools and colleges as being more student-centred than GCE A levels and as offering a coursework-based alternative to summative examinations. Again, further research will be required to investigate if the excision of explicit requirements for independent learning in the new courses impacts upon teaching and learning approaches.

Concluding remarks

Vocational courses are likely to remain peripheral to the practice of most Design and Technology teachers in schools. The take-up of full-time Design and Technology-related courses has been small and, although the changes brought about by the reform of advanced level qualifications in September 2000 may encourage greater provision, it is likely that most schools will continue to cater for students through the provision of GCSE and GCE Design and Technology. This is because the specialist vocational courses which are closest to Design and Technology are likely to be unfamiliar to most school teachers, and because they require specialist facilities unavailable in most schools. Despite this, vocational courses are of interest to students of the Design and Technology curriculum for at least two reasons. First, their history, rather like that of the National Curriculum, testifies to the problems and difficulties brought by a commitment to a highly specified, criterion-referenced, assessment-led curriculum. Richard Kimbell, while acknowledging the potential strengths of such an approach, also mounted a powerful critique against what he called 'atomized assessment' in which he outlined six difficulties brought by this approach:

- the danger of *exclusivity* as the process becomes a set of rituals prescribed by examiners;
- the associated tendency to transform creative *processes* into pre-specified *products*;
- the splintering of real images (real pupils) into digits of *meaningless detail*;
- the *proliferation* in assessment brought about by the splintering process;
- the uncertainty in knowing when a tiny bit of detail is a *no* or a *yes*;
- the confusion created by the inevitable *interaction* of the bits of detail.

(Kimbell 1997: 25–26)

Each of these features was evident in vocational courses in practice, although at a more pragmatic level it was the sheer unmanageability of the mastery-based assessment system which brought it down.

However, study of vocational courses provides a concrete reminder that the Design and Technology curriculum as it is known to teachers through the National Curriculum, GCSE and GCE could always be different. It is not inevitable that the curriculum should be built around a particular version of the design process. An alternative curriculum which is more knowledge-based, more vocationally-biased and which features a rather different variant of the design process is conceivable, although whether such a curriculum would be either desirable or feasible within the current context of schools is a moot point.

Note

1 In what follows excerpts are taken from the Advanced Vocational Certificates of Education in Manufacturing offered by Edexcel, which is the largest awarder of GNVQs. The other awarding bodies are AQA and OCR. The compulsory units are common across the awarding bodies but each offers its own choice of optional units.

References

Bates, I. (1998) 'The 'empowerment' dimension in the GNVQ: a critical exploration of discourse, pedagogic apparatus and school implementation', *Evaluation and Research in Education* 12(1): 7–22.

Bowe, R., Ball, S. and Gold, A. (1992) *Reforming Education and Changing Schools*, London: Routledge.

DES/DOE/Welsh Office (1991) *Education and Training for the 21st Century: Volume One*, London: HMSO.

DfEE (2000) 'Press Release, New Vocational GCSEs to raise standards: Blunkett', 6 July 2000.

Donnelly, J. and Jenkins, E. (1992) *GCSE Technology: Some precursors and issues*, Leeds: Education for Capability Research Group, School of Education, University of Leeds.

Edwards, T. (1997) 'Educating leaders and training followers', in T. Edwards, T.C. Fitzgibbon, F. Hardman, R. Haywood, and N. Meagher (eds) *Separate but Equal? A Levels and GNVQs*, London: Routledge. pp. 8–28.

Edwards, T., Fitzgibbon, T.C., Taylor C., Hardman, F., Haywood, R. and Meagher, N. (1997) *Separate but Equal? A Levels and GNVQs*, London: Routledge.

Gleeson, D. and Hodkinson, P. (1995) 'Ideology and curriculum policy: GNVQ and mass post-compulsory education in England and Wales', *British Journal of Education and Work* 8(3): 5–19.

Goodson, I. (1987) *School Subjects and Curriculum Change: New Edition*, Lewes: Falmer Press.

Helsby, G. and McCulloch, G. (eds) (1997) *Teachers and the National Curriculum*, London: Cassell.

Higham, J., Sharp, P. and Yeomans, D. (1997). *Constructing a New Curriculum: the Rise of General National Vocational Qualifications*, Leeds: School of Education, University of Leeds.

Kimbell, R. (1997) *Assessing Technology: International Trends in Curriculum and Assessment*, Buckingham: Open University Press.

Kimbell, R. Stables, K. and Green, R. (1996) *Understanding Practice in Design and Technology*, Buckingham: Open University Press.

Knight, P., Helsby, G. and Saunders, M. (1998) 'Independence and prescription in learning: researching the paradox of advanced GNVQs', *British Journal of Educational Studies* 46(1): 54–67.

Medway, P. and Yeomans, D. (1988) *Technology Projects in the Fifth Year*, Sheffield: Training Agency.

Pollard, A. (ed.) (1994) *Changing English Primary Schools: The Impact of the Education Reform Act at Key Stage One*, London: Cassell.

Raggatt, P. and Williams, S. (1999) *Government, Markets and Vocational Qualifications: An Anatomy of Policy*, London: Falmer Press.

Sharp, P. (1998) 'The beginnings of GNVQs: an analysis of key determining events and factors', *Journal of Education and Work* 11(3): 293–311.

Smithers, A. (1993) *All Our Futures: Britain's Education Revolution*, London: Channel Four Television.

Smithers, A. (1998) 'Improving vocational education: NVQs and GNVQs', in D. Shorrocks-Taylor (ed.) *Directions in Educational Psychology*, London: Whurr Publishers. pp. 311–27.

Yeomans, D. (1998) 'Vocationalising the Design and Technology curriculum: a case study from post-compulsory education', *International Journal of Technology and Design Education* 8(3): 281–306.

Yeomans, D. (1999) 'Exploring student-centred learning in GNVQs: case studies of classroom practice', *The Curriculum Journal* 11(3): 361–84.

6 The Design and Technology department

Gwyneth Owen-Jackson

This chapter describes how Design and Technology departments may be structured and orga-nized, and considers issues of personnel and accommodation. It is based on Technology Document 8, which was written by Frank Banks and formed part of the OU PGCE in Design and Technology.

Introduction

The first National Curriculum in England and Wales created a new subject, 'Tech-nology', which brought together a number of previously separate departments and required them to work as one:

> By creating a new subject area, work at present undertaken in art and design, business education, craft design and technology (CDT), home economics (HE) and IT will be co-ordinated to improve pupils' understanding of the sig-nificance of technology to the economy and to the quality of life.
>
> (NCC 1990: A1)

This led to the creation of a variety of departmental structures as schools developed different ways of working together to deliver the National Curriculum. (In North-ern Ireland the subject has never encompassed the study of Home Economics.)

However, since 1990 the National Curriculum has undergone a number of revi-sions and the subject has developed, as a result of which it now includes only those areas previously defined as Craft, Design and Technology and Home Economics. This does, of course, hide a more complex structure, as within these areas Design and Technology incorporates specialists in electronics, resistant materials, graphics, food and textiles. This became more complex with the introduction of vocational courses, such as Manufacturing, Engineering, Hospitality and Catering and Health and Social Care. Design and Technology departments now prepare pupils for a range of courses and organize themselves appropriately for these.

Another factor contributing to the diversity of provision was the belief that Design and Technology was a subject which contributed to the education of a better trained workforce and, ultimately, enhanced the economic well-being of the country. This led to the provision of extra government funding, some of a general nature and some targeted at specific schools which could act as 'centres of excel-lence'. City Technology Colleges (CTCs) were set up by government in partnership with industry and received additional funding to improve accommodation and equipment for the teaching of technology.

The consequence of the curriculum changes and government initiatives was a multiplicity of management structures, and a significant variability in resource levels, in different schools. Although there has been some reduction in the number of variations found, differences might still be seen in organization and practice, personnel, accommodation and resources within Design and Technology departments in different schools.

Organization and practices

In the early days of technology many different models of departmental organization and structure were developed in order to meet National Curriculum requirements: some of these are shown in Figure 6.1.

Now, however, with the development of the subject, and the reduction in the number of departments contributing to it, there are far fewer models to be found in schools. The majority of schools now teach units of work in each of the specialist areas, with some collaboration in planning and assessment to ensure coverage of the National Curriculum and coherence in pupils' experiences. During Key Stage 3, pupils are exposed to a range of specialized areas, usually including food technology, resistant materials, systems and control and textiles technology and sometimes including graphics. Links between these different areas may be made by some specialist teachers who have knowledge of what pupils have covered in other units, but this is not always the case. In Key Stage 4, pupils select one specialist area of study which they follow to examination level.

There are some advantages to this way of working, in that teachers have a depth of knowledge and expertise in their specialist area which allows them to teach more effectively. Pupils can be motivated by the short-term goals of a unit of work and they experience several specialist areas. The disadvantages, however, are that pupils may not perceive the links between the different specialist areas: for example, understanding that design development work can be carried out in the specialist areas, albeit in different ways. It may also be difficult for pupils to transfer common skills: for example, transferring their knowledge about developing a specification for a food product to developing a specification for a product made from plastics.

A further problem is ensuring that the specialist units of work allow pupils to progressively develop their knowledge and skills, rather than simply developing the same knowledge and skills in different material areas. This latter problem can be overcome with careful and detailed collaborative planning and assessment across the department.

Policy documents

Most schools have whole-school policy documents relating to issues such as equal opportunities and assessment. The Design and Technology department will also have its more specific policies which build on and incorporate whole-school policy, and are usually contained within the department 'handbook'. These policies will cover principles and practice in areas such as:

Model	Integrated project	Discrete specialist enrichment	Collaborative links between specialist areas	Modular approach	Specialist-specific units
Description	A full collaborative project across all areas. Pupils identify resource requirements	Collaboration on planning and some team delivery and assessment. Teacher identifies groups	Collaboration on planning of activities – separate delivery and assessment. Teacher identifies groups	Teachers from a range of specialisms deliver specific modules with common core foundation	Separate structured courses with some collaboration – planned units of work discretely delivered
Implications	Teams of teachers acting as consultants in a number of work areas. Pupils move to appropriate bases and resources	Group taught by one teacher. Pupils seek support from discrete specialist delivery. Then pulled together for project involving experiences across several specialisms	Common elements are delivered to pupils at same stage but by separate specialists. Links are made collaboratively between specialists by style and philosophy	Teams from a range of disciplines are each assigned to a specific module to be delivered once a year. All pupils follow the same core modules	Groups taught by individual specialists. Linear-structured courses with awareness of links with other specialists in the planning stages
Features	Great care needed in devising project specifications. Careful guidance for teachers and pupils to achieve progression in capability, teaching styles and roles, project budget and resourcing, team balance and expertise	Substantial overall programme needs planning. Discrete components must be devised to complement and link meaningfully and for relevant purposes	The philosophy of D&T must be interpreted and developed by the team through planning and then individually through delivery	Teams across specialisms with little linking. Management of coherent programmes difficult. Timetable structures straightforward. Limited cross-faculty linking	No opportunities for pupils to develop multimedia projects. Well suited to progressive development of capability but in a narrow experience, with little breadth and dimension to the activity
Advantages	Curriculum integration, accommodates wide interest range, ease of introduction of values	Fosters closer links between specialists. Reduces gender stereotyping. Requires planned assessment package. Involves pupil perception of whole curriculum area	Promotes links between specialists. Reduces gender stereotyping. Requires planned assessment package	Produces departmental co-operation. Reduces gender stereotyping. Improves pupil motivation through short-term goals	Enables some depth of experience in limited subject area. Requires little or no change from organisation prior to curriculum
Disadvantages	Difficult to manage, assess and map to PoS experiences. Increases gender stereotyping. Suitable for short-term goals only. Danger of shallow experiences	Management of directed time essential for team meetings	Can be a threat to traditional subject autonomy. Pupils may neither perceive links nor transfer common skills	Demands of co-ordination of core and modules lead to fragmentation of the curriculum. Difficult to standardise accreditation. May lead to a 'circus' of discrete elements	Reinforces gender stereotyping. Difficulties standardising assessment and in the building and transferring of knowledge and skills. Ensures very limited and narrow experiences

Figure 6.1 Design and technology federation delivery models

Source: Somerset LEA (1990: 82–3; adapted).

- equal opportunities
- examination entry
- assessment
- discipline procedures
- health and safety.

The extent of the policy documents will depend on the size and management of the school.

The department handbook usually contains information about the organization and structure of the department, job descriptions for teaching and non-teaching staff, procedures for working within the department, procedures for working with pupils, health and safety matters. It may also contain other information relevant to the school or department, and is a useful source of information for any new member of staff.

Personnel

Design and Technology departments consist of teaching and non-teaching staff. The number of teaching staff will depend on the size of the school and the organization of the department, but is usually comprised of teachers who are specialists in food technology, resistant materials, systems and control, textiles technology and graphics. Some schools teach graphics through other material areas, but Graphic Products is a specialist area at GCSE examination level. Some schools do not have a full complement of specialist staff; for example, not all schools teach food technology, textiles technology and/or systems and control. It is worth noting here that a 1999 survey by the Design and Technology Association (DATA 1999) found that at Key Stage 3, 8 per cent of schools were not offering food technology, 21 per cent were not offering textiles technology, and more than half the schools surveyed were not offering electronics. This is sometimes due to lack of specialist staff available, and sometimes to lack of school resources to teach these areas.

All staff will have job descriptions, and these may be found in the department or faculty handbook. The Head of Department or Faculty will have overall responsibility for the coordination and development of a cooperative team who share a common philosophy of Design and Technology. He or she will also have some specific areas of responsibility such as mentoring student teachers and new members of staff. In most departments or faculties, other members of the staff will also take on specific responsibilities, for example links with feeder primary schools, Key Stage 3 or Key Stage 4 courses, vocational courses or health and safety. Some areas of responsibility are linked to 'responsibility allowances' and can be a way of developing professional knowledge and skills in order to further develop your career: for example, taking responsibility for examination courses.

Non-teaching staff, or technicians, are important members of the Design and Technology department or faculty. The provision of non-teaching staff varies enormously from school to school, some having daily help, others having help just a few hours a week. The 1999 DATA survey (DATA 1999) found that the average number of technicians per school was one full-time equivalent, with 1.3 in technology colleges. The DATA recommendation is for one full-time technician to every three Design and Technology teaching areas.

Non-teaching staff can also be specialists, usually working either in the resistant materials/systems and control area or the food/textiles area. A good technician is invaluable in contributing to the smooth running of the department, by undertaking jobs such as the provision and checking of resources, the maintenance of equipment and the ordering of resources. This releases the teacher to concentrate on improving the quality of pupil performance and learning.

Professional development

Design and Technology is a subject in which there will always be new developments, in equipment, materials, manufacturing processes and products, and teachers will always need to think about keeping up to date. Professional development can take place in many ways, such as courses that teach new knowledge and skills, school-based training from colleagues to widen one's knowledge and skills, or individual development through practice and reading. New knowledge and ideas in Design and Technology can be gained from reading widely – not just professional journals but also good quality newspapers, magazines and books – and from watching relevant and appropriate television programmes. Professional development in Design and Technology can also mean different things: for example, either developing depth of knowledge in your specialist area or developing breadth of knowledge by learning about other specialist areas. It could also mean learning how to apply knowledge to new courses: for example, developing relevant vocational courses in a Design and Technology department by building on existing expertise and developing new knowledge.

During the first year of teaching, the induction year, new teachers should receive planned professional development, addressing areas identified at the end of the training course. After the first year most schools operate performance management, or appraisal, programmes, which provide opportunities to discuss professional development on a regular basis. These often allow teachers to identify areas for development which will contribute to school, department and personal goals, and should provide support for the attainment of these goals.

Health and safety training is of particular concern in Design and Technology. The Design and Technology Association has published *Health and Safety Training Standards in Design and Technology* (DATA 2000), which states what teachers must do in order to become registered. Registration and compliance with these Standards is not statutory but is recommended, and the Standards do comply with British Standard 4163 (2000) which outlines Health and Safety Training Standards and the Management of Health and Safety at Work Regulations 1999. After initially qualifying it is incumbent upon Design and Technology teachers to ensure that their health and safety qualifications and registration remain up to date. This can often be done through the school or Local Education Authority.

Professional development can also take place in your own classroom. Small-scale research is a way in which you can systematically look at your own practice, or at what happens in the classroom. There are many aspects of practice that could be observed: for example, the seating of pupils in a particular order and its effect on performance, the use of specific teaching strategies, or the use of specific resources. Whatever aspect you choose, if it is something that you regard as important to your teaching, then you will be more likely to follow it through. Your observations may lead you to change your practice: again, this can be done systematically and the results observed and noted. You may wish to work with other teachers on small-scale research, observing each other in the classroom and giving feedback. This does take time but will have benefits for your work in the classroom, and for pupils' learning.

Accommodation and resources

Many schools were built before the 1975 Sex Discrimination Act, which made it compulsory to offer the same curriculum to boys and girls. Consequently, accommodation for Design and Technology in single-sex schools is often restricted to either resistant materials/systems and control or food/textiles, and in mixed-sex schools Design and Technology teaching rooms for these specialist areas can be geographically separated. Increasingly, however, schools are using funds to develop the learning environment and to provide equipment to teach fully the requirements of the National Curriculum. The National Curriculum 2000 in England contains the statement:

> The Government believes that schools should be encouraged to look for opportunities to teach both food and textiles as part of the range of contrasting materials that pupils should use as part of the key stage 3 programme of study.
>
> (DfEE/QCA 1999: 17)

Design and Technology is an expensive subject, in that it requires specialist rooms, specialist equipment and consumable resources which constantly need replacing. Recent National Curriculum and examination syllabus changes, emphasizing the need to teach industrial practices and integrate ICT, have led to the need for the purchase of new equipment and resources. For Design and Technology departments to remain in the forefront of developing subject knowledge, it is likely that it will be a constant requirement to buy new equipment and resources, as well as to update and maintain existing ones. This is a fact of life that Design and Technology teachers have to live with.

The Design and Technology Association survey (DATA 1999) found that maintained secondary schools (excluding technology colleges) had £6.16 per pupil to fund their Design and Technology courses, while in technology colleges the capitation per pupil was £7.69. The figure recommended by DATA was £10.15, in order for schools to be able to provide the equipment and resources needed. Over half the schools surveyed said that they charged pupils for materials: this is a common practice but does influence what pupils may choose to make.

Design and Technology continues to be an area of concern for many influential pressure groups working with industry to improve the resource situation in schools. The Gatsby and Nuffield Foundations, for example, work to increase the facilities available to schools. They are also keen to widen provision beyond those institutions designated by government for special consideration. Schools can also benefit from partnerships with local business and industry.

Whatever the accommodation, equipment and resources a department has, they can always be enhanced by attention to the environment. Displays of pupils' work, work from other designers, interesting posters and well-displayed information can all be used to provide an interesting and stimulating environment for pupils. The use of clear signs and notices is also helpful, and all will help to convey a positive image of the subject and the department.

A well-organized and -managed department, with a cooperative team of teachers working together, can provide an interesting and motivating learning experience for pupils. This will encourage them to continue their studies in Design and Technology and help to create a positive spiral of improvement for both teachers and pupils.

References

DATA (1999) *A Survey of the Provision for Design and Technology in Schools 1998/99*, Research Paper No. 13. Wellesbourne: DATA.

DATA (2000) *Health and Safety Training Standards in Design and Technology*, Wellesbourne: DATA.

DfEE/QCA (1999) *The National Curriculum Handbook for secondary teachers in England*, London: HMSO.

NCC (1990) *Non-Statutory Guidance: Design and Technology*, York: National Curriculum Council.

Somerset LEA (1990) *Design and Technology: A Federated Approach*, Taunton: Somerset LEA.

2 Design and Technology in the classroom

7 Managing Design and Technology classrooms

Frank Banks and Gwyneth Owen-Jackson

This chapter begins a section on aspects of teaching Design and Technology by addressing an issue of concern to many new teachers: how to organize and manage pupils and resources in the classroom.

Introduction

In surveys of new teachers, it is classroom management and discipline that are of principal concern. The question always in the mind, if not actually articulated before the first teaching placement, is, 'Will I be able to keep control?' We believe that it is impossible to isolate classroom management from the way in which you attempt to teach and from the wider issues, attitudes and values with which you have to operate in school. If you have an ethos of how pupils and teachers should interact different from that prevalent in other areas of the school, then pupils will be unsure how to react in your classes. That is not to say you are wrong, just that it will take longer for the pupils to work out the 'ground-rules', and indeed they may never do so. As a trivial example, if you think that pupils should call you by your first name, but the rest of the school operates a more formal code, then pupils will be confused. In fact they may mistake such informality for a laissez-faire attitude to discipline. It is a mistake to try to work against the norms and routines of the school and department, and in isolation from the school support structures which surround you.

Norms and routines can work at a number of different levels. For example, for safety considerations, it is often the expectation that pupils will line up outside the door and wait for the teacher to signal entry before every lesson. It would be unwise to change this. As a new teacher, it will be important for you to follow the practice of the class you teach and to ensure that you are consistent in the way you sustain the code of practice.

Classroom management is not only concerned with pupil behaviour; it also encompasses the management of resources, the environment and your own teaching. This chapter will consider ways in which you might 'manage' the pupils and the resources, while the next chapter considers teaching strategies which can be employed in the Design and Technology classroom in order to ensure that effective teaching and learning can take place.

Preparing to teach

Good management begins before you enter the classroom. When lessons are planned in advance you have an opportunity to think through where problems might arise, and you can plan measures to reduce or deal with these.

Even before the lesson starts, how will pupils enter the room – will they line up outside or come straight in as they arrive? Each method has advantages: the first allows you to talk to the whole group, perhaps to calm them or remind them of safety matters, before they enter the room; the second allows you to talk to individual pupils as they enter, and perhaps to hand out work and comment on individual work rather than do this when the whole class is waiting to begin the lesson. You should think about the aims of the lesson, the group that you will be teaching, school or department norms and your own preferences when deciding which approach to use. In Design and Technology there are important health and safety issues to remember: for example, in practical rooms, where do pupils leave coats and bags, and are they required to wear protective clothing? These are simple but important management issues which will ensure a smooth start to the lesson.

Planning the lesson content will help you to think about where your management skills will be required. For example:

- Will pupils be engaged in practical activities? If so, you need to think about what resources will be needed. Are these sufficient and in place? Make sure you know how to deal with a broken hacksaw blade or sewing machine needle – small incidents like these can easily disrupt a lesson if not dealt with swiftly.
- Will pupils be doing written work? If so, make sure you have sufficient text-books or worksheets, and spare paper and writing instruments for those pupils who forget.
- Will you be showing a video? If so, check that the equipment works before the lesson starts and that the video is set to the correct point. Think about where pupils will sit to ensure that they can see, and to reduce the opportunities for disruptive behaviour.
- Will computer equipment be used? If so, again check the equipment and make sure that you are familiar with the software, and know how to deal with simple problems which pupils might experience when using the software. If pupils need a password to use the computer network, check what to do if a they have forgotten their password or do not have one. If work is to be printed out, check that printers are working and that there is sufficient paper.
- Will pupils be moving around the room, or even moving to other rooms? If so, think about how you will manage this: for example, giving clear instructions to avoid confusion and disruption.

Each one of these points can be considered and planned in advance to ensure that likely 'problem points' are kept to a minimum.

Teaching the lesson

Difficult times for a teacher in managing pupils are at the beginning and end of lessons and in transitions between activities during the lesson. We look at each of these 'hot-spots' in turn.

Beginnings

To help reduce the opportunities for misbehaviour, remember to:

- Arrive before the class
- Always make sure that the class is quiet, with bags put away and coats off before you begin
- Scan the whole class regularly (further reference is made to this in the discussion on 'whole class teaching' and 'demonstrations' in Chapter 8)
- Make eye contact with as many individuals as possible
- Keep the introduction short
- Make the first pupil activities clear and straightforward
- Be clear about the sequence of activities: 'What happens next?'
- Tell latecomers to sit down, don't let them interrupt your flow, but find out later why they were late for your lesson.

Endings

Again, you will be wise to draw on the usual school routines here, but it is essential in practical lessons that you leave enough time to pack away work and resources properly and clear up. It is still a source of amazement just how different the time for this is between pupils who are 11 years old and those who are just a couple of years older! Some points:

- Think how some of the 'ending tasks' can begin well in advance of the end of the lesson – perhaps you collect up some of the tools or equipment yourself, or perhaps a pupil who has finished early helps others
- Don't try to do too much yourself at the end
- If something took longer than you expected, don't try to rush to do everything you have planned
- Get everyone quiet at the end before they go and give a word of encouragement and praise
- Control the exit. This may be more important with a lively and large group of 12-year-olds, but even with older pupils make sure you are the one to dismiss the group.

Transitions within lessons

As described in the section above, a smooth transition from one task to another is down to planning and preparation. For example, if you are to use a video, make sure you can work the machine, know the channel setting for playback and have lined up the tape to the beginning of where you wish to start! Some general points:

- Make sure you are ready and have everything to hand before you stop a group
- Warn everyone that they only have a few minutes to finish what they are doing (and plan what you are going to say to those who have not finished – complete for homework?)
- It is easier to 'come round the front' or 'get into discussion groups' if this is an established routine.

Many teachers spend a considerable time at the start of the academic year establishing the classroom routines and procedures as it saves so much time later. As a new or student teacher you will not have had the opportunity to do this, but you can draw on the existing classroom routines to help you. It all soon becomes second nature when you are teaching, but at the beginning you will need to think everything through and plan explicitly.

Dealing with classroom management problems

The vast majority of schools are well organized and disciplined. Design and Technology appeals to most pupils – and particularly to the many pupils who have found the practical and realistic nature of the work a welcome change from the tasks set elsewhere in school. But you will meet some pupils whose behaviour is unacceptable.

The causes of misbehaviour, and how it manifests itself in the classroom, are numerous. Kyriacou (1991: 82) suggests that teachers most commonly have to deal with seven types of pupil misbehaviour:

- excessive talk or talking out of turn
- being noisy
- not paying attention to the teacher
- not getting on with the work required
- being out of their seat without good cause
- hindering other pupils
- arriving late for lessons.

It is sometimes a combination of these factors that creates a general feeling of unease and discontent on the part of both the class and the teacher. Sometimes what appears to be trivial misbehaviour, such as continual whispering throughout the lesson, can be the most irritating. This raises the stress level and leads you to forget where you are in your lesson plan – or that piece of advice you read about what to do with difficult pupils!

Unfortunately there is no 'golden rule' for establishing and maintaining classroom discipline. The planning discussed above will help you to decide when, in a particular lesson, you may need to pay more attention to this issue. However, most teachers would say that once you are established in a school, maintaining discipline becomes much easier, and give the following basic advice, which is far more sensible than the weary, time-worn shibboleths such as 'Don't smile till Christmas':

- find out the school procedures for handling disruptive pupils
- plan how you will deal with misbehaviour that you might come across (a behaviour management plan, see below)
- decide what you are going to accept as your basic standards of behaviour and politeness
- keep to those standards
- avoid confrontation.

A behaviour management plan is something that you could consider when planning the lesson. First, you would need to decide what behaviour would be acceptable and what would not (your basic standards of behaviour and politeness). This will vary as different people will tolerate different levels of noise, for example. When you have decided what behaviour would not be acceptable, you can think about how you will deal with it, and how you will deal with continual misbehaviour. For example, if a pupil is shouting out answers – which you find unacceptable – you may first give a general warning to the whole class; if the misbehaviour continues you could give the pupil an individual, quiet warning; you might then say that you will keep the pupil in over a break or lunchtime. The idea of a behaviour management plan is that you have a strategy for dealing with misbehaviour and do not respond inappropriately or inconsistently to it.

Remember, too, that praise can also be used in a behaviour management strategy. Giving praise to a whole class for good behaviour can have positive effects; giving praise to an individual pupil which can be overheard can work by having a 'ripple' effect on others. Some pupils, however, feel embarrassed by public praise, in which case talking quietly to them at the end of the lesson can produce benefits.

Using your voice

Regard your voice as a teaching tool – it can be very effective. The pitch of your voice can express a range of emotions, such as calmness, urgency, enthusiasm and displeasure. The pitch, volume and speed of your voice can be used to manage the classroom, for example, to speed up clearing away, to alert a pupil to danger, to prevent misbehaviour. However, if you continually raise your voice in response to misbehaviour it can become less effective, as pupils may bait you to respond in this way or may not pay attention. Sometimes it can be more effective to discipline pupils by speaking quietly and seriously.

Make sure that, however you use your voice, your non-verbal cues support what you are saying; for example, do not reprimand a pupil whilst smiling as the message is confusing. Your posture and facial expressions can indicate to pupils whether you are pleased or displeased with their behaviour, without the need for words.

Your position in the classroom can also be used to support your teaching; for example, watching a pupil or group of pupils will help you to see whether your intervention is needed or not, either to help or to stop misbehaviour before it starts. This can be particularly useful in practical lessons: when pupils are engaged with individual work try to position yourself so that you can see – and be seen and heard by – the whole class.

Conclusion

Design and Technology, because of its nature, may need more consideration of management than some other subjects. However, by planning and preparing for lessons, management should soon become second nature.

The following summary may be used as a checklist for organizing lessons in Design and Technology. For every lesson, have you:

- prepared and checked all the resources you need, including useful stimulus material
- worked out the routines of bringing the class into the room and settling them to work
- thought about the start of the lesson and how you will quickly get the class engaged and working
- shown clearly in your plan what you and the pupils are doing for each activity and the time you estimate each activity will take
- considered how you will change from one activity to another
- allowed for the differing needs of the different pupils in the group
- tried out any demonstration and any practical techniques you expect the pupils to perform
- worked out what you will say when giving instructions
- decided how you will distribute and collect resources
- planned the ending of the lesson, allowing time for the clear-up routine
- considered what the homework will be, either for the class as a whole or for individuals, as appropriate?

As you become familiar with the checklist you will need to refer to it less. However, as an aide memoire, it will help in your consideration of classroom management, and so help you be more confident in your teaching.

References

Kyriacou, C. (1991) *Essential Teaching Skills*, Oxford: Blackwell.

Owen-Jackson, G. (2000) *Learning to Teach Design and Technology in the Secondary School*, London: RoutledgeFalmer.

8 Teaching strategies for Design and Technology

Frank Banks

Following on from the previous chapter, this one considers the range of teaching strategies that could be employed in Design and Technology, and how they can be used appropriately.

Introduction

Why do you want to teach Design and Technology? I don't mean why do you want to *teach* – but why do you want to teach *Design and Technology*? What is it about the subject that makes it important enough for pupils to learn and for you to want to teach it? I asked that question to a number of student teachers and they gave a range of replies:

> … there are life skills involved with technology and too few people go through school obtaining these life skills. I mean you can have someone who's academically brilliant at maths, but yet at home can't change a plug, so I believe technology is really important …

Another said:

> I've a belief that everyone should follow technology with a business and a legal aspect … unless you know how much it's gonna cost, it's pointless designing something […] Can we make it? Far too often we find we design things which do not take into the remit […] realistic targets.

A third said:

> … my reasoning is that a lot of people should do technology up to a certain level so as they could maybe get the best out of a technological society later on.

These opinions, along with many others collected from both students and more experienced practitioners, show that Design and Technology teachers have different views as to what is the key purpose of their subject. David Barlex and I found we could categorize their views as follows (Banks and Barlex 1999: 226):

Aesthetics	The appearance is crucial. It says everything about the product
Communicating skills	Unless they communicate their ideas nothing will be accomplished
Design procedures	Without the procedural competence of design nothing can be achieved
Making skills	But if they can't make it it's a complete waste of time
Technical understanding	If it's not technically sound it just won't work
Values	Without an appreciation of the values implicit in the endeavour the whole exercise lacks worth.

All these opinions are valid and important, and one might say that taken together they would all contribute to a rounded and well-balanced Design and Technology curriculum. Figure 8.1 shows a cartoon of a department discussing a new scheme of work.

The cartoon may be a caricature, but it makes the point that teachers' personal beliefs about the subject are vitally important. However, if any one of these opinions predominates to the extent that teaching is done in such a way that other aspects of the subject are ignored, then the pupil's experience of Design and Technology becomes skewed. A balance is needed, and that means that we need to teach in a way that promotes all the different facets of the subject.

Manual subjects before the mid-1970s were largely restricted to the development of excellence in making skills. This was achieved by adopting pedagogy not so very different to the 'master–apprentice' model of a medieval guild. The pupil would be given a particular job and shown all the skills and techniques necessary to produce a (more or less) satisfactory outcome. It took a while for such one-sided teaching strategies to fade away and even in the late 1990s, one student teacher remarked:

> As I have been in school, I don't see the design process as important as I thought it was going to be. In a lot of classes it's put on the back burner and they're told what they are going to make and that's it. What I have seen is more skills based than design based.

The safe manufacture of such quality products is still important but is only one, restricted, aspect of technological capability.

It is clear that a traditional 'show and copy' apprentice model of teaching is inadequate and we need to select methods which match our broader aims for the subject. The methods must be both wide enough to embrace attitudes, skills and knowledge for life, as well as specific enough to cover the requirements of our local, national or vocational curriculum. And the teaching methods we employ will not be fixed and unchanging over our career. In recent times the work of Howard Gardner suggests that, rather than there being just one factor which we call 'intelligence', there may be a minimum of seven distinct intelligences: logical-mathematical, linguistic, spatial, bodily-kinaesthetic, musical, interpersonal, and intrapersonal (Gardner 1983). In

Figure 8.1 Developing a balanced approach

response to these views, teachers are increasingly taking into account the different preferred learning styles of their pupils. A limited repertoire of teaching strategies is unlikely to cater for the learning needs of the majority, who have a range of different sorts of intelligence and so respond to teaching in different ways.

So what teaching strategies *are* appropriate for Design and Technology? How can we help our students gain a capability in Design and Technology, both designing and making, but also appreciate the values that impact on them? What is the best way to use the support that a technician can offer? What can we do to encourage interest and enthusiasm and ensure good behaviour in the workroom?

This chapter will tackle these questions and offer some advice.

Teaching techniques in Design and Technology

Initially, I would like to leave aside a detailed discussion about *when* different techniques are most appropriate and instead review a range of teaching strategies and the techniques of *how* to employ them effectively.

I will describe some strategies for teaching:

- a whole class
- pupils working in groups
- pupils working individually.

As you read this chapter and the different teaching strategies discussed, think about you in the classroom or workshop. What will you be doing and what will the pupils be doing? Just as important, think about what messages you convey about the nature of design and technology in the way you teach, and what cues the pupils will take from you about the value of the subject?

Teaching the whole class

Exposition

As soon as you have more than one person to teach, you need to consider the range of aptitudes, different levels of understanding and variations in motivation for what you want your pupils to do. Exposition, the teacher standing at the front and talking to the whole group, is sometimes denigrated as 'just chalk-and-talk' which does little to address the individualities of the students. It can, however, be very effective and efficient in the following circumstances:

- giving the stimulus or setting the context for a topic (for example, this might involve the use of a video and other audio-visual materials, or demonstration and class discussion of a range of artefacts)
- demonstrating a technique or process
- using a question-and-answer session to re-motivate the groups or to allow groups to inform each other
- setting general goals of what you hope the class will achieve by the end of the session
- stressing points of safety
- preparing for a visit or the reception of a visitor
- rounding off a topic and preparing for the display of the work.

When exposition is used, ensure that it is not a lecture at the class. Always interact with the class by asking questions and encouraging them to give their ideas and opinions. Eye contact is essential to check that all are paying attention and questions are being posed which challenge but do not baffle the students. Exposition is also most used at the beginning and ending of lessons to help establish teacher control of the group. Workrooms in schools are generally very safe environments and it is the duty of all of us to ensure that remains the case.

Demonstrations

A demonstration need not be a whole-class activity; sometimes it is better to demonstrate a particular technique or process to a small group or an individual who happens to need that skill. However, in balancing broader tasks to encourage technological capability with focused tasks to give specific knowledge and skills, a whole-class demonstration may be the most straightforward course of action.

Any demonstration must be:

- clearly visible to everyone – if it cannot be seen by the whole class split the group into smaller units

- competently performed so that it is clear and the pupils understand why they are being shown the technique
- interestingly executed to keep everyone's attention.

The best way to ensure a confident and accurate demonstration is to practise the procedure first. It is essential to go through the demonstration in private and ask a colleague to help get it right, particularly if the technique is new or unfamiliar. Only by rehearsing the demonstration is it possible to ensure that it can be done and that there are no difficulties with the school's tools or equipment, either in supply or in use. It will also give an idea of how long the demonstration will take.

Before carrying out the demonstration, organize the components and materials in advance. Make sure that the bench or table surface is cleared as other items can obscure the view and are confusing and distracting. Place the items you will need in a logical order and close by.

When performing the demonstration, keep the students involved. Make sure that they are close enough to see what is happening, but are not in a position to interfere with the demonstration's arrangements. Occasionally a pupil will need to be on the teacher's side of the table to see and interpret the demonstration from the same point of view, but this is the exception rather than the rule. Question the pupils about the materials or components and ask them to link the procedure to similar processes they might have seen before. Discuss what is being done and use diagrams on an OHP or board to help explain any important or intricate points. A good way to keep pupils involved is to ask individuals to help. They can pass items, take readings if appropriate and repeat certain tasks or techniques which have just been shown. The students can also suggest what should be done next and perhaps use a check sheet to keep track of the sequence.

At the end of a demonstration, summarize the important points and then control the pupils' return to their workplace. It is obviously a good idea for them to use the technique as soon as possible to reinforce what has been shown, so try to leave enough time for this and circulate around the class to help where necessary.

Questioning

Asking questions is naturally a vital part of the work of a teacher, and it is surprisingly difficult to do well. I have already made the point that eye contact helps to establish and consolidate the social interaction of the groups you teach, and particular questions targeted at individuals can stretch them and encourage all to participate and think through what they are studying. However, even very experienced teachers find it hard to come up with pertinent questions that are unambiguously worded, linked together in a natural sequence and which do not lead to misunderstandings. Pupils are not 'empty vessels' into which we can pour our carefully worded explanations. They have their own ideas, already worked out from when they were very young. For example, ideas like 'electricity' and 'energy in food' and 'power of machines' and 'waterproofing' will have already been thought about in some measure by all pupils, and their common sense ideas might contradict the accepted scientific view. Careful questioning does not simply elicit what they have done before, but what robust ideas they hold and believe, which will influence your explanations. Such key questions need working out before the lesson.

We have all heard about 'closed questions', which simply require one answer which the pupil either does or does not know, and 'open questions', to which there are a range of possible answers, some may be better than others. But there have been a number of more detailed studies about the type of questions teachers ask and the cognitive level required of pupils to answer them. For example, Brown (1975) categorizes lower-order cognitive type questions under the headings of Recall, Comprehension, Application, and higher-order questions as Analysis, Synthesis and Evaluation. Taking an example of a lesson on making a mechanical toy, here are some questions that might be asked using that classification:

Lower-order cognitive questions

Recall	What is the name of this type of saw?
Comprehension	Why do we use that type of saw for this type of work?
Application	If we are going to cut this complicated shape in this piece of hardboard, which saw should we use?

Higher-order cognitive questions

Analysis	To make this pull-along toy I need to cut out the different parts. What would be the best sequence to do that so that I can make sure they all fit together?
Synthesis	What will happen to the head of the pull-along duck if we use this cam and this rod together like this?
Evaluation	You've heard the different ideas from the different groups. Explain to me which of the suggested combination of cams and rods you think will be the most robust to work together to control the head and wings.

It is plain from this list that to get all pupils to fully engage in the lesson requires careful planning of questions. Simple 'naming of parts' might give the superficial impression that the pupils are 'with you', and have learnt, but the quality of learning will be low. Low-order questions do need to be mixed in with the higher ones, however, in order to maintain the social purpose of the interaction and keep all listening and contributing.

Perhaps more directly useful than a classification of question types is a consideration of why we use questions at different stages of a lesson. Cohen and Manion (1989) give a summary, see Table 8.1.

Questions can be used in settings other than whole class teaching, but when used creatively and with careful thought to purpose, questioning can give cohesion to a group and direction to a project, which can sometimes be lost in the long sequence of lessons where a product is being realized.

Table 8.1 Use of questions at different stages of a lesson

Stage	Questioning:
Introduction	to establish human contact
	to discover what the class knows
	to revise previous work
	to pose problems which lead to the subject of the lesson
Presentation	to maintain interest and alertness
	to encourage reasoning and logical thinking
	to discover if pupils understand what is going on
Application	to focus and clarify
	to lead the pupils to make observations and draw inferences for themselves
	to clear up difficulties, misunderstandings and assist individual pupils
Conclusion	to revise the main points of the lesson
	to test the results of the lesson, and the extent of the pupils' understanding and assimilation
	to suggest further problems and related issues

Explanations

Many people think that good teaching means the same thing as good explaining – keep it clear and simple and all will understand. In fact, some student teachers tell me that they get very upset when, despite their greatest efforts, the pupils just don't grasp what they have explained. When pupils just don't 'get it' they take it as a personal failure. This may not be down to poor explaining, however, as such a 'transmission' view of how people learn is not upheld by research. Rather than simply taking 'on board' new ideas and concepts told to them, however clearly, pupils construct their understanding by making what is new come together with what they currently understand. Finding out what they already understand, so that the explanation can dovetail with their views and challenge inconsistencies in their thinking by discussion and further questioning, is very important.

Of course, a muddled and confused explanation is to be avoided. When pupils are asked about the qualities of good teachers, 'can explain things clearly' comes very high on the list. The following points are worth keeping in mind:

- Be explicit. Rather than just beginning a conversation about something, say clearly what you are going to do: 'I'm going to tell you about how to use this equipment which is called a "vacuum former".'

- Plan the sequence of ideas that you intend to introduce. Most successful lessons introduce only one or two new ideas (Brown and Armstrong 1984).
- Avoid jargon. Words like *cam*, *gear* and *ergonomics* are easy to spot, but it is quite hard to keep in mind that words like *pitch*, *fuse*, *blend*, *strut*, *tie*, *lock*, and *follower* all have both common and specialized meanings.
- If you want to introduce some new vocabulary, treat it as a new idea.
- Keep sentence constructions simple. Avoid asides of detail.
- Remember that certain expressions, such as 'metres *per* second', are not so easy to grasp as a phrase like 'metres *every* second'. This isn't jargon exactly, it is thinking about the way the pupils themselves express themselves and using similar patterns of speech.
- If you find that a particularly neat turn of phrase produces that open look of comprehension, store it away for later use!

Just as with questioning, explaining is not only confined to whole-class teaching, but is equally applicable to work with groups and individuals.

It is important to encourage students to become independent learners and to consider a variety of means of gaining knowledge and skills rather than simply looking on you as the fount of all knowledge. It could be argued that students' technology projects require so wide a range of knowledge and understanding that one teacher could never hope to supply all that is needed. The individual needs of project work may also reduce the appropriateness of whole-class teaching, but when it is used well it can generate enthusiasm, give a topic a sense of direction and be efficient in both teacher and pupil time. Most importantly, perhaps, whole-class teaching can give a 'group identity' to which pupils can feel they belong.

Teaching using group work

Despite the rhetoric, it is not often that you will see a lot of group work going on in Design and Technology. The specification for GCSE has recently been amended to allow group work, although pupils must produce individual work for assessment, but so far such methods are rarely implemented. Design and Technology teachers like each pupil to make their own product 'that they are proud of and want to take home to show off', yet this laudable aim often results in a teaching style which neglects the wider issues and focuses on the opinions of the individual. It is also in marked contrast to the group nature of technology projects outside the school workshop or classroom.

Group work is valuable in encouraging cooperative work in planning, sharing responsibility and allocating tasks, and in fostering teamwork. Care has to be exercised if a group activity is part of teacher assessment of practical outcomes in giving credit for different aspects of the project to the appropriate pupils. Group work need not only be for practical tasks, however, and group discussion is a valuable way for students to consider how technology affects lives. Whatever the aims for group work a few points need to be kept in mind:

- Consider the make-up of the groups carefully. Is friendship grouping the most appropriate? If not, what criteria should be used to form more effective groups? Is the grouping a temporary measure or a more permanent arrangement which needs monitoring?

- Ensure each group has short-term strategies to achieve long-term goals. This is best achieved by visiting each group quickly once they have started, still keeping every group in view. The different groups must know that their progress is being monitored even though the teacher is principally occupied in a different area of the room.
- Make sure all groups are kept busy and on task. If a group appears too rowdy or too many pupils appear to be moving around on short excursions check that it is to do with the organization of their task (see Denton 1994).

Group discussion

When designing, many people find it difficult to think up novel ideas. Discussion techniques can aid creativity by allowing individuals to trigger ideas off each other. Brainstorming is one simple technique, but organizing groups for discussion or brainstorming ideas needs particular care. Pupils do not always discuss well without help.

Establish rules for brainstorming:

- Every suggestion is written down.
- Use words already on the sheet to spark off other ideas.
- No one's suggestion is discussed (initially).
- No one's suggestion is ignored or 'rubbished' (STEP 1993).

For younger secondary pupils an initial brainstorm of about five minutes is sufficient before the ideas are developed and explored further. Later, as pupils become more experienced, a more flexible approach may be possible. The techniques where students note ideas individually, then share them with a partner, then in a group of four and finally reporting to the whole group can work well; however, the agenda for discussion needs to be tight and the time kept short, especially if pupils are not used to this way of working.

Some teachers have found it valuable for pupils to work out their own rules for discussion work. It is clearly important to find out how much group discussion is already used in Design and Technology, and in other curriculum areas, before making a major organizational issue out of what might well be, for the pupils, a routine learning strategy. However, if little discussion work is used, and this is often the case in Design and Technology, taking it forward within an agreed framework in small steps is very desirable. (Group work techniques are discussed further in Chapter 13).

Some of the benefits that small group discussion can bring are as follows:

- It enables students to contribute their own ideas to less threatening scrutiny before exposing them to a wider audience.
- Pooling ideas can help half-formed opinions to develop.
- It helps the values of different experiences and cultural groups to be considered.

Some occasions where discussion might be useful include:

- product evaluation
- problem identification
- ideas generation
- sorting out roles for a batch production simulation
- exploring the values implicit in a technological solution.

Teaching individuals

Although pupils may share ideas, conduct investigations and brainstorm in groups, much of the detailed production of designs and the making of a product is commonly carried out on an individual basis. Teamwork is very important, particularly as it mirrors the way technology operates outside the school, but teachers always recognize the individual personal 'investment' pupils put into their work. Pupils gain an enormous sense of personal satisfaction when they feel that their project is worthwhile, but they may experience an equal degree of devastation and frustration when things go wrong. The key to success is the correct matching of a pupil to an appropriate task and ensuring that they have the necessary skills and knowledge to carry out what they want to do.

It may seem obvious, but a straightforward way to judge whether a particular design is too cautious or too ambitious for an individual is to talk to them about it! With experience, the matching will be more accurate, but even then a new group of pupils should be questioned about their ideas and plans.

The following are useful strategies when working with individuals:

- Visit each pupil while they are producing and evaluating designs to ensure they have thought through the implications of what they wish to do.
- Encourage pupils to be self-reliant and think for themselves. Do not do the work for them. Give them hints and ideas but encourage them to use planning techniques and design tools (such as image boards) to make their own decisions.
- Do not spend more time with pupils of one gender than the other; such action gives hidden messages of relative importance (see Riggs 1993). Catton reminds us that we often unwittingly have different expectations of boys and girls with respect to the design-and-make process, and that we should '[Praise] girls for good ideas and practical work as well as neat drawing work. Praise boys for neat drawing work as well as good ideas and practical work' (Catton 1985: 21).

Pupils will need individual help with making techniques and suggestions about procedures, especially when things go wrong. The practical advice which turns a disaster into a triumph is particularly welcome, but the need for such interventions can be reduced if attention is given to individuals when they select their intended design. Go through the plan with the pupil, sitting next to them rather than towering above them. Ensure that:

- their working drawing of what they intend to do is understandable by all involved, including you
- the plan is feasible in terms of materials, time and techniques which they possess or are likely to be able to learn in the available time
- it builds on previous work to ensure progress but is not too risky and likely to fail.

At the start of this section, I suggested that it was important to read about the different teaching techniques with the following points in mind: What will I as the teacher be doing? What will the pupils be doing? In what ways am I as a teacher conveying messages about this subject by how I teach it? The first question is important because, when planning to use a particular teaching technique, it is necessary to think through the implications of the strategy as well as the details for implementation. For example, when working with individuals on their designs, details such as the actual questions to ask, the appropriate standard of the working drawing required and the procedures to implement if anything is unsatisfactory need to be carefully considered. The implications of the chosen strategy also need to be covered. For example, what is the rest of the class doing while you are involved with an individual? Will the work hold their attention for the time needed? Can they help themselves if they get stuck? These details need to be explained to the whole class early in the lesson so that your discussion with an individual is not continually interrupted by simple management queries. In detailed planning both the teacher's work and the pupils' work need to be considered at times throughout the lesson.

The second question is also important. The way we choose to teach can often have 'value-added' spin-offs. As is clear from the introductory quotation, technological capability requires a sophisticated range of teaching and learning strategies. By choosing a range of techniques over the life of a project we are able to balance the contributory elements of technological education and teach not only the necessary knowledge and skills for practical outcomes, but also promote consideration of the relevant social, environmental and economic constraints.

Teaching for design and technology capability

Now I would like to leave the detailed discussion of the range of teaching strategies and the techniques one can employ in Design and Technology and consider *when* those techniques are most appropriate. In particular I want to talk about supporting pupils in doing their practical or project work.

The aim of encouraging pupils to become autonomous – able to plan, investigate and research aspects of their own project – has long been part of the rationale for design and technology education. It has been argued that project work is able to encourage people to 'create and do' rather than just 'know and understand' (see RSA 1984). Such capability is important in many aspects of life and particularly, it is argued, in industry and commerce. Central to the teaching of Design and Technology is the design-and-make assignment. A design-and-make assignment is a type of project work where:

- the exact outcome is unpredictable (although the framing of the task reduces the possible number of outcomes and the risk of failure and disappointment)
- the pupil takes responsibility for the conduct of the project as much as possible; it is based upon a need which the pupil can see and identify with, and is a 'real-life' situation.

There are some important differences, however, between what is manageable for a teacher with a large class of 12-year-olds compared with a small and self-selected group of older pupils. With younger pupils, assignments are usually chosen by the teacher to highlight aspects of the Programme of Study. The direction and outcome is more controlled than in the open-ended major projects typical of many GCSE schemes, so that skills and knowledge can be introduced progressively. One drawback is that greater control over the content and timing of what is taught reduces the autonomy of the learner, but the resultant controlled development of learning and successful management of the project development may be more beneficial. Clearly there is tension between the degree of prescription versus the degree of openness. The prior experience of the pupils, and your aims and objectives for the learning experience, will largely dictate your approach.

How are successful projects and related tasks organized?

Before considering the organization at a teacher-in-classroom level, the higher level of planning a 'scheme of work' (the collection of projects and associated activities) should be thought through by all the teachers involved. If learning in Design and Technology is to be meaningful, the work done must:

- be *differentiated* – able to be tackled at a number of levels so that individual pupils understand what is expected of them and the work makes appropriate demands
- build *progressively* on previous activities – a new project must offer new challenges which, at least at a general level, are supported by previous tasks; Design and Technology activities must not become a treadmill where pupils 'go through the motions' of a design process but learn few new skills or ideas
- be *relevant* to pupils – pupils must see the point of the project, particularly if it is more open-ended and steered by the enthusiasm of the individual.

Considerable overall planning is required to ensure that this happens in practice before the details of classroom planning and organization can be considered (see Owen-Jackson 2000, Chapter 9).

There is a 'chicken and egg' problem when teaching Design and Technology. Pupils may know what they want to do, but may not be able to realize their solution because they do not have the required knowledge or skills. More critically, when planning their work, pupils may not consider certain approaches to a problem because they are ignorant of the existence of equipment or a technique which might help them. For these pupils technological 'problem solving' is doing little more than applying their common sense. So what is the best approach? Should pupils learn skills in isolation, which might prove useful later but for which they perceive little immediate value? Should pupils learn skills 'as needed' within projects when they appreciate the usefulness of what they are learning but without a coherent structure, and without realizing that there was something new that they should know, to transfer to future work? The best approach is to steer a middle line. Provide a balance between a carefully planned selection of shorter projects or 'focused tasks' – to emphasize particular skills and techniques – and the longer, more open task – which allows pupils to develop technological capability by drawing on their accumulated experiences.

In these longer tasks, new skills and knowledge will have to be covered, just as the shorter tasks will need to be meaningful and situated in an appropriate context to make sense. Teaching skills for skills' sake – as sometimes happens when pupils have to move from teacher to teacher in a 'skills circus' – can be unsatisfactory as the point of the activity is lost on some.

The problem of balancing focused tasks and broader tasks was first recognized in the Nuffield Design and Technology Project which identified two sorts of task:

- Resource tasks, intended to help pupils acquire the knowledge, skills and values necessary for capability in Design and Technology. There are many types of resource task but all have a clear and definite teaching intention.
- Capability tasks, further divided into 'identified open tasks' where a pupil engages in a complete project which has been placed in a context created by the teacher, and 'spontaneous open tasks' where the complete Design and Technology task has been identified by the pupil.

The interplay between resource tasks and capability tasks enables Design and Technology capability to be developed progressively. If you set the context of the open task, the learning intentions remain clear. If pupils choose a project themselves, they may be more motivated to work independently and with interest but they may have insufficient knowledge and skill to complete it successfully. A teacher-decided project may be better suited to build progressively on the pupils' previous work, be more controlled in the materials and equipment needed to resource it, and easier to manage as part of a whole class's work, but pupils may not be so interested in what they have been asked to do. This issue assumes a great importance as pupils progress and are required to engage in more open project work, but the issue is still relevant in earlier stages. The careful introduction of the project is vital and ways in which the pupils can themselves identify a need to investigate and work on is important. Brainstorming work in small groups will help an individual identify a possible line of work, but a teacher's knowledge of a pupil's background and interests certainly smoothes the negotiation of a project which is worthwhile from everyone's point of view.

Organizing project work in the classroom

I use the word 'classroom' here generically to denote any space where design and technology education takes place. It has already been suggested that much of the strategic planning of project work could be done at a team or department level. What is left for you to organize? You will be responsible for the conduct of the project and the teaching and implementation of what many books refer to as the 'design process'. There are as many different interpretations and critics of this process as there are different definitions of technology! The criticisms centre on the simplistic use of process as a linear movement from 'identification of need' to 'ideas' to 'specification' to 'product' to 'evaluation of product'. People do not actually design like that. The design process is not linear but is a complex, iterative activity where new possible solutions and evaluations of current ideas continually circle back and permeate every part of the activity at every stage. The over-emphasis on particular aspects of the process, perhaps because of a need to give marks, can be unhelpful in the teaching of Design and Technology and leads to such distortions as pupils inventing 'initial ideas' after their design is finished! While accepting the shortcomings of the descriptors, many design-and-make projects will contain the following activities:

- Researching – finding out information from books, magazines etc.
- Investigating – experimenting with materials, processes etc.
- Specifying – stating clearly the criteria that the chosen solution has to meet
- Developing ideas that might make a contribution to the chosen solution
- Optimising ideas to formulate the details of a chosen solution
- Planning the making or manufacture of the chosen solution
- Making
- Evaluating.

(Barlex 1987: 18)

Your skill is to integrate these activities within the constraints of the materials and equipment available and the timetable restrictions. However, a well-planned scheme of work with a lively introduction, carefully prepared resources for skill enhancement and teacher inputs, and a good balance of activities will still produce disappointing results if there is insufficient attention given to the allocation of short-term targets within the long task. Crucially, there should be a clear purpose to *each* lesson. By helping pupils to know what they need to have accomplished by strategic points throughout the project, they can be guided to a successful outcome. This does not mean that all pupils should do exactly the same thing in a rigid, undifferentiated way, but you should be aware of the way pupils can get side-tracked by a particular facet of the work and lose sight of the whole task. Your role is to help by providing the targets and framework to guide them towards success. (The use and organization of project work is discussed in more detail in Chapter 14.)

Conclusion

The main message from this chapter and the previous one is that classroom management and classroom methods are closely intertwined. Good classroom teaching and good classroom management go hand in hand. This chapter has highlighted some teaching strategies which you may use; these need to be selected appropriately according to the work to be covered and the class to be taught. If you teach in an interesting way, catering for the aptitudes and motivation of your pupils, you will have the relaxed classroom atmosphere which enables you to handle people and equipment effectively. The best advice to people concerned about how to discipline pupils is, 'Make your lessons interesting and well organized'.

References

Banks, F. and Barlex, D. (1999) 'No one forgets a good teacher!' – What do 'good' technology teachers know?', *Journal of Design and Technology Education* 4(3): 223–9.

Barlex, D. (1987) 'Technology project work', *ET887/897, Units 5–6, Module 4, Teaching and Learning Technology in Schools*, Milton Keynes: Open University Press.

Brown, G.A. (1975) *Microteaching*, London: Methuen.

Brown, G.A. and Armstrong, R. (1984) 'Explaining and explanations', in E.C. Wragg (ed.) *Classroom Teaching Skills*, London: Croom Helm.

Catton, J. (1985) *Ways and Means: The Craft, Design and Technology Education of Girls*, York: Longmans for SCDC.

Cohen, L. and Manion, L. (1989) 'Questioning and Explaining', in *A Guide to Teaching Practice*, London: Routledge.

Denton, H. (1994) 'The role of group/team work in design and technology: some possibilities', in F. Banks (ed.) *Teaching Technology*, London: Routledge.

Gardner, H. (1983) *Frames of Mind*, New York: Basic Books.

Northern Ireland Curriculum Council (NICC) (1992) *Technology and Design Guidance Materials*, Belfast: NICC.

Owen-Jackson, G. (2000) *Learning to Teach Design and Technology in the Secondary School*, London: RoutledgeFalmer.

Riggs, A. (1994) 'Gender and technology education', in F. Banks (ed.) *Teaching Technology*, London: Routledge.

RSA (Royal Society for Arts) (1984) 'Manifesto of education for capability' *RSA Newsletter*, Spring.

STEP (1993) 'Card 47 – Brainstorming', in *Datafile for Key Stage 3*, Cambridge: Cambridge University Press.

9 Teaching and learning about design

Gwyneth Owen-Jackson

This chapter considers what is meant by 'design', the processes involved in designing and the issues involved in teaching and learning how to design. It is based on Technology Document 4, which was written by Robert McCormick and formed part of the OU PGCE in Design and Technology.

What is design?

The word 'design' is used in common language in a variety of ways, but two are of particular importance to design in schools. One way of using 'design' is as a pattern: for example, when we say that a fabric has a nice design. Another way is when we call a sketch of an object 'the design'. It is this second use of the word 'design' that is of most interest to teaching, namely design as an *activity* carried out by people such as architects, engineers, craft workers and textile designers. Despite the fact that they are all working in different ways and with different materials, objects and systems, they are all trying to create something by defining its form, structure, pattern or arrangement. All of these designers will be creating a new product, system or environment. These different creations lead to different kinds of design activity: for example, product design, systems design and environmental design. Of course, within each type there are many variations: for example, product design encompasses the contrasting areas of fashion design and engineering design. Fashion design will demand considerable creative flair with respect to patterns and forms compared to engineering design of an electric motor, which needs to be precise. However, both kinds of designer will need to have an understanding of materials and manufacturing processes. What is included in the 'design activity' for all of these kinds of designer depends upon what is being designed and, in particular, the relationship the designer has with the manufacturing process.

It is important to distinguish different kinds of design situations to see what is included in designing. For the craft potter, designing and making may be very closely linked. Ideas may be sketched, and card models may even be made if the potter is constructing an object, but it is likely that the design will be formulated and refined only during the making process. Architects, on the other hand, will finish their design activity with drawings or 3D scale models of the building they have designed; they will not work on even a prototype. The distinction of real importance, however, is whether or not the context is an industrial one. In product design, for example, designers relate to many other people (Figure 9.1), and invariably finish their design

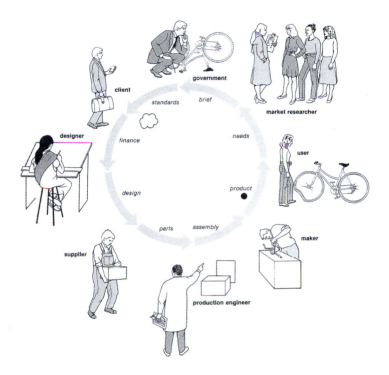

Figure 9.1 The product cycle

Source: Open University 1992: 47.

activity with drawings, 3D scale models or a prototype. A car body designer may make a full-size model of a motor car as the final step in checking the design, which would have been developed through other modelling techniques, such as sketches, formal drawings and computer images.

The distinctions of the different contexts in which designers work are not just of academic interest. For those teachers who were trained as craft teachers there is a great concern with making objects, with obtaining 'finish' and 'quality'. If what you want to teach is 'design', then the notions of finish and quality may be less important. Certainly, pupils must be able to realize their ideas and to see if they work, and in some circumstances that may mean making a prototype. The 'finish' on the proto- type may be important if, for example, it is necessary to judge the aesthetic qualities of the object, so these skills have some relevance to design. And it is, of course, quite reasonable to want pupils to be able to make things, but that is a separate aim from wanting them to be able to design. For the purposes of being able to design, all that is necessary is that pupils can model ideas appropriately to see if they are feasible. After all, the architect has probably never built a building in his or her life.

This does not deny that skill is required to produce clear and accurate drawings, whether by hand or by computer, and to carry out the various modelling techniques. When modelling is in three dimensions, some of the skills required will be identical to those needed in making – they merely serve a different purpose. It is this purpose that pupils need to be aware of.

Design and technology

An industrial setting for design brings up the need to consider the distinction between the words 'design' and 'technology'. Often they are used as a compound – Design and Technology, or Design Technology – as in the English and Welsh National Curriculums (in Northern Ireland, it is Technology and Design). However, it could be considered that there are aspects of technology that are not part of design: for example, the process of making stainless steel; and aspects of design that are not part of technology: for example, designing a logo or lettering. For practical purposes, design is better seen as a part of technology.

The compound 'design and technology' can be misleading, and represents a compromise to take in the design education lobby when the National Curriculum was initially being constructed (see McCormick 1993). It means that some design activities undertaken in schools are quite remote from technology, and leaves it to the teacher to make the necessary connections.

One of the arguments put forward as to why designing in all the different material areas in school is basically the same is that the activity of designing is the same in each case, whether designing a mechanical toy or a new food product. The 'activity of designing', in this sense, means the thinking processes that are involved. What is suggested is that designing a building, a fast-food product, an electric motor or a traffic-flow system requires the same basic process, and it is this process that we need to teach pupils. The assumption that the thinking processes are the same in each case ignores the interaction of such thinking processes with actions taken in the specific *contexts* of buildings, food products, motors, traffic etc. Whether you agree with this argument or not depends upon what you see as 'the design process'.

Models of the design process

There are several ways of representing the design process:

- as a linear sequence of stages, such as: identification of problem area, identification of control factors, specification, judgements and decisions, assessment of goal of achievement (Eggleston 1993)
- as a circular loop of phases, such as: detailing a problem, research, exploring possibilities, refining ideas, detailing a solution, planning the making, making, evaluation, detailing a problem, and so on (Schools Council 1975)
- as an interaction between thinking and action (Kimbell *et al.* 1991)
- as a process of exploring and defining the problem and the solution together (Cross 1982).

In looking at any diagrammatic model of the design process, you should ask yourself the following two questions:

1   What kinds of activities are being represented and what do the lines represent?
2   Is it all design, or are other processes included?

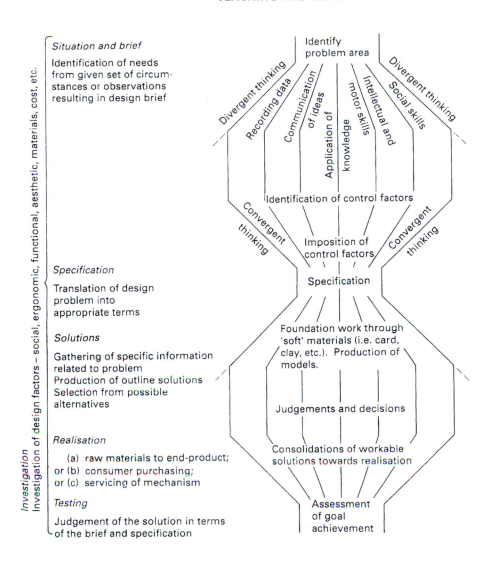

Figure 9.2 Design process: Design and Craft Education Project (from Design for Today)

Source: Eggleston 1993: 29.

Eggleston, for example, has two diagrams, one of the 'design process' and the other of the 'technology process'. The diagram of the design process (Figure 9.2) contains 'realization', which includes making and servicing. This model was taken from an early design and craft project, which may explain why it contains 'making' activities. Also, at the top of the diagram the lines are labelled to indicate 'thinking' and 'communication', but other lines refer to skills, such as 'recording data' and 'motor skills'. The diagram gives no indication that these lines continue to represent the same things throughout the process.

The technology process model shown in Figure 9.3 is one of those all-inclusive models that does not represent what a technologist does, but tries to show what the whole technological enterprise might be about. This model suffers from not being clear about what is being modelled. The core process – identify problem, propose solutions, implement and test – resembles the linear sequence of the design process in Figure 9. 2.

The model of design proposed by Kimbell *et al.* (1991) shown in Figure 9.4 tries to represent the relationship between the thinking and the realization of the design idea. This gives more insight into how design might be taught and learnt. In particular, it shows the interaction of the intellectual (reflective) processes and actions.

The sub-processes of design

Whatever way the process of design is represented, many of the models contain a number of sub-processes and these are variously described as:

- identifying a problem
- exploration or investigation
- specification
- creating or generating solutions
- evaluation.

These will now be considered in turn.

Identifying a problem

This process has two related elements: first, the identification of a context for a problem, which leads to the second, defining the problem clearly.

One design problem may arise from observation of the difficulty people have with opening jars of various kinds. The problem could be narrowed down to issues of grip and leverage and a variety of sizes and kinds of lids for jars. The 'problem' in this situation is relatively clear. However, if it had been a problem relating to, say, traffic congestion, the cause may be less clear. This problem would require further investigation, the subject of the next sub-process.

Exploration or investigation

Three kinds of investigation may be needed in a situation. First, if the requirements are ill-defined, as in the traffic congestion problem suggested above, then the investigation is part of the problem identification. Second, a thorough investigation of existing solutions and their shortcomings, including cost, should be undertaken. Such an investigation might include market research, if a commercial product is being considered. Third, factors which affect the solutions must be clarified, for example restrictions on size, cost, materials, manufacturing production methods. This kind of investigation also includes gathering knowledge, for example about possible materials, possible manufacturing methods, information about intended users and relevant legislation.

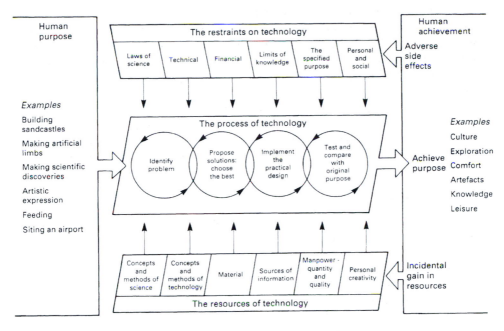

Figure 9.3 The process of technology: Project Technology

Source: Eggleston 1993: 30.

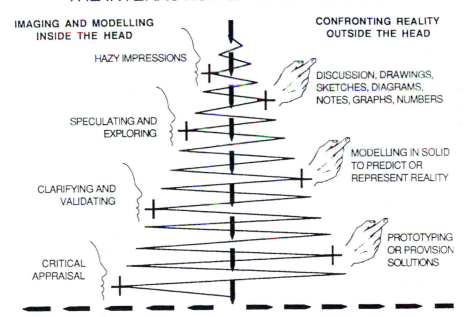

Figure 9.4 The Assessment of Performance Unit model of interaction between mind and hand

Source: Kimbell et al. 1991: 20.

These kinds of investigation should lead to a specification, the next sub-process. However, it is important not to see this as strictly linear, with the investigation occurring only at the initial stage. It is equally possible that suitable materials will not be defined at this stage but when the product is to be made (although in a manufacturing situation it is usually important that such decisions are made at an early stage).

Specification

This sub-process is crucial to all design but, unfortunately, is often not done well in schools. A specification defines the terms within which a solution will be acceptable: for example, cost, weight, finish. This brings together the clients' or customers' requirements, or the intended outcome if there are no customers, and the expertise of the designer. It provides the criteria against which evaluations of the design can be made.

Creating a solution

This involves generating various ideas for solutions, choosing a particular one, developing it into a practical solution and modelling it, for example, in a hand or computer drawing, scale model or spreadsheet. The concern to create a number of ideas helps to ensure that the designer doesn't get stuck in a particular groove. In practice, it is quite common for designers to focus on a particular idea and explore it, to gain a better understanding of the problem and possible solutions. However, they are usually prepared to abandon the idea later when it has served its purpose, something pupils are reluctant to do. With pupils, we usually insist upon a number of design ideas being explored to prevent them being too single-minded, but they often draw several ideas just to satisfy the teacher and only take their first idea seriously (see Hennessy and McCormick 1993, for a discussion of this). It is essential for pupils to understand why they are asked to produce alternatives and how they should evaluate each of them against the specification to choose appropriately.

Some descriptions of the design process (see Schools Council 1975) also include 'making' or 'producing the design' in the process of creating a solution. However, this making phase is not strictly part of design, unless it is seen specifically as making or producing a prototype or model. Without some kind of implementation of the design pupils cannot develop practical capability; they must be able to try out their ideas, and modelling – or building a prototype – fulfils that function.

Evaluation

Although the main emphasis for evaluation is often at the end of the process, this is not the only point at which it should take place. Indeed, it can be a starting point for the problem exploration, with pupils evaluating existing solutions as part of the investigation sub-process. Evaluation takes place throughout the process, and indeed constant refining and checking back to the problem or the specification are necessary. The basis for any evaluation is a comparison with the specification, once the problem has been explored and the specification arrived at. Modelling or developmental testing of prototypes may, of course, lead to modifications of the specification.

The point has already been made about not seeing the design process as a linear one, and the above sub-processes are not necessarily followed in a sequence. People think in a variety of ways and, while it is important to make sure that pupils are systematic about using the sub-processes, that should not mean a rigid follow-ing of a sequence. Cross (2001) has identified that the best designs come from those designers who work in a flexible way, but following some form of sequence or system, whilst the poorest work comes from those who are too rigid, or have no system at all. At the very least, pupils should be encouraged to start the design process from a variety of points. Thus, as suggested above, creating a new product could start from an evaluation of existing ones. From this, not only could ideas for new products be created, or modifications to existing ones, but a clear specification could be derived when the nature of the design problem has been clarified. In other words, the sub-processes can be undertaken interactively and perhaps even simul-taneously. Alternatively, it is possible to give a very clear specification to pupils and ask them to design a product based upon the specification. This is quite realistic, since manufacturers sometimes have a clear idea of the target market and the kind of product that would sell, along with knowledge of constraints of legislation, economy etc.

The holism of design

Following on from the above, however, some would argue that pupils starting to design from a specification is a denial of the holism of design – they would want to see all the sub-processes being undertaken in a design activity. The rationale for this kind of holism is to prevent pupils from being faced with tasks that are devoid of context, and from having to do a task, such as making a toy, without having first designed it. Although this has sound pedagogic sense, it can result in pupils being subjected to a treadmill of design-and-make activities where they always have to go through the same routine of defining the problem, investigating, creating solutions, making one and evaluating it. It can result in the same processes being undertaken but with no progression, because no time is given to developing pupils' skills at using the processes in increasingly more sophisticated ways. Thus, if you want pupils to be able to develop different methods of evaluation, such as user trips, formal tests of performance or surveys of use, then they must be systematically taught. This implies that tasks are set to emphasize, or focus on, evaluation.

Most schools teach using a mixture of holistic, design-and-make and focused tasks, with the last usually focused upon particular making skills or knowledge rather than the sub-processes of design. Before considering this further, however, let us first consider some of the issues in learning to design.

Learning to design

Design as problem-solving

The discussion above noted that not all design starts with 'a problem', and so some people do not see design as a form of problem-solving. Others, however, consider that as a general procedure is being employed to tackle design tasks it could be said to have a problem-solving approach. Hennessy and McCormick (2001) considered Design and Technology activity in terms of what the research literature had to say about problem-solving. They cast doubt on the idea of a general problem-solving capability that can be developed through activities such as those found in Design and Technology. They discussed several pedagogic implications, including allowing pupils to exercise the sub-processes and encouraging them to reflect on these, which teachers should bear in mind. Cross (2001), however, defends the place of design in education, stating:

> we can make a strong justification for design based on its development of per-
> sonal abilities in resolving ill-defined problems – which are quite different
> from the well-defined problems dealt with in other areas of the curriculum.
>
> (Cross 2001)

Pupils' and teachers' conceptions of tasks

Another implication arising from the work on problem-solving, and in particular from the work in Design and Technology activities done in school, is the importance of pupils and teachers sharing their understanding of what a task is about. The teacher may have a term's work in mind when setting a task but might not reveal it all at the beginning of the term, partly to prevent pupils becoming too 'outcome-focused'. The elements of the task may then be revealed as the weeks go by. For pupils, the conception of 'the task' will not necessarily be that of '*a task*' but rather a series of activities that are more or less connected, but which they cannot see the overall logic of or relationships between. For them, each lesson comes in a day where they have been doing several kinds of activities, in Mathematics, Science, History etc., and it may be separated from other Design and Technology lessons by several days, or even a week. Not only that, but the teacher may be evolving a view of the activity as pupils show what they can achieve.

Most teachers start off the lesson by giving pupils an overview of what they have to do, as well as giving specific instructions, and ask pupils if it is clear, or if they have any questions. This is to check the pupils' perceptions of the task, but teachers do this with a clear idea of where the pupils have come from and what comes next in the activity. Pupils will not necessarily have the same conception of the whole process, so some reflection may be necessary to clarify the task. Nevertheless, pupils will still interpret the task in a variety of ways.

Where a teacher wants pupils to be creative in thinking up ideas, for example, for kite designs, an individual pupil may see the task as 'to make a kite that will fly'. Thus, the pupil may see it as quite sensible to find a book that has a design he or she likes and copy it, whereas the teacher may see this as short-circuiting the intentions for creative thinking.

Similarly, a teacher may think it is important to produce a scale drawing of the kite, to encourage forward thinking about some of the details of construction and to allow a scale model to be built, but may not communicate this clearly to pupils. Some may then become frustrated about the purpose of the activity, and certainly will not see it in the wider context of the term's work. In addition, the difficulties that pupils may have with scale drawing, and the associated arithmetic, may transform the task to one of solving these particular mathematical problems, rather than being part of the task of designing their kite, which is the teacher's intention.

Teachers cannot always anticipate how pupils will interpret a task, but must try to spell out their own thinking to pupils, involve them in reflecting about the nature of the task, and check as much as possible what pupils are making of it. In particular, pupils' 'mistakes' may have to be seen as legitimate, if different, interpretations of the task.

Meaningful contexts

Another of the findings from the problem-solving literature discussed by Hennessy and McCormick (2001) is the importance of creating meaning in the problem-solving activity. Experts and novices alike use specific methods of solving problems that relate to familiar contexts. Trying to get pupils to use the sub-processes of design in some mechanical way in tasks that are not familiar (pupils do not usually design toys) can be counter-productive. Design and Technology teachers have long recognized the importance of pupils tackling problems that they have some stake in, or 'ownership of'. So they will ask pupils to design a toy for their younger brother or sister, or some child they know, but this may only help at a superficial level of motivation. It does not necessarily tackle the more difficult issue, of making their learning meaningful in the kinds of problems they regularly meet. The design of the toy will still be a school activity and will only have meaning if pupils realize that school is all about such activities and that, to succeed, it is necessary to suspend normal operation and do what the teacher says.

Pupils will never attain the commitment to the task that a toy designer, whose livelihood depends upon the design, will have. Creating this sense of meaning and reality is very difficult within the context of school Design and Technology. Any approach is, therefore, a compromise. One approach would be to construct within the school a company, or design consultancy, and relate the design task to a real, or at least a tangible, company. This was done by a school in Suffolk, who invited the local supermarket manager in to talk about a perceived gap in the savoury snack foods market. The Food Technology class was then set the task of developing new food products to meet this need, and the solutions generated were looked at by the supermarket manager. A similar idea is pupils designing and making costumes for the school play. The staff involved in producing the play could talk to the pupils about what is required and could be consulted by them throughout the process. This approach creates meaning in the activity, and a sense of involvement with a real customer. (Chapter 25 discusses ways in which the local community can be involved in Design and Technology projects.)

Another approach would be to spend time discussing with pupils possible situations and involving them in creating a suitable one: for example, their own needs for storage containers; these might range from storage for CDs to magazines or photographs to fishing tackle. The more involved pupils are with the context of the design, the more likely they are to work well to produce quality outcomes.

Teaching design thinking

This section will consider teaching design thinking through discussion of the sub-processes described earlier. The sub-process of identifying a problem has been referred to above, in relation to creating a meaningful context, and exploration or investigation is reasonably straightforward, so here we will concentrate on aspects which are more problematic.

Specifications

Pupils need to learn several things about specifications. First, they need to know what a specification is and why it is important. Second, they need to know how to create one. Third, they need to be able to work to one and, in particular, to be able to use it to evaluate a product. This order does not imply any sense of progression to these different aspects. As a teacher, you should plan activities bearing these different aspects in mind.

Creating a specification can be done in a variety of ways. Pupils can:

- individually define requirements
- collectively try to define requirements
- individually ask their own family what they would want and then, perhaps, pool their findings
- investigate a wide range of real users' requirements.

The method used will depend upon what the product is, and pupils' experience of the situation within which it has to be used, but it will also depend upon their experience of creating specifications. The list above shows progress from an egocentric view of the individual pupil to one which involves potentially a large number of other people. With familiar objects, such as sandwiches, young pupils can use simple market research methods to find out other people's tastes, even if only within the context of the school. The crucial point is to involve a customer or client, and where 'real' ones are not available, try to create one. A teacher can easily act as a customer giving out a considerable range of requirements that match the experience and achievement of the pupils. This is particularly important when the teacher wants to control the project so that it stays within the skills of the pupils, for example when making, and the resources of the school, for example the materials available. The teacher could, therefore, as a customer give a specification which states the materials to be used, and it is common practice for designers to base specifications on standard components or standard stock materials.

It is also important to control what is included in the specification. Thus, if you want to focus on social and environmental factors you can highlight them in the specification; for example, book supports could be designed for wheelchair-bound readers or textile items could be created using recycled materials, or off-cuts from other processes. (Environmental issues in design are discussed further in Chapter 22.) Similarly, if manufacturing techniques are important, specifications can be created with this in mind; for example, plastic items which need to be vacuum-formed could be required.

A critical feature will be the level of generality of the specification, in other words, the amount of detail that is given. For example, if a hat is to be designed the specification could say 'it must be visible' or 'it must be colourful'. Equally, if the hat is for a particular company, the specification might say 'it must be yellow'. Pupils are likely to move up and down the levels of specificity, sometimes making design decisions and sometimes simply putting general constraints on the product. It is a simple jump, in designing a hat, from 'it must fit a range of people' to 'it must be adjustable', but these are two different levels of specificity.

Teachers often create a specification at the beginning of a lesson for pupils to design a product: for example, drawing up a list of requirements for a storage container. They may not call this list a specification, nor be systematic in using it in the evaluation of the product. Teachers, therefore, should think through carefully when to introduce the specification, make correct reference to it, and ensure that it contains appropriate detail and is referred to during the designing and making stages, as well as at the end for a final evaluation.

Creating ideas

There are two inter-related meanings for creating within design: having ideas and bringing into being. They are inter-related because modelling provides a way of exploring a problem or situation *and* creating new ideas; indeed it has been suggested that modelling and testing of tentative solutions are crucial to the design process (see Owen-Jackson 2001).

One phase of having ideas must be creative, in the sense of not initially checking whether the ideas are feasible. This generation of ideas is thus unconstrained and divergent, leaving their evaluation until later. This speculation may not produce practical ideas but will encourage pupils to think about possible solutions, so it is important to give them opportunities to speculate, without the constraints of evaluation.

Brainstorming is one such opportunity, where pupils generate ideas without trying to see if they are feasible. The crucial element is a good climate where pupils can generate initial ideas without feeling that they will be criticized, even if their ideas seem silly. It may be appropriate to use artificial activities, such as getting pupils to think of as many uses for a paper clip, a house brick or a washing-up bottle as they can. It is important, however, that pupils are then encouraged to reflect on the process of idea-generation, rather than the outcomes. (See Owen-Jackson 2001 for further techniques for generating ideas.)

Modelling

In some ways, modelling is closely related to creating ideas. Indeed, one of the functions of modelling is to try out ideas by sketching (2D modelling) or by constructing (3D modelling). It is a common mistake to think that sketching is the designing phase and making is the implementation phase, when all the design problems have been solved. Some people prefer to model in three dimensions and, for some problems, it is essential. Certainly for younger children, 3D modelling helps them to explore and try out their ideas, as they are often not able to translate into 2D, or from 2D to 3D, when they come to the making stage.

Modelling has a second function, that of communicating design ideas to others. For example, when someone else has to make the product, a detailed technical drawing may be necessary. Architects have scale models built for their clients so that they can see what is being created, and approve it, before work commences. If a group is working on a project, drawings and sketches are a good way of ensuring that everybody in the group has the same vision of the design.

Two things are important in teaching modelling in schools: when are the modelling skills to be developed, and who are the pupils communicating with? If we focus on 2D skills, these can be developed either before they are needed, for example, with a basic graphics course, or they can be provided on a 'need to know' basis. The latter requires some kind of independent learning if the teacher is not to be continually tied down helping individual pupils with basic skills. One problem with this, though, is that pupils do not always know what they 'need to know', so the teacher will need to ensure that work is planned to cover what pupils will need to learn. It is also important to realize that skills take time to develop and need to be practised so time will have to be built in for this.

Putting pupils into teams is one way of encouraging modelling for communication purposes. The separate teams need to be set up in such a way that communication is a requirement: for example, they have to produce connected parts, or one team does the drawing and another does the 3D modelling. This, in turn, may mean specific instructions need to be given on how to use diagrams to communicate, for example, getting pupils to produce visual instructions on how to change a fuse in a plug, open a box or pack something in a special container.

Modelling not only allows a way of thinking through the design, and communicating it to others; it also provides a means of evaluating the design before it is manufactured.

Evaluation

Evaluation normally means assessing the quality of a design in meeting the specification once it has been completed. It can also refer to assessment *during* the process of design, when its purpose is to improve the design as it develops.

Product evaluation helps pupils to develop a critical view, and to develop their skills it is probably better to start with existing products, preferably everyday objects. Younger pupils can ask a series of straightforward questions in relation to the product:

- What is it for?
- How does it work?
- What are its good and bad points?

If pupils work in pairs or small groups they can do simple 'user trips', one pupil using the product as normal with others observing. This should stimulate sufficient ideas about how it works, and for good and bad points to be discussed. This could be extended as a homework activity, with family members using the same product and the pupil observing, which would also highlight different uses by people of different ages. Discussion of pupils' findings could lead to ideas about how the product might be improved. You might also want them to discuss whether the product should 'look good', to encourage a consideration of aesthetic criteria, and whether other countries have similar or different products to do the same job, to encourage an awareness of other cultures. Examples of products that could be evaluated in this way include lemon squeezers, writing instruments, calculators and scissors.

Pupils' development in evaluation techniques will lie in their ability to formalize the techniques. Quantitative measurements will be more difficult than qualitative judgements, and as pupils develop their scientific investigation skills they can employ them to test the performance of products. For example, lemon squeezers can be judged qualitatively by users for their ease of use, and this could be put on to a rating scale. In addition, the amount of juice obtained could be measured (although pupils would also need to know about the principle of 'fair testing' when the juice measured would be from different lemons).

Another aspect of pupils' development will be in their ability to deal with an increasing range of criteria, so this must be done alongside the development of the sub-process of developing specifications. Initially, pupils might be asked to consider a limited range of factors, such as those described above. Older pupils could be asked to think about additional factors, such as the materials used, the cost of the product, its reliability or maintenance issues.

Such evaluations allow pupils to develop techniques which they can then use on their own designs and products, and make them more critical and aware of everyday objects. They can also allow them to consider the social, cultural and environmental aspects of technology, if these are brought in to evaluation discussions. (The use of value judgements in design evaluation is discussed further in Chapter 20.) When using evaluation for pupils' own products, you will have to overcome their reluctance to criticize their own work, especially when they have invested considerable time in producing it. That is why it is beneficial to build up their evaluation skills through looking at the designs of others.

Central to any evaluation is the specification. For others' designs, pupils usually don't have access to this but have to imagine what it might have been. With their own designs, they should be encouraged to use the specification as the basis for their evaluation. This does not deny the fact that the specification may develop as the pupils come to understand the problem and how they have solved it. There is no harm in improving on the initial specification, but avoid introducing new elements, especially those which were simply forgotten at the inception!

It is common practice to have an evaluation session at the end of a project, where the whole class takes part in evaluating the various products. This is a useful way of involving pupils actively and giving them experience of a wide range of solutions and designs. However, it is important to avoid humiliating or embarrassing pupils, and focusing on modifications and improvements may be a way of encouraging constructive criticism. The aim is to create a balance between a lively and interesting session and serious and meaningful learning. What you will want to achieve is a state where pupils have internalized the need to evaluate as they go along, with constant reference to the specification.

Progression in design

The first important step in thinking about progression in pupils' performance is to identify the dimensions along which pupils can progress. The list of sub-processes described here gives a starting point but within each of these further dimensions can be identified. For example, in creating a specification there are several aspects: what a specification is, how to create a specification, using a specification (especially for evaluation).

What a specification is can be defined in terms of the number and range of criteria it contains, thus pupils will initially deal with a few criteria and progress to working with many. Similarly, they can deal initially with simple functional criteria and progress to working with more complex social and environmental ones. This need not be a linear progression, nor does it assume that only pupils who have reached a high level of achievement can deal with social and environmental criteria. Depending on their knowledge and understanding of the situation and the product, pupils may be able to cope with more or less simple or complex criteria.

The other sub-processes described are also made up of different aspects, for example identifying problems and defining them. Exploration and investigation involve defining requirements, investigating existing solutions and considering constraints. All of these can be done at simple or more complex levels. Creating ideas can be done in different formats, and using the specification when creating ideas. Modelling can be done in 2D or 3D, using different media and selecting an appropriate form of modelling for its intended purpose. Evaluating requires pupils to move from an egocentric view to considering the views of other users, varying the factors that they evaluate, using quantitative as well as qualitative judgements and selecting techniques appropriate to the product and purpose of the evaluation. (See Kimbell *et al.* 1996, Chapter 5, for a discussion on progression.)

Conclusion

Any attempt to spell out in a formal way the nature of designing, and how it should be taught, is fraught with dangers of over-formalization and artificiality. We know little about how experts and pupils carry out design processes and so we must remain cautious about our proposals for teaching it. A balance has to be struck between offering a structured and systematic approach that will help pupils in their experiences of designing, and allowing them to harness their creative and imaginative capabilities without giving any support.

These cautions mean that you have to be flexible in what you teach and in what you expect of pupils. There are likely to be considerable individual differences in styles of working, and your skill as a teacher will be to be sensitive to the individual styles and specific strengths of pupils. This will require you to employ a variety of strategies and approaches to meet their needs and to develop their capabilities to the fullest extent.

References

Cross, N. (1982) 'Designerly ways of knowing', in *Design Studies* 3(4): 221–7.

Cross, N. (2001) 'The nature and nurture of design ability', in G. Owen-Jackson (ed.) Teaching Design and Technology in Secondary Schools, London: RoutledgeFalmer.

Eggleston, J. (1993) 'What is design and technology education', in F. Banks (ed.) *Teaching Technology*, London: Routledge.

Hennessy, S. and McCormick, R. (2001) 'The general problem-solving process in technology education: myth or reality?', in G. Owen-Jackson (ed.) *Teaching Design and Technology in Secondary Schools*, London: RoutledgeFalmer. First published in F. Banks (ed.) (1994) *Teaching Technology*, London: Routledge.

Kimbell, R., Stables, K., Wheeler, T., Wosniak, A. and Kelly, V. (1991) *The Assessment of Performance in Design and Technology*, London: Schools Examination and Assessment Council.

Kimbell, R., Stables, K. and Green, R. (1996) *Understanding Practice in Design and Technology*, Buckingham: Open University Press.

McCormick, R. (2001) 'The coming of technology in England and Wales', in G. Owen-Jackson (ed.) *Teaching Design and Technology in Secondary Schools*, London: RoutledgeFalmer. First published in F. Banks (ed.) (1994) *Teaching Technology*, London: Routledge.

Owen-Jackson, G. (2001) *Developing Subject Knowledge in Design and Technology: Developing Planning and Communicating Ideas*, Stoke-on-Trent: Trentham Books.

Schools Council (1975) *Education through Design and Craft*, London: Edward Arnold.

10 ICT in Design and Technology
Gwyneth Owen-Jackson and Louise Davies

Information and communications technology is now being used across the school curriculum. In Design and Technology its use is particularly important because the subject should reflect industrial practice, which now relies on ICT for many different operations. This chapter discusses how ICT can be effectively integrated into Design and Technology teaching, and its impact on pupils' learning.

Introduction

The use of information and communications technology (ICT) is growing rapidly, and in the world of industry and manufacturing it is transforming the way that products are designed and made. If Design and Technology is to remain relevant and contemporary, then it is important that pupils are taught how ICT has transformed industry, and how they can make use of it when designing and making in the classroom. Many of the pupils that you teach will be familiar with computers and their many uses, and you will be expected to integrate ICT into your lessons to enhance pupil learning. Information technology is not a separate branch of Design and Technology, it is a tool which everyone can use to make learning more effective.

… It is important to remember, though, that you will have to make decisions about when it is appropriate to use ICT and when it is not. There may be times when ICT facilities and resources are available and you decide not to use them. This is as important as using them appropriately, as you have to decide which resources will best help the pupils to achieve the learning objectives that you have set. […]

Information and communications technology which may be used in design and technology includes:

- design software, 2D and 3D
- drawing and art packages
- graphics software
- CAD/CAM software
- databases
- spreadsheets
- word processors
- desk-top publishing
- systems and control software.

By using a variety of programs and applications, ICT can help improve teaching and learning by:

- aiding creativity in designing
- giving access to more information for research
- speeding up aspects of the making process
- improving the quality of work
- helping pupils to understand its business and industrial uses.

It is assumed in this chapter that you have some basic knowledge and understanding of computer use, that you can switch on and load a machine, use a mouse, run a program, save work to hard and floppy disc, word-process and print out work. If you are unsure about any of these then talk to your mentor, or the ICT technician, and ask to be shown. It also assumes that you have a basic working knowledge of databases, spreadsheets and word-processing.

Planning to use ICT

[…] Your planning will obviously depend on:

- how many computers there are in the department, or available for use elsewhere in the school
- where computers, or other ICT resources, are located
- whether computers are linked to other design and technology equipment, such as plotters, lathes, milling machines, sewing machines
- whether the computers are networked, or if they all operate independently
- whether any computers are linked to the internet; if so where are they and what are the procedures governing their use.

You will also need to find out what the pupils already know and can do using ICT. It is likely that you will have to take account of different levels of skills and abilities, but you should try to plan so that each pupil is able to make progress, both in their learning of design and technology and their use of ICT. It will be useful for you to look at any governing guidelines (for example, in England and Wales there are National Curriculum Programmes of Study for ICT), as these will help you to judge what is an appropriate level of expectation.

The following sections consider the various aspects of design and technology and how ICT could be incorporated to aid pupils' learning. […]

ICT and research

When pupils have been set a design brief, or have identified a problem or an opportunity for themselves, very often we then ask them to find out more about that particular situation. This can be done through research in textbooks and journals, surveys and practical investigations. It can also be enhanced through the use of ICT, for example searching for information on CD-ROMs or the internet. The internet, and email, can also be used for pupils to communicate with others; these may be other schools, companies or practitioners, who may be anywhere in the world. This direct contact would allow them to ask for information or advice, or ... to enter into discussion with others which will let them find out more about other contexts, other possible solutions, other values.

Databases can be used to search for information, and can be used by pupils to store their own information. CD-ROMs, which are examples of large databases, are available from commercial organisations. These may be general reference ones or encyclopedias, such as those produced by Dorling Kindersley, or they may be specific to areas of design and technology, such as those produced by the Technology Enhancement Project (TEP). It is also worth remembering to look at CD-ROMs produced for other curricular areas, such as science, art or personal and social education, as these may have sections that are relevant to design and technology. Commercially produced databases contain vast amounts of information, but these will have been structured in a particular way and you will need to become familiar with each one to discover the best way to access the information – for example, the particular words used in a search: does 'wholewheat' produce the same results as 'wholemeal'? Examples of using databases in design and technology include researching information on designers, the properties of materials, ... manufactured foods, ... components available to use in a printed circuit board. [...]

You may create a database yourself, for example of materials held in stock by the school. This could contain information about cost, uses and suggested alternatives and pupils could use it when selecting materials for their own work. A database could be compiled which contains diagrams of components, for example in electronics. Pupils could then look through the database for information about the components, their size, shape, uses and properties, before deciding which to incorporate into an electronic circuit being designed for a particular purpose.

Pupils can also construct their own databases to hold information which they have collected through surveys, questionnaires or practical investigations. This could then be used to help them produce graphs and charts, compare information and make decisions about their designs. Information from databases, their own or others, can be used by pupils to justify their decisions in planning and making, when evaluating and when writing reports.

When compiling your own database, or asking pupils to construct one, you need to take time to plan the work carefully. Guidance on compiling a database can be found in the booklet *Using Databases in Design and Technology* (DATA 1998).

A word of caution here about allowing pupils to use the internet, or databases, to gather information. Searching these resources for information is a skilled activity; pupils will need to know how to conduct a search, what questions to ask and how to ask them. They will need to be taught how to discriminate in the information that they find. Allowing pupils free access to these search facilities may lead to hours of 'surfing the net' without producing any worthwhile results, so as a teacher you need to guide them. Table 10.1 shows a number of ways in which you can do this, ranging from very structured guidance to more open access.

If the school has the facility to connect to the internet, then it will also be possible for you to communicate electronically. This will allow the pupils to communicate with other pupils, either in the same country or anywhere in the world. This facility can be useful when they are researching: for example, finding different bread recipes

Table 10.1 Using the internet in your teaching, from tight control to open use

Method	Advantage	Disadvantage
You find the information, print it off and copy it, hand it out.	You decide what the pupils see, there is no waiting at the computer and little cost.	The material is not designed for individual pupils. Pupils do not develop information-handling skills. It is less exciting for pupils.
You find the information and download it to your computer, edit it and hand it out.	The information can be matched to the needs of groups of pupils. You can create up-to-date teaching materials.	As above.
You download a website onto your computer system and give pupils access to it.	Pupils begin to learn how to access information for themselves. There are no on-line costs.	Pupils have limited access to the site and will not be able to make links to any other sites shown.
You create a limited list of websites and ensure that pupils only access these.	Pupils can begin to learn how to search available information. The sites are real.	Pupils' work is limited by the sites you select. There will be costs for on-line use of the internet.
You create a bigger list and allow pupils to choose which they access.	Pupils have greater freedom to conduct a search and have to make decisions.	As above.
Pupils are taught how to use a search engine and how to get the information they want.	Pupils can access a huge amount of information, can develop information-handling skills and have to make decisions.	You may need to 'police' some of their searching, to keep them on task and away from unsuitable sites. There will be costs for on-line internet use.

Source: Adapted from Davies, 1999

from different parts of the country or the world; finding out what kind of seating is used in different places; or discovering what kinds of fabrics clothes are made from. At the design stage, pupils can send their design ideas to other pupils from different cultures for them to comment on. Pupils can develop not only their design and technology knowledge and skills through this sort of activity, but also their interpersonal skills and their awareness of other cultures and values. […]

ICT and designing

Designs can be produced by pupils using computer-aided design (CAD), drawing, art or paint packages. The benefit of pupils using these are that their designs can easily be modified without endless redrawing or redrafting, and they can explore using different shapes, scales, proportions, colours and typefaces. Also, designs can often be more accurate and drawn to scale more easily, and they can be used to produce templates for the making process. These benefits encourage pupils to experiment more with their design ideas, and are especially helpful for pupils with poor drawing skills.

Some pupils, though, will find it just as difficult to sit in front of a blank screen and produce design ideas as they would to sit in front of a blank piece of paper. For these pupils, there are programs, called clip-art files, which contain designs and drawings which they can bring on to their computer screen to provide a starting point for their own design work.

Other ways of starting pupils off would be to give them an image on screen as a first step. This can be done through 'scanning' an image, a picture or photograph. This is similar to taking a photocopy but it is transferred straight on to the computer screen. Digital cameras can be used to take photographs which can then be transferred straight to the computer screen; video-clips can be digitized in the same way. All of these methods would produce an image on screen which pupils could then manipulate and modify to create their own designs. If you are not sure how to use these methods, the school ICT technician should be able to advise you.

Computer-aided designing offers pupils the opportunity not only to create an image, but also to develop a deeper understanding of the product and how it might be manufactured (Davies 1999). […]

ICT and modelling

'Modelling is a creative process at the heart of designing and making' (Davies 1999). It enables pupils to:

- try out their ideas to see if they will work
- think about ways in which their ideas can be improved
- visualize their ideas
- develop their ideas before making final decisions.

Modelling using ICT also offers pupils opportunities to analyse materials, procedures, structures and processes in order to gain a better conceptual understanding of what is happening.

Modelling is often taken to mean producing a three-dimensional 'mock-up' of the intended product. This still has its place in design and technology, but it can be expensive in terms of time and resources, and should only be used when appropriate. Other forms of modelling, using ICT, include producing 3D models on screen, producing simulations on screen and producing information which can be manipulated, for example in a spreadsheet. This could be part of the designing, researching or making process.

When designing, modelling could be done through producing a 3D diagram on the computer, to allow the pupil to 'see' their proposed solution. The model could then be modified, for example in scale, for the pupils to discover what would happen if they made different decisions about size, shape, structure, material. This type of modelling allows sophisticated 'what if ...' questions to be asked and answered, and can help pupils to develop high levels of analysis and understanding.

One particular type of program, a parametric design tool (PDT) can be used to analyse components and structures in space. This allows for the component parts of a design to be created on the computer screen and moved around to check that they fit together when the product is made. Modelling in this way saves pupils' time and school resources.

Modelling can also refer to the use of art or paint packages which allow pupils to look at their designs with different colourways, different lettering, different patterns. This modelling can contribute to the design decisions to be made, to the evaluation process and to the making process.

A spreadsheet is also a good modelling tool which allows pupils to see 'cause and effect'. For example, amendments can be made to ingredients in a food product and the effect on its nutritional value can be seen; or the material used for a product can be changed and the effect on its weight or cost can be seen. A spreadsheet could be used to design a manufacturing process, allowing pupils to manipulate it to find out how decisions about changes to the process, or changing the number of products made, would affect the time or cost of manufacture. This would give them an insight into industrial production processes.

With some software it is possible to link a spreadsheet to a drawing, or computer-aided design, and by animating the drawing, a chart or spreadsheet can be produced which models the way in which the design will work (Davies 1999). [...]

ICT and making

Traditionally, Design and Technology has involved pupils in making hand-made, one-off products, or small quantity batch-production. Where large-scale manufacturing is mentioned, the one-off product is referred to as a prototype, but pupils do not really get the opportunity to consider how the prototype would work in scaled-up production runs. With the introduction of ICT in the making process, pupils can be involved in producing products in larger quantities.

Computer-aided manufacturing (CAM) is often linked to CAD work. In the making process, computerised milling machines can be used to shape wood, metal or plastic, and they can be programmed to make products that pupils would be unlikely to be able to make by hand. Computers can aid in the engraving or etching of a printed circuit board. Computerized sewing machines can produce complex pieces of embroidery, direct from the computer design. These machines are reducing in price and more schools are finding that they are affordable and worth buying.

One of the advantages of using CAM is that it allows pupils to make a number of products to a more consistent quality than would be possible through the traditional hand-crafted methods of making. It helps them to understand commercial manufacturing processes and everyday products. It is not always necessary to have this equipment yourself. If the school has appropriate industrial links, it is possible to set up a situation where the pupils create a design on CAD/CAM software in the school, which is emailed to a linked manufacturing company who load it on to their CNC (computer numerically controlled) machine, manufacture the product and return it to the school. This is known as 'remote manufacturing'.

If you have limited access to specialist equipment it is still possible to produce good work with a computer and printer. Some printers or printer drivers allow images to be 'tiled'. This means that several sheets of A4 can be fixed together to produce large posters or patterns for making. Patterns produced on the computer can be printed out, laminated and stuck on to products to give a finish (Davies 1999).

Graphics and desk-top publishing programs can help pupils to produce packaging and promotional materials for products they have made. Desk-top publishing and word-processing programs can be used to produce instructional leaflets to accompany products.

There is a website which allows pupils to practise computer-aided designing; this is at http://www.dtonline.org Here they can use design tools and software to produce electronic circuits, nets for boxes and design work for use in textiles projects (Davies 1999).

ICT and evaluation and presentation

Evaluation work can take place at any point in a pupil's designing and making activities. It can involve testing materials, collecting results from user trials, making modifications to their designs, plans or products. Information and communication technology can be a useful aid to many of these processes: for example, conducting tests on the computer which would not be possible in real-time; recording results from tests and trials and analysing and manipulating them; using a spreadsheet to model changes to their ideas.

Pupils are often asked to produce reports describing the context of their work, outlining the work that they have done and evaluating it. Word processors can be used here to help pupils draft work and to edit it until they are satisfied. They can produce the report alongside the work and save it on the computer each week until their work is finished. Desk-top publishing packages and some word-processing programs would allow them to incorporate diagrams, tables and pictures into their report.

Presentations are one area that pupils often find difficult. Frequently they write what they are going to say on a piece of paper and hold it in front of themselves whilst reading it to the class. The use of ICT, from simple overhead projector transparencies to sophisticated multi-media presentation tools such as Powerpoint or Persuasion, would allow them to produce a presentation with tables, diagrams, models and pictures to support their text. Remember, though, that pretty presentation should not be taken as evidence of understanding or good quality work. Evaluation and presentation work should be read for content and for evidence that pupils' knowledge and understanding have progressed.

ICT and pupils' learning

The use of ICT should have an impact on pupils' learning. It is your job as a teacher, though, to assess what learning has taken place. This may mean that you need to reconsider the way in which you teach when using ICT. For example, when pupils are working at a computer screen you need to be able to see what they are doing in order to be able to judge the progress they are making. When pupils are working in groups or pairs at the computer, which is a common occurrence, you need to be able to judge how much each pupil is contributing and how they are interacting. If pupils are encouraged to save their work as it progresses, you will be able to see how pupils have arrived at their outcome, rather than just the outcome itself. This can be done even more easily if you ask pupils to print out their work as it progresses and annotate it to show their thinking. This will help you to judge if the pupil has understood the underlying principles and concepts involved in the process they have been through. It will be helpful if you have learning objectives and criteria relating to the design and technology work, and which are made clear to the pupils, to guide you in your assessment of their work.

Pupils themselves should be encouraged to evaluate the effectiveness of using ICT in their work. In your teaching encourage them to think about whether using the ICT resources made their work quicker, easier, more creative or of a better quality. Ask if it helped them to understand the knowledge, skills or processes involved in the work.

Using ICT can help you differentiate the work for pupils; for example, high-ability pupils may be moved more quickly through a program and be given more demanding tasks to do, whilst others may review sections of their work on several occasions.

Computers and other resources can help many pupils to take part in design and technology activities, where previously they would not have been able to, owing to physical or educational difficulties. For example, visually impaired pupils can use a computer program to produce designs in enlarged sizes. Pupils with poor manipulative skills can draw and design with more accuracy. Pupils with physical disabilities can use computers to help with designing and drawing; they can use computer-controlled machinery to help in the making of products, and their work need not suffer in quality.

Most, though not all, pupils are motivated to learn when using ICT, as learning can be made more interesting and more fun. You should always ask yourself, though, what is the purpose of this lesson, what are the pupils learning, and is using ICT the best way of bringing this about? Don't be afraid if the answer is no – ICT is a wonderful tool, but it cannot teach everything and sometimes other ways will promote your learning objectives more effectively.

The assessment of pupils' work, when they have used ICT, can be difficult. It is inappropriate to assess only the finished work as pupils may have made many changes along the way, all of which could be part of the learning process. Some points to consider are:

- listening to pupils while they are designing and making
- observing and responding to pupils while they are designing and making
- reflecting with pupils on the products during all stages of the designing and making
- involving pupils in the assessment and encouraging them to generate evidence which shows what they can do (Davies 1999).

Recording these types of assessments can be difficult. You may find it helpful to keep notes of questions or comments, or to annotate pupils' work as a reminder.

Assessing what pupils have achieved will mean being clear in your own mind about what you expect from the lesson, and what part ICT will play in this. You should be clear about particular outcomes that individual pupils may achieve. The following points may help you to think about these:

- How will access to ICT resources affect what you expect the pupils to produce? For example:
    — Do you expect them to produce more?
    — Do you expect them to work more quickly?
    — Do you expect them to produce work of a better quality, and what will that mean?
    — Do you expect them to show more understanding, make more decisions?
- How will you determine the achievement of individual pupils when they are working together? This may be done through observation, questioning, setting individual tasks, homework tasks, pupils keeping a log of their own work.
- What criteria will you use when assessing achievement? (For example, are these related to aspects of design and technology or are they related to ICT?)
- How will you ensure that you assess learning in design and technology rather than the availability and knowledge of ICT? (For example, it is relatively easy for a computer-literate pupil to produce a well-finished piece of work, word-processed and with graphics, but you will still need to assess it for content, understanding and suitability. Remember that some pupils will have access to high-quality computers and software and may be extremely computer-literate, but this should not overshadow the content of their work and the understanding and learning which it demonstrates (Davies 1999)).

[…] There are some things that you can do that will help to make assessment easier. The following offers some guidelines:

- Encourage pupils to save their work frequently so that they can explain its development more clearly.
- Talk to pupils about their work and listen to their views and opinions; this will help you in making judgements.
- Encourage pupils to review their own work so that they can justify decisions made and actions taken.
- Ask pupils to build up a portfolio of their work which will help you to follow the process and help them to evaluate their work.
- Annotate pupils' work to remind you of activities, comments or achievements that are not written down but which indicate progress or learning (Davies 1999).

As with all teaching, after teaching a lesson using ICT it will be useful for you to reflect on it and evaluate its effectiveness. Consider whether or not ICT was appropriate. Did it help in the achievement of the learning objectives? Did pupils understand some aspect of designing and making in a better way through using ICT? Was ICT work well integrated with other work? Be honest in your evaluation and consider whether the learning could have been improved through other methods, other software, other tasks. Improvement is always possible, and as ICT continues to develop it will be important to keep on reviewing your use of it, to keep up to date with software and equipment, in order to continue to provide good learning experiences for the pupils.

Classroom management issues

The management of ICT can often be very different from the management of a design and technology practical work area, yet in some ways they are very similar. Before working with ICT, as with other equipment, you should make sure that you know how the machines work and be able to use them proficiently. With ICT this means knowing where sockets and leads are, checking the software you intend to use, checking on any passwords that might be needed (if pupils have their own password, find out what to do if they have forgotten it), check any peripherals such as printers (which computer it is connected to; who supplies the paper), floppy disks (who keeps them – you or the pupils; where do you get new ones?). It is important to make sure that you know, and follow, any virus protection procedures that the school may have in place. Make sure that you know how to save pupils' work: is this to the hard disk, or will you need floppy disks? This is all preparation which will help you to feel more at ease with the teaching.

You also need to make sure that you are familiar with any health and safety regulations, and that you carry out a risk assessment, for example if the ICT equipment is located near dusty areas or water, as then you will need to take special precautions. All the equipment used will mean a variety of leads, plugs and wires; you need to make sure that these are not trailing or a danger to the pupils and that they are in good condition. Pupils should be able to work comfortably at the machine, so you should check desk and chair heights and that the lighting levels are sufficient. Before working with ICT, check the school and department policy on its safe use.

During the lesson you will need to consider where pupils are seated, which pupils are using ICT resources and which pupils are just watching, and how pupils are interacting. As with any other design and technology work, you have to try to manage each pupil's experience and activities and allow them to work to a level that meets their needs and from which they can make progress. This may mean planning differentiated activities, just as you would for any lesson. You may have basic tasks which you expect all pupils to complete, others which you expect most pupils to complete, and yet others which you know only the more able pupils will be able to do. However, it may be that when it comes to computer use the 'more able' pupils are not those you would normally expect and you should be prepared to respond to individual pupils. It is more difficult to do this with ICT as you cannot always 'see' what pupils are doing. You may have to listen to conversations, or ask questions, to check progress and understanding. […]

There may be occasions when you use whole-class teaching, for example to demonstrate a new piece of software to all pupils. You can do this either by using an ICT suite if the school has one, so that all computer screens can show what you are doing, or by connecting one computer to a large screen so that all pupils can see it. If you use this technique you will need to check that pupils have understood, by asking them questions or, better still, get them to use the software for a specific purpose.

Pupils should be encouraged to 'plan' what they are going to do on the computer: for example, if carrying out a search they should think through what key words might form their search; if they are designing, they should consider basic shapes and sizes, possibly even measurements; if writing up work, they should have notes from which to work. This planning and preparation on their part saves wasted time and helps them to realise that the computer is there to aid their learning and thinking, not to take it over!

If resources are insufficient for the whole class to work with ICT, you may need to plan activities that do not require its use but are an important and integrated part of the work. This may be done through rotating pupils through a number of activities, or by the pupils working in groups with each group undertaking a different activity. If this happens there should be sufficient suitable workspace for the variety of activities being undertaken. Also, remember to check that different pupils have access to ICT in different projects, and that it is not the same ones each time who use the equipment, as these are the ones who are most likely to be proficient already in its use.

Another way of making the management of resources easier is by putting limits on the design work that pupils do; for example, you may limit the size of their designs, or the number of colours or shapes that they can use. By doing this you can save time and storage space without any loss of effective teaching. […]

Summary

This chapter has suggested various ways in which ICT can be incorporated into the teaching of Design and Technology and some of the benefits which may result. We hope, however, that it is merely a starting point for you and that you will go on to explore for yourself the many other ways in which it can be, and is being, used. Remember, though, that you are a teacher of Design and Technology and that whenever you plan to use ICT it should result in some learning outcome which enhances pupils' learning or understanding of design and technology. It is as important for you to know when *not* to use ICT as it is to know when it is appropriate.

As with all areas of design and technology, ICT will continue to develop and change and it will be important for you to keep up to date with the equipment and resources available. You will be able to do this through contact with your professional organisation, through reading relevant journals, through becoming familiar with new software packages as they are produced and through practice, practice, practice.

References

Davies, L. (1999) 'ICT in the teaching of design and technology' in The Open University/Research Machines (1999) *Learning Schools Programme*, Buckingham: Open University Press.

Design and Technology Association (1998). Publications include: *Using Databases in Design and Technology; Using Drawing Packages in Design and Technology; Using DTP in Design and Technology; Using Spreadsheets in Design and Technology*, Wellesbourne: DATA.

Further reading

Bates, R. (1997) *Special Educational Needs: a Practical Guide to IT and Special Educational Needs*, Oxford: RM.
Qualifications and Curriculum Authority (1998) *Information Technology – a Scheme of Work for Key Stages 1 and 2*, London: QCA.

11 Taking risks as a feature of creativity in the teaching and learning of Design and Technology

Trevor Davies

Design and Technology is not a straightforward subject with easy answers – it requires pupils to make decisions and commit themselves to their decisions. They sometimes have to take risks when designing or when deciding which materials or processes to use. Teachers, too, take risks when selecting projects and when deciding when and how to support or 'push' individual pupils.

This chapter considers the nature of risk-taking, and its place in the teaching and learning of Design and Technology.

Introduction

The arguments for technological education as a specified component of the National Curriculum are at the vortex of change in schools.

> Technological education is the only subject in schools that has ever followed an experiential pedagogical philosophy – one that is in harmony with the natural and manufactured worlds and with the way societies adapt to their environments.
>
> (Hanson and Froelich 1994: 192)

Traditionally, in secondary schools, technology education has been associated with a craft paradigm linked to vocational determinants or to applied science. Here the purposes are clear, the skill and knowledge base easily definable. …

Currently, the demands are for greater transferability of knowledge and skills to work in different meaningful contexts, based on integrating cognitive and practical abilities.

The main concerns with design and technology problems are likely to hinge around the following questions:

- Will the outcomes work efficiently and safely?
- Can the job be done within cost and resource constraints?
- Will approval be given by the client and others likely to take an interest?

- Will it be beneficial? In the event of problems being encountered, what will be the nature and measure of failure and will losses be recouped? Over what term?

The commercial rewards for originality are huge for industry dealing with a sophisticated customer base such as those in western societies. This is always a requirement to deal with associated risks.

Since the inception of National Curriculum Technology, teachers have been subject to many influences with respect to how the subject should be taught. Many problems have resulted which have often been linked with shallow learning experiences and sometimes coupled with 'creativity'. In the current political climate, there is caution about how much freedom should be given to schools, teachers and learners to be creative. There are concerns that:

1 it might not show immediate gains in knowledge skill and understanding
2 valuable time might be wasted
3 creative success is difficult to measure and not subject to universal agreement.

It is argued by Richard Kimbell:

> that the dead weight of a national curriculum runs the risk of placing a dead weight on innovation – discouraging imaginative teachers and schools from developing their curricula with the consequence that pupils develop a narrow view of their world unrelated to their society.
>
> (Kimbell 1996: 99)

This is despite an economic imperative driving the recognition of the need for Design and Technology to be present in the curriculum. It is apparent that amongst industrial and commercial bodies that 'creativity and problem-solving are desirable qualities for citizens of the 21st Century' (Joyce *et al.* 1998: 113).

It is within this climate, against a backcloth of debate about the role of creativity in school Design and Technology that this article examines how teachers and their students deal with risk and uncertainty in the teaching and learning of Design and Technology.

Human responses to risk

In order for an individual to take risks, outcomes have to show potential benefit to the individual through identifiable gains. Risk thresholds are personal, resulting in 'high risk-taking' to 'risk aversion'. Facing risk implies emotional exposure and adrenaline flow and it is likely that responses will reflect the general capacities and tendencies of individuals to face, and cope rationally with, stress. Responses are also 'context-based' in that people are prepared to tolerate and actively manage different types and degrees of risk dependent upon the situation. Literature on risk indicates that responses to risk are frequently irrational, reflecting their multidimensional nature but Singleton and Hovden believe there is in general 'a close correlation between perception and behaviour' (1987).

... Knowledge and personality ... directly affect our response to risk-taking, which is always associated with the making of choices and decisions, which can change a course of events. This can include the option of not making a choice or decision, whenever a problem is presented to be solved.

Creativity and its contribution to design and technology

Children and creativity

Children begin their lives with a strong disposition to explore and develop an understanding of the world around them. Links are forged between the components of their understanding as it evolves and the desire to experiment and gain wide experience in divergent areas. Propositions concerning the nature of convergent and divergent thinking and their relationships to creativity emerged as a result of the work of Hudson, Torrance and Guildford. Guildford (1957) states that young children are largely locked into divergent thinking, which is essentially creativity-based. As world experience increases for children, so does the propensity for analytical thinking, as their depth of understanding of domains and fields increases. Based on this, Beetlestone (1998) refers to 'little' creativity, or creativity for all, which is particularly pertinent in classroom situations:

> In considering creativity it is important to establish that all children have equal rights to be creative and to have full access to opportunities within the creative areas of the curriculum.

> (Beetlestone 1998: 34)

She recognizes that creativity has cultural dimensions and that children do not all respond to creativity in the same way:

> We do not perceive that all children have equal gifts and indeed we may ascribe differences to perceived notions of ability, class, race, gender and able-bodiedness.

> (1998:34)

Creativity in classrooms

The opportunity for children to grow creatively in classrooms would appear to depend critically upon how support (scaffolding) is maximized through teachers, peers and parents. This is an area little researched and understood in design and technology, but defined and discussed generally by Vygotsky (1978), Gardner (1995), Rogoff (1990), and in specific classroom terms by Fryer (1996) and Beetlestone (1998).

Characteristics associated with creativity, particularly in the affective domain such as doggedness and singlemindedness, can result in disruptive classrooms. It has been known that particularly creative individuals are often very demanding of themselves and committed to their task. They are often 'difficult' individuals, sometimes surrounded by tragedy and often marginalized from 'ordinary' communities. Selfishness, intolerance and stubbornness are often present and there is an enjoyment of complexity and asynchrony which, if not present, is sought (Koestler 1964; Feldman *et al.* 1994). Teachers can find it difficult to sort out more random disruptive behaviour from that associated with children taking up creative challenges. If teachers are limited in their own creativity, what impact will this have on children? Given the often identified 'domain specific' nature of creativity, what relationships and values develop as a result of children's experience of creativity in the different subjects of the curriculum? Gardner clearly posits separate 'types' of creativity associated with each form of intelligence (Gardner 1995). […]

Educational writers such as Alexander *et al.* (1992), Beetlestone (1998) and Shallcross (1981), suggest that the ultimate endeavour of teachers, is to promote creative acts and release creative potential. They, however, recognize the levels of difficulty in achieving the conditions with respect to the characteristics of individual children, the domain within educational settings and the values associated with the field.

Creative designing

Creativity is a little used term in the field of design and technology education (although it is becoming more widely used) but problem-solving isn't. … Hilgard proposes two major approaches to addressing design problems through problem-solving and creativity:

> the first of these relates problem-solving to learning and thinking, as a type of higher mental process or 'cognitive' process. The second approach, supplementary rather than contradictory to the first, sees creative problem-solving as a manifestation of personality and looks for social and motivational determinants instead of (or in addition to) purely cognitive ones.
>
> (Hilgard 1959: 162)

Technological problems are human problems and involve taking risks to improve lifestyle and the general good of society. David Wann (1996) argues that all things in the natural world are interconnected: in framing a solution to a particular human problem, its impact on other systems must be considered in order to address matters such as pollution, erosion, congestion and stress. Design decisions in today's world should only be taken after full consideration of the impact on human beings. This implies consideration of people's values, beliefs, concerns and fears in addition to consideration of their cognitive, physical and emotional attributes. Fundamentally, the question always to be asked concerning any design problem is: 'Am/are I/we prepared to pay the costs?' The decision will depend on whether the gains are seen to be worthwhile and consistent with visions and hopes.

Creativity and risk-taking in Design and Technology classrooms

Design and Technology education is concerned with learners developing the skills, knowledge, understanding and attitudes associated with producing and using technological outcomes. To most learners, the effectiveness of their work is judged by the quality of the products they make whilst teachers are also concerned about development of the processes. Students are not exposed to the accountabilities of having products that customers depend upon. Failure is not likely to be catastrophic and no litigation is likely as a result of inappropriate product specifications. Indeed, most outcomes tend to be concrete or functional models. Additionally, this means that students do not share the motivating advantage of seeing their products usefully used, serving purposes. Their ability to appreciate the worth of taking risks is therefore limited to balance their investment of time and application of effort. This is particularly so if Design and Technology is not held in appropriately high esteem. […]

The role of 'significant others', particularly teachers and/or parents, … can make the critical difference between failure being a negative or positive learning experience.

The research context for examining risk-taking by teachers and students

The findings from my research into the contribution that creativity makes to design and technology education has established the need for more deliberation about risk assessment and risk management. The way that teachers work with students, their approach to the organization and delivery of the subject and the way students react to their situation has been investigated. A field study was set up with a girls' secondary school in a small town in the Home Counties. The methodology used was tailored to identifying creative acts associated with students' design and technology work, then to have in-depth, semi-structured interviews with teachers and students concerned. The personal construct theory of George Kelly (1955) informed the data-collection process which allowed me to gain access to the constructs (personal creations of meaning) of the respondents. From the data, it is possible to make causal connections between what the respondents understood and believed and the actions they were responsible for in teaching and learning situations.

The teachers were initially invited to select six products created by students that they thought were interesting. They were 3D in the main, occasionally 2D, but gave a focus for discussion about the processes that both students and teachers were involved in to produce the outcomes. Towards the end of the interview, two or three products were chosen as having an interesting aspect of creativity associated with the process of production. Each student 'owner' was subsequently interviewed about them. …

Interviews with two Design and Technology teachers … and three students are used to illustrate the findings from the research.

Risk-taking by teachers of Design and Technology

Institutional constraints affect the degree to which teachers are prepared to trust students and construct challenging tasks and contexts for them to work in. All of the teachers interviewed recognized fully the self-limitations that exist in design and technology teaching situations. They also felt the need to be self-critical about their professional effectiveness in order to enable learners to maximize their potential. All teachers perceived, however, that projects offering challenge were 'high risk' to support. This was because of their desire to ensure that students achieved success, which was their dominant concern, in order to produce a positive, engaging climate.

The major accountability influencing each teacher's role and approach includes encouraging students to opt for examination courses and subsequently succeeding in them. A direct implication of this need is encouraging students to value their experiences and make progress in line with course expectations. Teacher X recognized that in order to obtain the best from her students, she had to push them often beyond what they thought they were capable of achieving. Logistical constraints of curriculum organization and delivery often cause failure without any consequent opportunity to turn this into a learning experience, e.g. to run out of time on a project is always likely with often 'unfriendly deadlines'. She felt that the penalty she suffered was students blaming her for their failure and consequently becoming negative about the subject. 'Safe' work with students offers them tasks that are tightly constrained, in turn creating security. This approach precludes an experience of the motivating effects of success and recognition of progress beyond self-expectation:

Interviewer When girls come up with ideas of their own which they want to develop how do you deal with that?

Teacher X Well I usually say 'Is it possible to do this?' and then I talk through the various problems that might occur. I need to be convinced that they have thought through the issues and done the necessary research and will they be able to finish in time – the practical things. I think occasionally where someone has thought of a good idea, I want them to have a go at this and sometimes they don't quite finish, they are disappointed and I find it very difficult to make them feel better about the quality of the work that they have done – I feel I carry a lot of 'blame' for this then.

X understood how important her leadership and credibility were with students and the fragility of the trust they place in her. In a school culture which can mitigate against 'practical learning', she realized that her task was a difficult one. For personal success, she needed her students to gain rich rewards. She tried to value them as individuals and challenge them constantly but in a supportive framework that attempts to minimize the senses of 'loss' and 'fear' associated with failure. A way she tried to achieve this was to keep open 'two-way' lines of communication and to be closely involved with each individual's work from the ideas stage.

Teacher X … they don't want to fail. I had one girl who made a hair-band – she was Year 7 and doing the healthy heart project and it wasn't as good as she thought it would be and said 'I could do so much better now'. And she was quite disappointed with the result. But she thought it through and that was very rewarding for me because she had actually learnt so much and knew that she could do better. It was a disappointment for her, but we did talk it through and she was fine then. But you can learn a lot through failure.

X's overriding confidence in her work meant that she consciously tried to make progress with the difficult problems facing her. She sought to know more, see more and understand the cause–effect relationships that existed. ... She was conscious of managing risks with student values, attitudes and motivation.

Teacher Y found students' value systems difficult to deal with, particularly in the light of their frequent rejection of the subject at the end of Key Stage 3. She felt pressure from teaching a subject which the students compare, often unfavourably, with other subjects, due to value systems outside her control. She had to define the stages in her own teaching where she felt able to trust students to undertake different levels of open-ended activity, but questioned whether or not sufficient opportunity was created for student creativity. Her own judgements were based on maximizing the impact of her own teaching to account for the needs of each whole class, not the individuals within them:

Teacher Y   ... Where also the groups are smaller for design and technology – perhaps 15 and they can act more independently. At a lower level briefs will be set in such a way that they have to be more constrained in their responses.
... I just wonder whether we maximize our opportunities for creativity or not in the tasks that are set. At times it feels – this is quite a difficult one to put into words – but – it is whether we use the materials to best advantage with the children.

Failure in the student's eyes is construed to be a product that didn't work or did not look nice. Her planning and teaching were constructed on the basis of reducing the possibility of this occurring. [...]

Y's professional interpretation of her subject was such that creativity was an important element, for which her own and student motivation was crucial. She frequently stated the need to set up tasks and encourage students in ways that develop motivation. She felt that boys were more capable of creative activity than girls because they are more prepared to take risks.

Risk-taking by students

The response of students to their handling of risk appears to depend on what had been gained through prior experience. Examples of the responses from three students indicate comparative stances on risk-taking and links to environmental factors and influential relationships. For Student A, observations of the world about her resulted in an appreciation of the need for risk-taking and risk management. Her experiences, however, left her frustrated, and in some senses were the cause of what she perceived as her inability to reach her potential. This was, however, within the context of how she interpreted the objectives of design and technology as skill-based. She spoke confidently about the circumstances when she was prepared to take risks:

Student A I am quite prepared to take risks with some things. I think on the tie-dying as well, I didn't know – I had never – I didn't know how it was going to turn out – instead of the string, I thought if I used elastic bands it might be quicker. I didn't know whether it would turn out naff but it worked out alright.

Interviewer Yes, so that is one example – you said it wasn't much of a risk, but do you think that was a big risk for you as an individual?

Student A I think it could have gone wrong if the elastic band hadn't worked. I could have ended up with nothing.

The main inhibitor to following her inclination for risk-taking is her mark profile and concern for examination success.

B was used to thinking carefully about her projects, but not when they were closely prescribed. She, however, also enjoyed changing direction mid-project and the surprise element of unexpected success. Indeed, she associated this with the production of her best and most inventive work. Interestingly, she was the least positive about her best planned project which was food-based:

Student B I hated repeating the various bits to get the result I needed.

Being driven by a dislike of mistakes and failure, she was prepared to apply time and effort to ensure success. There was a sense in which she detected the anxiety of teachers who tried to ensure her success through offering solutions that she found unacceptable. She reacted negatively to this in response to the way in which she herself weighed up risks and planned her activities:

Student B I won't do what I think is just acceptable for the teacher. I like to try and go for what I think will be an interesting project. […]

In rejecting a teacher's advice, she was comfortable in using diplomacy skills with her teacher to achieve her objective even though she knew what the limits were. Whilst examination success was a factor in her thinking, it was not so pervasive as to prevent her from challenging a teacher's judgement. If she failed to persuade a teacher of the merits of an alternative approach, she rejected the worthwhileness of the project:

Student B If I think I am right I will argue the point with her. I will try and get out of following her instructions if I don't see the sense in them.

Interviewer Do you complain about the decisions, the way the teacher tries to control all of what you do?

Student B Sometimes, I try through reasoning and making other suggestions.

C was a risk manager and understood some of the basic requirements to avoid the pitfalls of failure in the subject. She recognized that attention to detail was important and that quality complex solutions to problems were difficult to create and, because of confidence limitations, tended to go for simple solutions:

Interviewer How much of a risk do you think you take when you make things out of clay and plastic and the other materials you use?

Student C I am not really very confident. I prefer it to be simple than hard and not turn out very well.

Originality is a highly fraught area which demands creative leaps which don't always work for her. From her observations of teachers and parents successfully predicting her potential to deliver outcomes, she recognized that she lacked some key analytical skills. Creative solutions demand inner confidence and she perceived, rightly or wrongly, that some of her peers were better at it than her. This resulted in a cautious approach with her preparation and when tackling innovative solutions to problems resulting from difficulties with affective factors. The responses she made to tasks usually left her satisfied due to the good levels of support and mentorship she received, which she positively acclaimed. She also expressed her enjoyment of surprise in the subject, which she claimed was important to her. Novelty value was sometimes added through surprise results.

Interviewer So tell me about product no. 3 then. What was novel about that – you told me about getting rid of the scratches and it surprised you. You used the word surprise – it surprised you. In what way?

Student C I was surprised that the scratches went so easily after filing and using the wet and dry paper on them. All of the scratches just went. They went with just an extra bit of work.

Interviewer And it was that which made you feel good about the project?

Student C Yes.

Sometimes when risks were taken successfully, they secured a pathway to a more difficult problem resulting in greater satisfaction and higher standards. Claiming ownership of a task and exercising responsibility appeared to be a major motivating force for risk-taking in certain situations.

Interviewer … if your teacher told you that it was important for you to get good marks for your work, would that affect how much of a risk you were prepared to take?

Student C Probably to a certain extent but I wouldn't do something really, really simple just for that. I would still take risks but not probably the biggest ones which I would take without that mark.

Interviewer If the teacher advised you not to do something because they thought it wasn't appropriate but you really wanted to have a go at something, what would you do?

Student C I would probably do it.

Interviewer You would still do it.

Student C Yes.

Risk-taking with the task was actively managed where products were being made for particular purposes or clients. C was very articulate about the measures she takes involving paper-planning and discussion to ensure a result that would be likely to succeed in meeting with approval. Sensitive support from mentors and the closely related clients, for whom she produced work, gave confidence to C. This enabled her to both experiment further and increase the sophistication of the procedures she was using, to generate high-quality responses.

Pride and enjoyment were often gained from success with simple skill-based tasks. Several students admitted low confidence levels and backing off high-risk strategies that contained a chance of failure. Where confidence levels were high, they were sufficiently confident to learn from failure. Some intellectualized the relationship between learning and failure, but did not feel strong enough to face real challenges for their ability. They satisfied themselves by minimizing risk working within the domain of 'personal creativity'.

Emergent issues

The professional qualities that teachers possess and their approaches to classroom management and learning are important in assessing and managing risks with teaching and learning. There is a need for teachers to recognize when and where students are required to take risks in their learning, and the impact that failure might have on their attitudes, values and dispositions. Risks with relationships, both inside and outside classrooms, can often influence student behaviour and response linked to their progress and attainment. This emphasizes the importance of developing a classroom climate in which risks in the following categories are exposed and faced:

Teachers' professional qualities

- lack of personal skill and aptitude designing and/or making will randomize and not rationalize students' exposure to risk in their learning
- values form the baseline for working – but whose values? If the teacher promotes a narrow system of social or subject-based values, they can induce hostility and promote rejective stances amongst students.

Student needs

- low levels of capability in the core skills of literacy and communication can prevent a student from asking questions, enlisting support from others and developing a well thought-through solution to a problem
- individual learners require responses to their own difficulties and problems which reflect both their knowledge and feelings
- recognition of success and giving constructive, measured feedback to learners is important to enable students to develop risk management strategies
- inability to achieve personal expectations can lead to frustration and a feeling of helplessness
- lack of success over time with the range of tasks and activities can be accumulatively damaging to student motivation.

Teaching approaches

- avoidance of decision-making is often perceived to be the easiest response to a dilemma but the one that can lead to the least effective solution
- if teachers choose to make decisions on behalf of a student, they might not necessarily act in a student's best interests overall. If teachers and learners share the risks associated with the learning process, better quality learning is likely to be achieved.

Teachers' expectations

- rich, varied contexts and appropriate expectations of performance can promote interest, ownership and appropriate risk-taking
- teachers sometimes misconstrue or ignore the prior learning and experience of students
- teachers feel that there are likely to be differences in the dispositions and responses of boys and girls towards risk-taking.

Curriculum structure

- a fragmented curriculum structure can reduce motivation levels
- the requirement to complete a project within the boundaries of time and materials which exist in schools can be very limiting. Even though rich progress might have been made, the learner who does not have a polished outcome to show for their endeavour might still perceive failure
- inability to match product quality to initial ideas in either function, form, or both, can lead to frustration and rejection.

Relationships

- loss of face with peers, which may be covered-up by a 'don't care' attitude, leaves an emotional scar and negative attitude if not attended to and faced through a teacher/learner relationship
- loss of face with teachers. Whilst students usually work hard to satisfy a teacher's expectations, they would not do so at the expense of going against the peer-group culture which might be 'anti-learning'. Students will do enough to get by without becoming a 'swot'
- group work placing expectations on individuals. Whilst offering the opportunity to share risk-taking, the exercise of control by one student can limit achievement for others according to the nature of the social hierarchies operating.

Conclusion

A life without adventure is likely to be unsatisfying, but a life in which adventure is allowed to take whatever form it will, is likely to be short.

Bertrand Russell (quoted in MacCrimmon and Wehrung 1986: 3)

Whenever choices are made about paths to follow in any human endeavour, judgements are required and risks are incurred. It is likely that some paths will lead to short- term benefits, others longer-term. The benefits of success are balanced by the impact of failure through any decisions taken. Creative work when designing and making is likely to bring about novel, or different, knowledge which will incur risk-taking through 'exposure to loss, the chance of loss (a sure loss is not a risk) and will require consideration of the likely magnitude of any losses' (MacCrimmon and Wehrung 1986: 9).

It is up to every educationalist with an interest in design and technology to weigh up the costs and benefits for themselves and reach considered views.

References

Alexander, R., Rose, J. and Woodhead, C. (1992) *Curriculum Organization and Classroom Practice – A Discussion Paper*, London: Des.

Beetlestone, F. (1998) *Creative Children, Imaginative Teaching*, Buckingham: Open University Press.

Feldman, D., Csikzentmihalyi, M. and Gardner, H. (1994) *Changing the World: A Framework for the Study of Creativity*, USA: Praeger Publishers.

Fryer, M. (1996) *Creative Teaching and Learning*, London: Paul Chapman Publishing.

Gardner, H. (1983) *Multiple Intelligences: The Theory in Practice*, NY: Basic Books.

Gardner, H. (1995) 'Creativity: new views from psychology and education', *RSA Journal*, May.

Guildford, J. (1957) 'Creative abilities in the arts', *Psychological Review* 64: 110–18.

Hansen, R. and Froelich, M. (1994) 'Defining technology and technological education: a crisis or cause for celebration', *International Journal of Technology and Design Education* 4: 179–207.

Hilgard, E. (1959) 'Creativity and problem-solving', in H.H. Anderson (ed.) *Creativity and its Cultivation*, USA: Haarer Professional and Technical Library.

Joyce, M., Franklin, K., Neale, P., Kyffin, S. and Veronesi, B. (1998) 'What stimulates the creative process?', *Journal of Design and Technology Education* 3(2): 113–16.

Kelly, G. (1955) *A Theory of Personality*, NY: The Norton Library.

Kimbell, R. (1996) 'The role of the state in your classroom', *Journal of Design and Technology Education* 1(2): 99–100.

Koestler, A. (1964) *The Act of Creation*, London: Pan Books Ltd.

Krimsky, S. and Golding, D. (1992) *Social Theories of Risk*, Westport: Praeger.

MacCrimmon, K. and Wehrung, D. with Stanbur, W. (1986) *Taking Risks*, USA: The Free Press.

Singleton, W. and Hovden, J. (1987) *Risk and Decisions*, London: John Wiley and Sons Ltd.

Shallcross, D. (1981) *Teaching Creative Behaviour*, Buffalo, NY: Prentice Hall.

Rogoff, B. (1990) *Apprenticeship in Thinking*, NY: Oxford University Press.

Vygotsky, L.S. (1978) *Mind in Society*, Cambridge: Harvard University Press.

Wann, D. (1996) *Deep Design: Pathways to a Liveable Future*, Washington: Island Press.

12 Managing problem-solving in the context of design-and-make activities
Reflections on classroom practice
Jim Newcomb

This chapter describes a project, set in a primary school, which was intended to help teachers and pupils to develop a better understanding of the 'design-and-make' process and how practical problem-solving might be managed to secure effective results in the pupils' work. The project was carried out with pupils who had little experience of designing and making, or of the resistant materials used. Although based in a primary school, this chapter describes issues relevant to the lower secondary school.

Introduction

Defining 'problem-solving' is problematic and this article does not intend to belabour this issue. Rather, along with the suggestion of Fisher (1987) below, I would like to focus upon what it usually involves, in the context of design and technological activity, and how teachers can best support the development of pupils' associated knowledge, understanding and skills. In broad terms then:

> What problem solving involves is thinking and doing, or acting for some purpose. It is a way through which we can learn, practise and demonstrate essential thinking skills and knowledge.

These thinking skills include, for Fisher, creative aspects (seen to be associated with areas of performance such as: the consideration of a range of possibilities, being prepared to look at a situation in different ways etc.); critical or analytical aspects (for example, a willingness to reflect on experience, to explore the consequences of preferences, to value time etc.) and strategies such as observing, designing, decision-making and team-working.

However, whilst aspects of performance and associated benefits may both be identifiable and appreciated, they need to be considered in the context of understanding the need for both general and subject-specific problem-solving strategies to be effectively taught. As Bransford and Stein (1993) suggest, our ability to solve problems is not simply equivalent to a set of general problem-solving skills but often depends upon specialized knowledge in a discipline. Indeed, effective problem-solvers utilize a great deal of specialist knowledge and skills that allow them to understand why, how and when to apply specific strategies.

In this case study, for example, it was hoped that the use of three-dimensional modelling, judged to be an effective strategy for initially exploring the first task that the children were set, would help to signpost both 'how' to go about such a task (procedural knowledge) and 'when and why' the strategy was appropriate (conditional knowledge).

A number of authors – Meadows (1993), Hennessy and McCormick (1994), Stephenson (1997) – have stressed the importance of supporting the development of children's procedural abilities which can be seen as a means of aiding them as 'novices' toward more 'expert' forms of practice. Indeed, reference to the analysis of problems into a sequence of appropriate sub-problems (tasks), and the need to teach such problem-solving strategies in contexts where they are useful, is seen as critical to the development of 'capability'. As Hennessy and McCormick (1994) stress:

> Design-and-make activities that always include an holistic process, with little or no focus on particular sub-processes (such as generating design ideas) are likely to make it difficult for pupils to build up their understanding and skills at using such processes.

What knowledge and skills, then, are important? Though there is no intention here to undervalue the important interplay that exists between different forms of knowledge and skill, the focus for this article will be on procedural knowledge and skills. The 'knowing how' rather than the 'knowing that'; developing children's understanding of the ways and means by which they can, for example, explore problems, generate and communicate ideas through a range of modelling strategies and plan effectively etc. In short, the thinking behind the doing!

Children's first task, when presented with a practical problem to solve, will be to understand the problem, to clarify intended goals and to recognize how best to get started and to develop their proposed solution(s). Teachers have a responsibility to assist pupils in this endeavour, and this will require them to:

- help pupils to recognize how a global problem might be broken down into more manageable steps
- help them focus on aspects that are significant, but may not always be obvious
- help them to develop a wide range of communication and modelling strategies from which, in time, they can choose efficiently.

Bearing these points in mind, the intention of the approach taken in this case study was one of attempting to provide these essential 'clues' by, on this occasion:

- guiding the children through a number of related sub-tasks rather than leaving them, as novices, to tackle a global problem – the design and manufacture of a coal cart – by themselves
- introducing them to a range of communication and modelling techniques, to increase the range with which they were familiar

- offering focused practical tasks to develop related, subject-specific, knowledge and skills.

As Rogoff (1989) suggests, by structuring learning activities in this way children can be helped to focus on 'manageable' aspects of a task through which they can extend current knowledge and skills to a higher level. Indeed, if the development of knowledge and skill is seen to involve the discovery of what is best paid attention to, borne in mind and acted upon, in an appropriate goal-achieving sequence, then the suggestion here is that teachers must take responsibility for developing in children appropriate strategies for doing just that.

The focus here was to help the pupils toward being able to operate more as 'experts' might. In line with Kimbell *et al.* (1996) the project was seen to be assisting the pupils in the skills of 'self-management' by their learning to take greater responsibility for the efficient progress of a project. However, I also recognize that, over time, the degree of guidance must be gradually reduced to facilitate the children's growing confidence in their decisions and actions. ... At this stage, the aim was not to simplify the tasks to be undertaken by the pupils but to simplify their roles. That is, to 'scaffold' their involvement by structuring a series of steps toward their eventual goal, whilst encouraging and extending their current levels of knowledge and skills in tasks which continued to offer appropriate levels of challenge.

Summary

The interim conclusions which can be drawn from the discussion so far are:

- it is vitally important for teachers to consider that practical problems, inherent to design-and-make activities, may need to be appropriately broken down into manageable sub-tasks to aid effective teaching and learning
- that in so doing, teachers and children can come to better understand how best to use elements of task-associated conceptual and, in particular, procedural knowledge and skills. For example, developing the ability to choose the most efficient means of communicating and generating ideas
- that over time, children can be moved toward more expert levels of performance requiring greater responsibility for the decisions and actions they make and take.

Description of project

The project, stemming from work in history, required pupils, working eventually in teams of three, to design and make a coal cart. Here, the global problem was broken down into three inter-related areas:

- the design and manufacture of the cart's **container**
- the design and manufacture of an associated **chassis**
- the design and manufacture of a suitable **wheel and axle assembly**.

In structuring the project in this way it was felt that the pupils would be sign-posted to the essential features of each task and helped to recognize that the means of communication and modelling ideas can be varied to suit the task in hand.

Introduction

The class (30 Year 6 pupils) was initially divided into five mixed-gender teams of six pupils, reflecting the normal ability groupings for the class. As such, they were used to working together. It was stressed that the progress of their work, and a successful conclusion to the project, depended much upon them being able to organize themselves effectively and to be willing to take as much responsibility for their decisions and actions as possible. [...]

Most of the work was carried out within the classroom, with all the children working at the same time. A small number of children ... also used a workspace in the adjacent corridor, where glue guns were based.

In the main, children used square section timber, doweling, MDF wheels, card, paper and assorted found materials, together with a limited range of associated hand tools and equipment.

An on-going display of all elements of the children's work was regularly updated by the class teacher, vital to the children recognizing the value of both the process and the product.

A brief description of the work is provided below.

Week 1

- The project began with a whole-class discussion about the general nature of child labour during the Victorian era, building upon previous experiences undertaken during topic work.
- Three A3 photocopies of mining trucks were then used to stimulate discussion about the way in which the vehicles were hauled, the materials from which they had been manufactured and the difficulties associated with pulling them through the darkness of the mine.
- At this point, the children were introduced to the materials from which their own trucks were to be made and asked to think about which they might prefer to use and why.
- The children were then given their first problem-solving task, the design and manufacture of a suitable container for the coal truck. This centred on three-dimensional modelling in card. In order to constrain the overall size of these models the pupils had to produce a container that would hold a set amount of dried peas (used to represent a quantity of coal) displayed in 250g coffee jars.
- The pupils, seated in their groups of six, began by working individually to produce paper nets ... based on their estimation of the required shape and size of a suitable container. Completed models were temporarily sellotaped to allow them to be tested by emptying the contents of the coffee jar into them. This encouraged all pupils to modify initial ideas and to work towards an 'optimum' solution in a meaningful way.

- They were also encouraged to add brief notes to ideas which did or did not meet the criteria, thereby suggesting a reason for a solution's rejection or selection.

Week 2

- At this stage the groups were divided to allow teams of three to continue with the project.
- Their first task was to select one of their individual models to act as a template for the next stage of the work. They were then asked to carefully unstick the paper model and transfer the design onto grey card to produce as accurate a model as possible.
- They were then asked as individuals to produce a sketch of this model in both two and three dimensions. This work followed a short blackboard introduction to rudimentary elements of orthographic projection (front and side elevations) and isometric drawing, using an underlay and the classroom windows as a 'light box'.
- Each individual had then to decide how to enhance these drawings by adding suitable surface details in order to develop the design into a more lifelike representation of a coal cart.
- On the plan and end views pupils were free to draw around actual pieces of material, for example, square section timber or lollipop sticks, to achieve an accurate result. Samples of the materials chosen were also stuck onto their design sheets as a simple form of 'planning'.
- The three-dimensional view of their design was similarly enhanced.
- Each trio was then asked to make a further choice by selecting what they believed to be the most appropriate design within their group. Having done this, the teams began to measure, mark, cut and fix their resistant materials to the card model in order to complete the coal cart container.

Week 3

- This was a practical session, including relevant focused practical tasks, during which the children, working in their groups of three, concentrated on enhancing their card models to make them look as realistic as possible. The children were encouraged to make regular references to their design drawings and planning work and to discuss any changes that they made along the way, giving reasons for their choices/decisions.
- During the session pupils cut and fixed lengths of square section timber (10mm and 8mm), doweling (5mm) and lollipop sticks. With additional support they also manufactured their own simple cutting jigs.
- During this time a number of groups found opportunities to further enhance their ideas by the inclusion of additional detail, often based upon prior experiences. For example, containers were manufactured to allow one of the sides to open and close. This required a simple hinge and locking mechanism to be made that was based upon simple systems employed on, for example, tip-up trucks. As such, 'differentiation' was clearly exhibited by outcome.

Figure 12.1 Example of completed model

Week 4

- Having completed their container sections, attention was turned to the design and production of a suitable wheeled chassis to which the container could be fixed. This included the design and manufacture of a simple wheel and axle assembly.
- The pupils were first introduced to the Jink's method of frame construction and asked to think about appropriate dimensions for their own chassis – taking into account the size and shape of their container, and the most appropriate materials for the task.
- Time was also spent, during both whole-class and group demonstrations, considering ways in which the children might manufacture realistic wheels for their carts to enable them to run along a short length of track that the groups were to make.
- During this part of the project the pupils designed through discussion and direct manipulation of materials. They did not draw and/or model their suggestions in three dimensions.

Week 5

- Pupils concentrated on making a simple length of track from square section timber. On the surface this seemed to be a very straightforward task. In reality it proved to be more difficult than I had expected. Essentially the children had to decide upon a suitable gauge for the track, working from the dimensions of their own trucks, and construct the necessary sleepers and lengths of rail. Complications set in when the pupils confronted the necessity of keeping the rails parallel to facilitate the efficient running of their carts. A number of modifications were required before all was well.

Week 6

- Whilst the pupils had been evaluating throughout their work, they also undertook an end evaluation of both process and product, first as part of a whole-class, group-based discussion, and then individually. It was clear from the group feedback that, with one or two exceptions, the children had really enjoyed the chance of working as part of a team and that they were very pleased with the results obtained. Generally, they expressed the view that they had relished the opportunities provided for them to take responsibility for their own progress and, within the parameters set, of organizing their own actions.

Week 7

- At the end of the project, and under the direction of their class teacher, each group was encouraged to display their work in a life-like, three-dimensional dioramic setting (Figure 12.1). This additional responsibility for displaying the final product helped to maintain the sense of ownership that children had developed for their work.

Conclusion

The development of pupils as capable designers and technologists will, in large part, be associated with a willingness on the part of teachers to provide them, in an appropriately progressive manner, with greater opportunities to explore a problem and develop suitable solutions with the minimum of teacher intervention. However, to support this aim it will be necessary, at certain times, to take appropriate control of pupils' oversight of the process by structuring their work into more manageable sub-tasks. In this manner, they can be encouraged to work in a methodical way, interacting with and coming to value important sub-elements of the process, thereby developing associated conceptual and, most importantly, procedural and conditional knowledge and skills.

This does not mean that work should be overly teacher-directed. Rather, each task should provide sufficient challenge to both motivate the children and inculcate the new knowledge and skills that the teacher deems necessary for effective progression to take place.

In all of this it is essential that the children are aware from the outset of the ultimate goal of any particular design-and-make activity and that they are able to see how sub-tasks fit into the overall structure and development of their work. Moreover, it is crucial that teachers are aware of, and plan effectively for, the knowledge and skills that should be developed to help children to progressively extend the repertoire available to them.

In this case study the children were told at the beginning that they would be designing and making a model coal cart and that it would consist of a number of parts that would need to fit accurately together: these being the **container**, **chassis** and **wheel and axle assembly**. This helped to focus their attention from the outset and provided a clear and single goal for all groups to work towards. Moreover, it provided guidance from which the pupils could begin to perceive a framework or structure for tackling design-and-make activities in a competent manner.

Here, I was attempting to concentrate on what I believe are two important strands of design and technology 'capability'. First, a recognition, on the part of teachers and pupils, of the advantages to be gained from breaking down a global problem into more manageable sub-tasks. And, second, recognition of the importance of being able to choose wisely from a widening repertoire of subject-related knowledge and skills. That is, to know not only 'what' strategies to use, but 'when' and 'why' to do so in order to proceed, in an efficient manner, from initial ideas through to an optimum solution – to develop 'procedural and conditional knowledge' to good effect.

These issues will need to be considered carefully in teachers' planning. If pupils are prompted to tackle a problem in its entirety they may be overcome by uncertainty and not know what to attend to first or how to logically sequence the activity to ensure optimal success. Teachers will need, for that reason, to consider the extent to which support is required, bearing in mind the age and experience of the children in question. It may, therefore, be essential, when devising a scheme of work, to begin by establishing how a particular project might be effectively broken down in order to provide a suitable pathway through the activity yet still encourage independence and a challenge within each of the linked sub-elements. This will help children to construct local expertise by focusing their attention on relevant and timely aspects of the task and by highlighting things they need to take account of. It also breaks tasks down into a sequence of smaller tasks which children can manage to perform, and orchestrates this sequence so that pupils eventually manage to complete the whole activitvy successfully.

At the same time, pupils' knowledge and skills can be developed, in the context of each sub-task, so that they begin to appreciate the means by which such tasks may be efficiently accomplished. The examples in this case study include three-dimensional modelling for initial ideas, simple orthographic sketches for ideas development and discussion and the direct manipulation of materials when developing the wheel and axle assembly. This sort of approach is certainly essential as a means of moving beyond the view that 'designing' is simply synonymous with 'drawing'.

This form of teaching has had the metaphor 'scaffolding' attached to it. Built well, such scaffolds help children to achieve heights that they could not reach alone. In effect the teacher aims to simplify the child's role, rather than the task, by means of offering graduated assistance – this will include structuring the activity into manageable steps, demonstration, drawing attention to previous work or associated concepts, simple encouragement, etc. What is important is that assistance should be adjusted as a direct response to children's level of performance and perceived needs.

As Wood (1996) notes:

> Children, being novices of life in general, are potentially confronted with more uncertainty than the more mature and, hence, their abilities to select, remember and plan are limited in proportion. Without help in organising their attention and activity, children may be overwhelmed by uncertainty. The more knowledgeable can assist them in organising their activities, by reducing uncertainty, breaking down a complex task into more manageable steps or stages. As children learn, their uncertainty is reduced and they are able to pay attention to and learn about more of the task in hand.

[…] The significant issue here is that children, as 'novices', need thoughtfully structured direction as an aid to 'capability'. From this basis children will be able to work toward more 'expert' approaches and exhibit a knowledge of not simply 'what they know', but why, how and when it is best to exploit that which they have at their disposal.

References

Bransford, J.D. and Stein, B.S. (1993) *The Ideal Problem Solver*, New York: W.H. Freeman and Company.

Fisher, R. (ed.) (1987) 'Introductory Notes', *Problem Solving in Primary Schools*, Oxford: Blackwell.

Hennessy, S. and McCormick, R. (1994) 'The general problem-solving process in technology education: myth or reality?', in F. Banks (ed.) *Teaching Technology*, London: Routledge.

Kimbell, R. Stables, K. and Green, R. (1996) *Understanding Practice in Design and Technology*, Buckingham: Open University Press.

Meadows, S. (1993) *The Child as Thinker*, London: Routledge.

Ritchie, R. (1995) *Primary Design and Technology, A Process for Learning*, London: David Fulton Publishers.

Rogoff, E. (1989) 'The joint socialization of development by young children and adults', in P. Light, S. Sheldon and M. Woodhead (eds) *Learning to Think* (1991), London: Routledge.

Stephenson, P. (1997) 'Children's learning using control information technology', in A. McFarlane (ed.) *Information Technology and Authentic Learning*, London: Routledge.

Wood, D. (1986) 'Aspects of teaching and learning', in P. Light, S. Sheldon and M. Woodhead (eds) *Learning to Think* (1991) London: Routledge.

13 What is cooperative group work?
H. Cowie and J. Rudduck

Group work is an important teaching strategy in Design and Technology because it reflects the practice found in many industrial and commercial organisations. Here, the various forms and techniques of group work are discussed, together with some consideration of how group work might be assessed.

The distinctive potential of group work

We found little evidence that teachers shared a common conception of the distinctive features of group work as a form of learning. In our view, whatever the form in which group work operates, there are certain fundamental principles that must be respected. The whole point of group work, and its central feature, is *the opportunity to learn through the expression and exploration of diverse ideas and experiences in cooperative company*. It is cooperative in the sense that no one in any one working group is trying to get the best out of the situation for him or herself; it is not about competing with fellow members of the group and winning, but about using the diverse resources available in a group to deepen understanding, sharpen judgement and extend knowledge.

Groups that are working effectively will have the following characteristics:

- group members are, between them, putting forward more than one point of view in relation to the issue or task that confronts them;
- group members are at least disposed to examine and to be responsive to the different points of view put forward (in role play and simulation, this will occur implicitly during the event but can be made explicit in the review or debriefing);
- the interaction assists with the development of group members' knowledge, understanding and/or judgement of the matter under scrutiny. (See Bridges, 1979, pp. 16–17.)

What matters is that teachers frame the task in ways that support the distinctive potential of learning through group work. The task should also be one that all members of the group think worthwhile to explore together.

Effective group work also depends on a shared understanding among the members of the group of various social and procedural rules. Group activity should reflect such values as reasonableness, orderliness, openness, freedom to take risks with ideas, equality, and respect for persons. Quite often the normal experience of pupils … does not equip them for interactions which support such values. It is important that teachers who are keen to develop group work consider (a) ways of helping pupils to understand the social and procedural rules that underpin group work, and (b) provide some opportunity for sustained experience so that pupils begin to appreciate and feel comfortable with the new way of working.

Different forms of cooperative group work

Group work has many guises; in classrooms it mainly takes the following forms:

Discussion

Here a larger group of pupils and their teacher, or a smaller group of pupils without their teacher's constant presence, work to share understandings and ideas. The focus may be the interpretation of something which is ambiguous (an unknown product – such as a porridge stirrer, an 'old' product or one from another country), the sharing of experiences, the pooling of ideas, or the eliciting of opinions on an issue of common interest (for example, the use of packaging, or recycling of materials). Discussions may lead to enhanced individual understanding, or they may require negotiation in the interests of arriving at a group consensus.

Problem-solving tasks

These usually depend on the discussion of alternatives as a medium for constructive interaction. Often the same task is set simultaneously to a number of small groups of three or four pupils, and there may be a final review of solutions with mutual evaluation.

For example, a class could be divided into groups with each group taking the role of a design company. The groups could all be given the same task, say, of designing a table lamp suitable for children aged 8-12 years, and each design company is asked to submit proposals, as would happen in the real world. The groups would all be working to the same task, and with the same constraints and considerations, but would have the freedom to develop their own designs. Each group could present and justify its proposals, with the rest of the class acting as the customers and asking appropriate and relevant questions. There could then be a final evaluation of all the proposals, not only of their aesthetic appeal but also of how safe they were and how well they matched the constraints and considerations identified.

A bigger example of this is where schools run 'activity days' or 'industry days'. On these days the timetable is usually suspended and pupils are grouped into 'teams' or 'companies', each with its own name and identity. Each team is then set the same task, often the production of a batch of items. The team has to divide into 'departments', with different pupils taking responsibility for areas such as production, packaging, advertising, catering and finance. Often local industrialists can be persuaded to take part, as managing directors or consultants, and their participation may influence the products being produced. The groups are expected to work as company teams, to produce quality outcomes within agreed constraints, which will be judged against the outcomes of the other groups. To ensure that pupils learn from this experience it is important that the activity is followed up with evaluation and reflection on their learning.

Alternatively, an overall problem might be identified as a framework in which groups of pupils work on different aspects of the task and the different contributions are then brought together and reviewed. For example, the whole class could be set the task of producing a range of items to launch a new fast-food bar. Each group could work on a different aspect of the launch, for example: the menu; the decor/appearance of the bar; uniforms for the staff; items such as serviettes and place mats; advertising. All the groups would have to liaise to ensure that a consistent image was created.

Production tasks

These are slightly different from problem-solving tasks in that there is usually a concrete outcome: that is, pupils might be working in teams to produce, say, a set of masks for a school play, with one team responsible for the research, one for the design work, one for the production, etc. Or pupils might work in small groups to design and make a bookstand that even if only partially full holds the books upright! Here, like the problem-solving task, there may be a communal, whole-group review of the progress of different bits of the task, or there may be a comparison of products and even a judgement as to the best.

Simulations

In these, pupils take on the situation or task of a supposed real-life group. They might, for instance, become a company that has to market a new product in order to stay solvent. Or they might, in smaller groups, work to a brief, sometimes against the clock, which puts them into realistic competition with other groups; the situation might be one in which different companies put in competitive bids for a contract to design and build, say, a new children's playground. Within simulations, pupils are often free to contribute from their own strengths or perspectives, although sometimes they may be assigned quite specific roles and the simulation then merges into our next category, role play.

Role play activities

These are activities in which each pupil is given a character or perspective within the framework of an event or situation. The role becomes, as it were, a mask and the characters interact according to their interpretation of the given role. Roles are usually assigned to reflect different perspectives on an issue or event: for instance, the issue of putting antibiotics into animal feed might be debated by a farmer, a vet, a supermarket owner, a doctor or a low-income parent.

Techniques involving group work

'Techniques' should be distinguished from the more fundamental 'forms' of cooperative group work outlined in the previous section. Techniques, of which buzz groups, snowball groups, and cross-over groups are the most common, are ways of promoting interaction – of getting ideas flowing – in the interests of collaborative group work. They clearly embody the key characteristics of group work in that they bring small groups together to pool ideas in a framework which positively encourages people to interact and to be creative or to take risks with ideas. However, they are limited and are not, in our view, a substitute for the sustained interaction and depth of understanding that cooperative group work supports.

Buzz groups

To provide an opportunity for greater participation by individuals the teacher may invite pupils to turn to their immediate neighbours and, in threes or fours, spend a few minutes exchanging views about, for example, things they don't understand; things they disagree with; things that haven't been mentioned, and so on. As Jaques (1984) says: buzz groups enable pupils 'to express difficulties they would have been unwilling to reveal to the whole class without the initial push of being obliged to say something to their neighbours. Taken by itself, the buzz group has little meaning. Yet in the context of a large (i.e. whole-class) event it can rekindle all sorts of dying embers.'

Snowball groups

The principle here is that groups of two or three people, with a very tightly defined task that they have to discuss in a very short time, form a partnership with another group and compare ideas. The quartet then joins another quartet to form an eight. Sometimes the culminating task is to arrive at some consensus. This is then reported back, from each of the eights, and an overall position arrived at through further exploration. The advantage of this approach is that it prepares pupils to participate confidently in the final plenary discussion. There are two disadvantages in practice. First, pupils may not always be good at managing the negotiation which allows the pairs to reach a common view and then the quartets to reach a consensus. A consensus may be arrived at through domination rather than through reasoned discussion. Second, pupils may switch off as they find themselves going over the same ground. To avoid this second problem, the sequence of stages can be differentiated. (See Table 13.1 below which is based on Jaques, 1984, p. 92.)

Here, the task at each stage is slightly different and the danger of repetition is to some extent avoided.

Cross-over groups

If teachers find that the final plenary sessions are not working, or that they need an alternative structure to avoid repetition, the cross-over system can be useful. Pupils are divided into groups on a mathematical basis: for example, if there are 27 pupils in

Table 13.1 Example task – to find out whether there is a shared perception of school rules

Stage 1	0 + 0	Brainstorm, and record your ideas in a list
Stage 2	00 + 00	Share lists and select six that all four of you agree are school rules
Stage 3	0000 + 0000	Share lists; identify those rules that are common to both lists and list them in order of importance. Appoint a spokesperson
Stage 4	00000000 + 00000000 + 00000000	Plenary session: review reports and discuss areas of agreement or disagreement

the class, there will be nine groups of threes (three As, three Bs, three Cs, three Ds, three Es, three Fs, three Gs, three Hs, three Is). In order to consolidate the sense of 'home-base', the A, B, C, etc. groups will need to meet for a briefing before mixing so that they establish their identity and control over the agenda. Groups then reform as threes (an A, B, C in each of three groups; an E, F, G in each of three other groups, and so on). Then, after a specific time on their task, they go back to their base of As, Bs, Cs, etc. Again the task needs to be one that can be handled within this format, and also one that gives responsibility to the home-base teams for reviewing the different experiences that the three members will have had in separate groups.

Forming groups

Whereas the logic of the lecture is easily translated into familiar and relatively unambiguous roles and physical structure, group work is more diverse. Group size may vary but it should not be so large or so small that it undermines the fundamental principle that group members may learn through easy interchange with each other. Groups that set out to use discussion to explore ideas or experience will not normally work effectively with more than 12 members, while six to eight is often thought of as a good – though in education not always affordable – size. But where interaction supports the pursuit of a problem-solving task or product-oriented task, then an effective group size is usually three or four.

The physical placing of participants should be such as to allow easy interaction: a circle, square, rectangle or arc of chairs will reflect the kind of interaction that discussion is designed to foster. This physical grouping or movement is not always possible in design and technology teaching rooms, but consider whether pupils can sit around tables or benches. As a last resort, you may even consider moving to another classroom.

Groups may be formed from volunteers or may be constructed in order to ensure that different kinds of experience or skills are represented. Teachers are now much taxed by the issue of whether small groups should include both boys and girls and whether they should bring together pupils of different cultural backgrounds. This is something which you will have to decide on personally, taking account of school and department policy and your own experience and knowledge of the pupils. The topic or technique may also influence your decision.

Discussion-based group work and the teacher as chairperson

Discussion groups may or may not, depending on pupils' experience of this form of learning and their capacity for disciplined activity, benefit from having a teacher as chairperson. In our experience, teachers underestimate the complexities of discussion-based group work and tend not to appreciate the expertise required of group members and the group chairperson. Pupils may need to experience good chairing in order to learn how to behave constructively in group work. Although the chairperson is not the fount of wisdom, nor intended to be the main contributor, the role is not an inactive one, for the chairperson will try to see that discussion flows freely across the group and not just between the chairperson and individual members.

The chairperson will encourage non-contributors without bullying them, and indicate that their comments will be listened to and treated with respect. The chairperson will help students to avoid arriving at easy judgements and try to understand views that other group members express. The chairperson will generally favour a thoughtful style of discussion rather than an argumentative style where members are quick to arrive at judgements and are bent on defending entrenched positions. The chairperson will help pupils to express their views freely and without ridicule. The chairperson will be a good listener, will appear supportive but firm, and will signal that all members of the group are important.

The main types of spoken contribution to discussion made by successful chairpersons seem to be these:

- asking questions or posing problems;
- clarifying, or asking a group member to clarify, what has been said;
- summarizing the main trends in discussion;
- keeping the discussion relevant and progressive;
- helping the group to use and build on each other's ideas;
- helping the group to decide on its priorities;
- through careful questioning, encouraging reflective criticism.

Of course, as pupils learn to work effectively together they will assume and share responsibility for these functions. But too often, in our experience, pupils are expected to learn in groups without adequate briefing about procedures, roles and responsibilities.

There is a difference of opinion concerning the need for a chairperson. On the one hand, a chairperson can improve the quality of discussion by acting as a model of an enquirer who shows respect for other people's contributions. But on the other hand, a chairperson who is a teacher and who is perceived by pupils as behaving in an authoritarian or otherwise teacherly manner may inhibit the easy flow of talk – in particular, the kind of talk that is expressed in a register that the participants find they can most easily handle. Barnes and his colleagues therefore explored the use of small, highly interactive groups which gave the pupils more freedom to construct their own meanings and to work things out in their own ways. They concluded, after analysing tape-recorded discussions, that without a teacher present pupil interaction through talk is very different. Pupils are more ready to embark on an enquiry using language to test out the limits of their knowledge and to reshape it collaboratively, often drawing on personal experience as a way of making progress in understanding (see Barnes, 1976).

Aware that teachers who act as chairpersons in discussion often find it difficult to relinquish familiar patterns of classroom behaviour, Stenhouse, in a curriculum project developed in the early 1970s, offered the support of a strong self-monitoring framework. Teachers were encouraged to tape record discussions and listen to them, bearing in mind questions such as these:

- To what extent do you interrupt pupils while they are speaking? Why and to what effect?
- How many silences are interrupted by you?
- Are you consistent and reliable in chairing? Are all the pupils treated with equal respect?
- Do you habitually rephrase and repeat pupils' contributions? If so, what is the effect of this?
- Do you press towards consensus when consensus is inappropriate?
- Is there evidence of pupils looking to you for reward rather than to the task?
- Do you generally ask questions to which you think you know the answer?

(Stenhouse 1970)

Bridges (1979) observes that it is difficult to conduct discussion in school if pupils are afraid to speak freely, if teachers do not think that pupils' opinions are worth attention, if pupils are rudely intolerant of opinions that they disagree with, if pupils feel it improper to express a personal opinion, or if pupils are not amenable to the influence of reason, evidence or argument. Bridges adds, wryly, that in our education system the conjunction of all these conditions is not at all uncommon! We think, however, that the situation is changing.

Small group work and the teacher as facilitator

[…] A teacher who has in his or her charge the progress of a number of small groups of children has first to be confident that the tasks set are clear and engaging. Pupils must understand the structure and timing of the session so that they can pace their work; they must also understand what demands will be made of them for sharing their work or reporting back on what they have done.

A common phenomenon is for teachers to intervene either too much or in the wrong way. Galton (1981) (which although based in primary schools is relevant here) documented a dilemma: the teacher, it seems, when 'calling in' on a small group at work did not listen long enough to know where the group was up to, and his or her interventions consequently tended to move the pupils' thinking backwards or to divert it. The research showed that the teacher asked more intellectually challenging questions in whole-class activity, presumably because he or she knew where the corporate understanding of the group was at. The lesson for cooperative group work is twofold: first, wait until you are called – without feeling guilty about not doing your job as a teacher – and help pupils to feel comfortable about seeking advice when they need it; and, second, abandon the idea of 'getting round' to each group in turn and spend long enough with the groups that you do join to make sure you understand the pattern and direction of their thinking. If the teacher plays a 'drop-in' role, pupils can perceive him or her as fulfilling a policing function – always checking up because of some deep-rooted mistrust of pupils' capacity to get on on their own.

Some pupils in a local comprehensive school, who for the first time had the experience of working collaboratively in small groups on projects in integrated design, made the following comments about the teacher's attempt to manage his new role:

'If only he (the teacher) would let us get on with it and not keep calling round.'

'If he didn't have so many talks and let us get on with it.'

'The staff should stop talking and let us get on with it.'

For their part, pupils who are working in small groups that are not under the constant surveillance of the teacher tend to experience or exhibit the following problems:

- reluctance to value the contribution of some members of the group;
- the persistent dominance of one or two pupils. Sometimes the dominant ones may do most of the talking (boys are sometimes dominant in talking in a mixed gender group) or they may assert their dominance by assigning low status tasks to other members of the group while maintaining higher status tasks for themselves;
- the breaking up of the group into two slightly hostile sub-groups or two completely separate sub-groups;
- the tendency to proceed from a particular perspective, without adequately examining the alternatives that are available within the group membership. This results in one-sidedness or conservatism;
- the failure of one or two pupils to allow themselves to become part of the group. Other pupils in the group sometimes accuse such pupils of being idle, or of being passengers and doing none of the work;
- inequality in the acceptance of responsibility for the group's work or aspects of it. This is sometimes a product of other forces at work in the group (see the first three points above);
- the acceptance of an over-easy agreement in the face of complex issues. This is often because pupils are anxious about the time and concerned to 'finish' before the bell goes, or because they have not been helped to see uncertainty as a legitimate state;
- inactivity and lack of interaction, whether arising from uncertainty, resistance or boredom; boredom may be caused by a task not engaging the pupils or the pupils failing to perceive the depth and challenge of the task as set. [...]

Assessing group work

Examination work, at any level, usually values individual achievement over group or team achievement. There are provisions now to encourage group work in GCSE but teachers will require guidance on the complex problem of assessing group achievement. The most recent specification assessment criteria for GCSE Design and Technology (December 2000) state that:

> Internal assessment must facilitate candidates working in groups without excessive duplication of evidence, however, each candidate must produce a uniquely definable and assessable contribution.
>
> (Williams 2000)

All we will say here is that there seem to be different criteria for different purposes; some criteria relate to the *products* of learning, while some criteria relate to the *process* of learning, with teachers increasingly ready to judge the success of group work in terms of such things as engagement, enthusiasm, and participation levels, comparing their pupils' response to group work with their response to more traditional teaching approaches.

Here are some of the dimensions of the problems of assessment.

Short-term and long-term gains

It is sometimes difficult to measure the immediate short-term gains of group work. As we saw in one school, the readiness of pupils in a unit for the 'disruptive' to share their food was regarded as a breakthrough by their tutor, but it did not appear until they were two or three months into the course. Out of context, it might not even be taken into account as a significant, let alone measurable, change in behaviour.

Personal development in the group

Some of the qualities which are facilitated by cooperative work are by their nature hard to quantify. Take another example from the disruptive unit. When pupils, rather than the teacher, took responsibility for the antisocial behaviour of one individual and showed sensitivity to his needs, they showed the beginnings of an empathy which up to that point had often been lacking in their social relationships. In the teacher's words:

> We had a 'runner' – somebody who came in one door and went out the other. He was not there one day and they sat down and said that he ought to be kicked out. 'Get rid of him. He's no good. He's wasting his place here; he's not doing anything.' And we were just about to say, 'Is that fair?' when – you get that you sort of hesitate – one of the kids said, 'Well, I don't know. He's all right when he's doing so and so' and then the conversation got round to not 'we ought to kick him out because he's letting us down' but 'what can we do to get him back?' ... Eventually, they agreed not to nag him when he came back but to say 'Oi! You missed something and we've put your name down for this ...' It's

much better to come from them … 'How can we support somebody because he's one of us?'

The assessment of the individual in the group

We are concerned that, although in theory group activity is endorsed in examination syllabuses, there is often a requirement to identify the contribution of each member of the group and to assess it individually. This in our view contradicts the very essence of group work! However, the issues are real and some teachers would disagree with us because of inequalities, within groups, in contribution. Some pupils opt out by letting the keen members of the group do all the work. Are they to get credit for the end product? A related problem is the tendency of group members to adopt different roles and therefore not to develop skills in areas where they are weak. A Science teacher commented:

> It wouldn't worry me if I thought that they took it in turns to play the different roles, but they don't. It always tends to be the same one that will get up and collect the apparatus, do the measuring, do the weighing, whatever it is that they have to do. It will be the same ones that sit and watch, or not even get involved at all.

How can teachers assess the various levels of participation?

> You can make it difficult by insisting that everyone tries to do an equal share of whatever it is that you are asking them to do. It would be easy to sit back and say that as long as that group came up with some results it doesn't matter provided they can interpret these results and use them. But maybe the watcher gets as much out of it as those using their hands …

Although the contribution of some individuals may be greater than others, it might still be difficult to give due credit to a contribution which represented a considerable achievement for that particular pupil even though in objective terms the contribution to the overall task was not very great. Take the example of Jenny, a withdrawn 15-year-old who opts out of class work and is often tired and listless. During a class debate in which different groups present their own point of view, Jenny twice asks a question. For her this is an achievement although, taken in isolation, her contribution is not noteworthy.

Some pupils talk a great deal in the group context and seem to be very involved. Yet how do we assess the contribution of Mary who observes silently for a whole lesson until, right at the end, she makes a statement which clarifies the problem and enables the group to make a quick completion of the task?

There are ways in which group productivity and cohesiveness can be monitored, but many teachers see monitoring as likely to undermine the spontaneity of group activity. The awareness of being assessed could be inhibiting. Furthermore, it could act against the very qualities which group work aims to achieve, since individual competitiveness could sabotage group cooperation.

Despite the difficulties of assessment, the benefits of group work to pupil learning make it a useful and important teaching strategy. This is discussed further in Chapter 8. [...]

References

Barnes, D. (1976) *From Communication to Curriculum*, Harmondsworth: Penguin.

Bridges, D. (1979) *Education, Democracy and Discussion*, Windsor: NFER.

Galton, M. (1981) 'Teaching groups in the junior school: a neglected art', *School Organization* 1(2): 175–81.

Jaques, D. (1984) *Learning in Groups*, London: Croom Helm.

Stenhouse, L. (1970) *The Humanities Curriculum Project: An Introduction*, revised by J. Rudduck (1983) Norwich: University of East Anglia Press.

Wagner, B.J. (1979) *Dorothy Heathcote: Drama as a Learning Medium*, London: Hutchinson and Co.

Williams, I. (2000) 'New GCSEs in Design and Technology' – paper at Engineering Council Seminar, London, September 2000.

14 Organizing project work
David Barlex

Project work is an integral part of Design and Technology, and it helps pupils to develop many important skills. This chapter considers how project work contributes to pupils' learning, and how teachers can plan effective project work.

This chapter is an edited version of a much longer booklet on project work written for the Open University course 'Technology in Schools'. The advice offered is clear and 'down to earth' but not linked to any specific National Curriculum document or examination syllabus.

Since the chapter was first written project work has become an integral part of Design and Technology courses in both primary and secondary schools, in the form of designing and making assignments (DMAs) as specified by the National Curriculum for Design and Technology. The importance of project work to pupil learning, and the contribution of Design and Technology to this, was recognized in a speech by the Chief Executive of the Qualifications and Curriculum Authority, who said, 'We need to revive project work in schools to help pupils develop the skills they will need in the knowledge economy' (Hargreaves 2001).

Why project work is important

Project work has been seen to be important in a number of curricular areas, but particularly so in technology. This is because it provides the opportunity for pupils to experience genuine technological activity. The activity can be in response to a human need or problem; it can use technological processes (e.g. design or systems analysis); it can be multidisciplinary. The extract below highlights some of the reasons for the inclusion for project work in technology courses:

Project work in technology develops:

1 skills in the application and use of knowledge and expertise in solving particular problems
2 the ability to work with others
3 divergent and convergent thinking by giving due consideration to intuitive inspiration, guesses and accidental developments as well as those achieved by means of logical step-by-step progression

4   self-discipline and responsibility, as the success or failure of the project is pupil-centred

5   creative abilities and encourages enterprise and dedication

6   speculative thought and exercises ingenuity.

(Cross and McCormick 1986: 254)

It is worth noting that underpinning the fact that project work is centred on the individual pupil and pupils take responsibility for their own work is the idea that pupils will be self-directed in tackling much, if not most, of the learning. Although other teaching methods might individually develop the features quoted above, project work is seen as particularly valuable because, under self-direction, pupils integrate these into a capability demonstrated by successful completion of the project.

Clarifying the learning in project work

Project work involves the following categories of learning – knowing, understanding, skills, attitudes and values. Black and Harrison propose the idea that task-action-capability depends on three related features:

1.   *Resources* of knowledge, skill and experience which can be drawn upon, consciously or subconsciously, when involved in active tasks.
2.   *Capability* to perform, to originate, to get things done, to make and stand by decisions.
3.   *Awareness*, perception and understanding needed for making balanced and effective value judgements.

(Black and Harrison 1985)

It is important for you to be clear on what you wish to achieve by project work and one way to do this is to try to relate these three features – resources, capability and awareness – to the categories of learning. Figure 14.1 attempts to do this. As you can see, most of the categories contribute to more than one feature.

At the beginning of a project pupils will start with their own individual collection of resources, awareness and capabilities. It is then important to ask whether there is any progression, during the time a project is tackled and completed, in the extent to which a pupil possesses these three features. Engaging in the project will enable pupils to utilize their existing resources and, in so doing, reinforce and extend their skills in using them. If, in addition, successful completion of the project requires a pupil to acquire new resources then progression will have taken place.

In applying values to a project, pupils will also become aware of their own existing values – if these are reassessed in the light cast by the project, then progression will have again occurred.

The demonstration of an existing and, perhaps, unsuspected capability and the acquisition of a new capability as the project moves forward will show progression in capability. It is in this area that personal qualities are so important and it is through project work more than any other form of learning that such qualities are revealed.

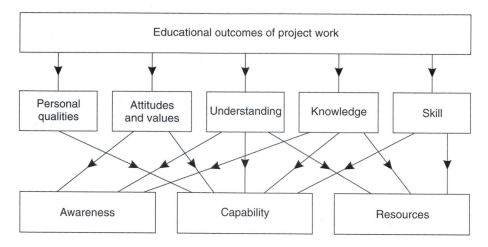

Figure 14.1 Categories of learning related to resources, capability and awareness

Planning projects

In this section I shall examine how the design of a project is governed by the educational outcomes you, as the teacher, require from the project. When planning project work it is important that you are clear on the following:

1 the capabilities, resources and awareness that pupils are likely to bring with them to the project
2 the resources the pupils will reinforce and develop by means of the project
3 the capabilities the pupils will be required to demonstrate by means of the project
4 the awareness that will be highlighted by the project.

I shall examine one typical 'beginners' project in which the last three features were deliberately orchestrated by the teacher in order to achieve particular educational outcomes. I shall also discuss the consequences of this orchestration in terms of the organizational decisions that teachers planning project work have to make – how much time is to be devoted to the project, what facilities and materials are needed, which parts of the examination syllabus will be covered, etc.

Educational outcomes for a Key Stage 3 project

The control project you are to consider is typical of many carried out in upper primary or lower secondary schools. The brief given to pupils might read:

Design and make a ring-can buggy which:

1 uses an electric motor, battery and belt drive to move it

2   can be controlled – start/stop at least; forwards/backwards, fast/slow, left/right

3   is visually pleasing and/or has an element of 'fun' in the way it works.

Skills

The practical skills are:

- simple but accurate measuring
- comparing and marking out
- the cutting to length of a wooden strip, metal rod and plastic tube
- drilling for tight and sliding fits
- cutting, scoring and bending paper and card.

Many lower secondary pupils have these skills when they reach secondary school. The use of pupils who do have the skills to demonstrate to those who do not is one way to cope with a class of mixed ability.

Intellectual skills

Most of the intellectual skills listed below will be utilized.

KNOWING

Pupils will need to know about simple circuitry and the use of an on and off switch. The desire to control the buggy will drive some pupils to investigate reversing switches, steering mechanisms and speed control. They will learn to appreciate the use of a belt drive with reduction in speed of rotation, which will, perhaps, lay the foundation for later work on belt drives and gears.

UNDERSTANDING

Design and problem-solving figure largely in this project. The design can be tackled in two phases (chassis/control and the visual/'fun' elements), although they are clearly related. It is likely that pupils will develop visual ideas quickly and then hold them in abeyance while they design and produce a chassis to which the visual elements may be added.

Two extreme approaches are possible with chassis design. First, pupils may be given a standard chassis design which they all make. This will specify the materials to be used and the positions of the axles/ring-cans, motor and battery. Once the chassis has been made, pupils can add their own control features and visual elements.

This approach will leave little room for problem-solving in chassis design. Where do I want the cans? How does this affect the position of the axles and the motor? Have I got room for the battery? It precludes any investigative 'tinkering' but it has the advantages that pupils will take less time to construct the chassis and there will be little risk of failure. Designing the control features may then become the major focus of the design activity.

The other extreme is to give pupils almost complete freedom over chassis design: simply specify the materials available and then leave it to them. Pupils will spend a lot of time attempting to solve problems, but the chances of failure will be high.

A middle approach might be to establish with the class important critical dimensions (ring-can size, clearance, motor size, battery size, belt drives available) and develop a chassis design that takes these into account and can be altered to suit individuals' particular needs. This leaves considerable room for problem-solving and investigative tinkering, but reduces the risk of failure.

ATTITUDES AND VALUES

In deciding on the overall appearance of their buggies, pupils will bring a wide range of visual values to bear. The 'fun' element may be due to overall appearance, or may be achieved by building in mechanical devices, such as cams to make wings flap or off-centre axles to simulate wave motion.

If the teacher wishes pupils to explore a wide range of visual possibilities then stimulating materials must be provided and the time for their use must be built into the schedule. Similarly, the inclusion of a mechanically driven 'fun' element will need to be supported by the pupils' existing resources. They will need to have already been taught about levers and linkages or cams and followers, say. Otherwise, provision will need to be made for them to acquire the necessary knowledge and understanding within the project's schedule.

PERSONAL QUALITIES

Clearly, the successful completion of this project requires the integration of the areas already discussed. To achieve this, pupils have to operate in a self-directed way, moving through the different phases of the project as is appropriate for their own designs. This means that they will be deciding for themselves what to do now, what to do next and how to do it.

To help them make sensible decisions the teacher can develop a timing scheme for the project in which deadlines for the completion of various stages are identified. This can, and should, be shared with the pupils at the outset of the project. Pupils will then be in a position to organize their own progress through the project.

The success with which they do this when they are new to project work will depend on their personal qualities – industriousness, perseverance, realistic appraisal of their own abilities, meticulousness and confidence. It is only by giving pupils the chance to demonstrate such qualities that they can be revealed or seen to be lacking and, more importantly, developed.

As pupils become more experienced in project work they can begin to negotiate their own deadlines for completion of the stages in the project and eventually plan the entire timing for a project.

It is almost impossible for one single lower secondary school project to feature equally prominently all the characteristics of technological activity. Clearly, the ring-can buggy project fails to meet the following considerations: economic criteria; manufacturing as opposed to making; issues concerning the interface between technology and society; working as part of a team and the necessary communicating and cooperating.

As such, the buggy project needs to be complemented by other projects in which the above and other elements are considered and enhanced, while those adequately covered in the buggy project can be featured less prominently.

Developing progression in successive projects

In the project just analysed, the path taken by the pupils was clearly laid out by the teacher, although pupils were for much of the time operating in a self-directed manner within these constraints. The whole range of skills needed for self-directed project work was, however, *not* used. This was deliberate, as a 'beginners' exercise should build confidence by gradual initiation into the skills required for project work.

To achieve gradual progression through a series of projects, each project needs to be analysed in terms of the types of task to be performed. Below is a list of the activities that need to be tackled in order to complete a constructional technology project:

1   *Researching*   Finding out from second-hand sources such as books, journals or magazines.
2   *Investigating*   Finding out by experiment and observation.
3   *Specifying*   Stating clearly the criteria that the chosen solution has to meet.
4   *Developing ideas*   that might make a contribution to the chosen solution.
5   *Optimizing ideas*   to formulate the details of a chosen solution.
6   *Planning*   the making or manufacture of the chosen solution.
7   *Making/manufacturing*.
8   *Evaluating*.

In planning for progression it is useful to look at each activity and to see the extent to which it is promoted in a particular project and over a sequence of projects.

For example, at first sight there seems to be little scope for researching in the buggy project. However, consulting scrap books and printed resource sheets are the first steps in developing research skills. Eventually, this can lead to a pupil being able to visit a public library and use catalogues and the Dewey decimal classification to find and make notes from books written at a level appropriate to a project's requirements. It is possible to use the internet for this research activity, visiting a range of websites to gather images that might inform the appearance of the buggy or websites providing technical details that can be used to inform design decisions about battery choice or transmission systems. In fact, if you compare the buggy project and the activities listed above you will see that all the activities are present in the project to some extent.

For any technology project you could present, by means of a bar chart, a profile of the project in terms of the depth of engagement associated with each of the activities. The length of each bar will be an indication of the depth of engagement. For the buggy project the profile might look like Figure 14.2. It is whether an activity is present or not and the relative, rather than absolute, depths of engagement that are

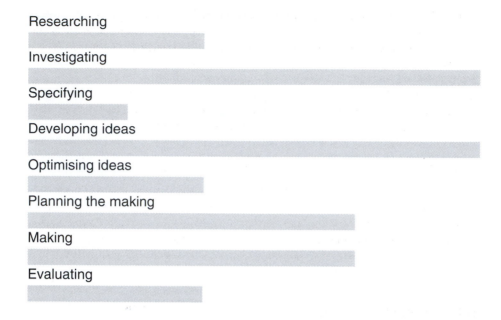

Figure 14.2 Project profile for the ring-can buggy project

important. A clue to the depth of engagement will be how long pupils spend on a particular activity.

Of course, it is possible to deliberately enhance a particular activity within a project in order to give pupils a deeper experience and appreciation of it. This will be an important strategy for developing the competence of pupils to undertake project work. I think it is preferable to attempting to advance on a broad front across all aspects of project work by, say, making successive projects more demanding all round. This latter approach makes it difficult for the teacher to concentrate on a particular activity and requires pupils to get better at everything all the time.

Project briefs for GCSE

There are several approaches to developing project briefs. Conditions have changed since this article was written and some teachers now set a common brief to all the examination candidates in a single class. In such cases the choice open to the candidates is much more limited than that envisaged in the following discussion. However, it is important to keep the possibility of student choice on the agenda, especially in the context of developing the Design and Technology curriculum with a view to enhancing student motivation.

Teacher-decided projects

Many pupils of lower ability often experience particular difficulty at the initial stage of choosing a major project. Two extreme responses are often encountered: 'I can't think of anything', or the over-ambitious, completely unrealistic proposal, 'I know, Miss, I'll do a rocket-powered, remote-controlled skate board!' A list of briefs suggested by you, the teacher, may prove very useful in starting a discussion with such pupils.

It will be important to develop ways of probing a pupil's commitment to a brief drawn from such a list. There is considerable danger that a pupil coerced into tackling a project chosen by the teacher will not be sufficiently committed to it to maintain interest and motivation in the face of problems and difficulties.

Briefs derived from knowledge bases

One way to engage pupils in the formulation of their own project briefs is to consider briefs from the view point of the knowledge base they are likely to use. With this approach, it is possible to deliberately exploit areas of knowledge acquired in curricular areas other than that in which the project is taking place. One danger, however, is that it is all too easy to fall into the trap of carrying out a project that is technically interesting, but has no wider appeal.

Briefs arising from events

Using the unexpected or accidental event as a starting point for a project has a great potential for motivation, but the attendant problems of the need for a rapid response and of ensuring appropriateness can be overwhelming. There is, however, no reason why a planned event may not stimulate a discussion from which a problem may be identified. Visits by a whole class or a group are clearly such planned events.

It is possible for all the pupils in a class to concentrate on one of the briefs and to develop their own unique response. Equally, pupils may be allowed to choose from the range of briefs generated. In this case, it looks as if there will be organizational problems similar to those encountered when a project is stimulated by an accidental or unexpected event. This is not so, because the teacher will have chosen the visit with the revelation of particular problems in mind – problems that will generate project work that meets syllabus requirements. After the visit there will be several follow-up lessons in which discussion will lead to briefs being formulated. This slow build-up identifying a brief gives you the chance to assess the likely needs of the briefs as they emerge and to pan the provision of materials and equipment accordingly.

Briefs derived from pupils' interests

You have seen that considerable motivation can be achieved if a project is concerned with a pupil's personal interest or hobby. There is sometimes the danger that the project can become too technically focused, but there are ways to avoid this.

A situation in which a large number of very different hobby-based projects were being tackled within a single class could present organization problems. However, it is possible to envisage a situation in which one or two pupils were pursuing such highly individualistic projects while the rest of the class were following a brief derived collectively from, say, a visit. The motivation resulting from the hobby will enable the pupils to operate independently from the rest of the class.

In summary, four ways to help pupils decide on briefs for major project work have been explored:

1   *Teacher-decided projects*   Important for less able pupils, but with the risk of motivational problems due to coercion.
2   *Briefs derived from knowledge base*   There is the risk of being too technically focused.
3   *Situation-derived briefs*   With the possibility of control by the teacher over the diversity of briefs to be tackled within one class.
4   *Briefs derived from personal interest*   These have high motivational possibilities.

Whatever approach is used, and it is likely that more than one will be needed for a whole class, it is clear that the pupils' involvement in any decision, and their commitment to it, are essential.

Support in the face of difficulties

It is a consequence of pupils being self-directed and taking on responsibility for their work that they experience disappointment and frustration when pursuing promising ideas that prove unsuccessful. One of the problems facing teachers supervising major project work is the disillusionment, and consequent loss of motivation, that can then occur.

As a teacher, you may see struggling through a 'sticky patch' as an important part of the learning process but for the pupil this can cause great dismay. It is here that the teacher–pupil relationship is vital. Encouragement and support from the teacher, that helps pupils solve the difficulties for themselves, are required rather than the teacher's instant solution. On some occasions, however, it might be important to provide a solution in order to prevent a pupil floundering. It is worth noting that pupils can help each other with their problems and an atmosphere that encourages pupils to share their experiences will provide support.

A clear commitment to the project from the outset is also important. Some schools insist that the decision as to which project to tackle is taken by both pupil and parents together, particularly when it appears likely that expensive materials or components may be involved. There can be little doubt that parents' awareness of project work, and the support and encouragement they can give, will, at times of crisis, help teachers maintain a pupil's commitment and motivation.

Possibilities for involving parents are:

• as consultants to technology projects
• as sources of cheap or free consumables materials
• as fund raisers for equipment
• as visitors who talk to pupils pursuing project work.

Pitfalls to avoid are:

- consultants who mislead pupils
- free consumables that are stolen goods
- clients who will be very disappointed when a project succeeds educationally, but fails to produce the desired artefact.

Project assessment for GCSE

This concerns the assessment of the performance of pupils *throughout* a project. It is clearly more complex than evaluating a product, but it is of particular importance if pupils are to develop an overall view of their experience of technology project work. It is also important that you should actively engage pupils in this type of assessment.

In assessing a pupil's performance on the various stages of a project you have to consider *when* such assessment should take place in addition to *how* it should take place. Ideally, the assessment should take place as the project develops. In this way the rose-coloured hindsight of both pupils and teachers can be avoided, although the reality of the situation is often that all concerned are so busy with the tasks in hand that a conscious, on-the-spot assessment does not take place. However, given that clear markers concerning likely progress through a project have been established with pupils, it is possible for both teacher and pupils to use a simple check list to assess a pupil's performance continually. This could be used as a reminder when assessing a pupil's overall performance at the end of a project.

When assessing performance at the end of a project, using data collected during the project if possible, it is important for pupil and teacher to share their perceptions of the pupil's performance. The most significant learning will occur when there is a mismatch in perceptions, *and* the opportunity to resolve it. I think it is important to share such a marking scheme with pupils taking the examination course, but it is highly unlikely that they will make any sense of it unless they have been regularly involved in both evaluating what they have made and assessing their own performance over a long period of time.

Clearly, it makes sense to try to introduce this performance assessment in the lower school and one school's attempt to provide a form for making an assessment at the end of project is shown in Figure 14.3. You should note the following features:

- it is much simpler than that used for examination purposes
- both teacher and pupil use the same criteria
- pupils are required to assess their performance before the teacher
- any mismatch in perceptions of a pupil's performance is highlighted and can form the basis for discussion.

The use of a folio or workbook written by the pupil to 'tell the story of the project' is common to much project work and is an essential element in assessing pupils. The London and East Anglia Examination Group's regulations for CDT technology stated:

Candidates will be required to produce a folio on their project. The folio should give a full account of the whole design process, including an analysis of the problem, research carried out, possible solutions, design details, problems

Name _____

Tutor Group _____

		PUPIL	TEACHER
FINDING OUT Did you find out	a lot?		
	a little?		
	not much?		
USEFULNESS Was what you found out	very useful?		
	useful?		
	not much use?		
IDEAS Did you have	lots of ideas?		
	a few ideas?		
	only one?		
CHOOSING How many reasons did you give for deciding which was your best idea	lots?		
	a few?		
	only one?		
MAKING PLANS Are your plans	very clear?		
	clear?		
	a bit muddled?		
THE PRODUCT Is it	well made?		
	well finished?		
EVALUATION Does your evaluation include	how well it works?		
	how good it looks?		
	things to improve?		

Figure 14.3 Assessment format for lower secondary school project work

encountered and modifications made during the realization of the solution and an evaluation of the whole project. Information from a wide range of sources should be available and evidence of reference to it recorded. Candidates should be encouraged to evaluate continually their project work as it progresses and to use a variety of presentation techniques, including colour.

Compare this to the current description of folio requirements from the EdExcel Examination Board concerning their Design Technology Resistant Materials Technology Full GCSE course:

Students must place evidence of work relating to the design and make task in an A3 portfolio or a hard copy of the equivalent ICT evidence. The A3 portfolio should consist of approximately 15 pages. The assessment criteria are:

1 Identify needs, use information sources to develop detailed specifications and criteria.
2 Develop ideas from the specifications, check, review and modify as necessary to develop the product.
3 Use written and graphical techniques including ICT and computer aided design (CAD) where appropriate to generate, develop, model and communicate.
4 Produce and use detailed working schedules, which include a range of industrial applications as well as the concepts of systems and control. Simulate production and assembly lines using appropriate ICT.
5 Select and use tools, equipment and processes effectively and safely to make single products and products in quantity. Use CAM appropriately.
6 Devise and apply tests to check the quality of their work at critical control points. Ensure that their products are of suitable quality for the intended use. Suggest modifications that would improve performance.

It is clear from both these quotes that it has always been the intention of the workbook to reveal the pupil's thinking and decision-making as it has developed through the project. It has not been the intention that it should be produced retrospectively once the practical work has been finished, although such practice is, unfortunately, common. If the workbook is to meet these requirements it is important to establish clear guidelines for pupils to encourage written and graphic work that is appropriate.

For pupils, assessing their own performance will be even more intimidating than evaluating a product they have designed and made. The relationship with the teacher will probably be the most important factor in building the confidence to tackle this. In developing technology project work it is therefore important for you to build into the project sufficient time for both its evaluation and assessment.

While product evaluation can be carried out by group activities it is essential that a pupil's performance is assessed individually with the teacher. This poses interesting logistical problems. If, at the end of a project, you allocate each pupil five minutes for a personal tutorial and have 20 pupils in your class, this assessment will take the best part of two double lessons. At any one time there will be 19 pupils working on their own while the teacher deals with the tutorial.

Preparation for the next project is a useful way to deal with this potentially difficult situation. Three possible activities are:

1   comprehension exercises – newspaper or magazine articles to be read, with questions to answer which are relevant to the next project
2   making up questions to ask during 'user trips' appropriate to the next project
3   making entries into a Design and Technology scrap book.

There are many problems about project assessment yet to be resolved. Even what is known about these problems tends to be locked up in teachers' and examiners' heads and so it is only possible to point to some of the issues.

How do you take into account, if at all, the help given to a pupil by the teacher? It would be a tragedy if the prospect of being penalized in assessment prevents a pupil from asking for help at critical stages in a project. Apart from the effect this has on the relationship between the pupil and the teacher, and hence on the learning, it does not reflect the way people are expected to work in industry, which projects are at least in part supposed to simulate.

The second problem concerns the pupil being penalized for the fact that the problem chosen does not allow him or her to exhibit the criteria being used in the marking scheme. The scheme assumes that every project has each of the stages identified. What, though, of the pupil who starts with a specification and puts considerable work into solving detailed problems and aspects of realization, but has not carried out the problem recognition and analysis stages? A pupil who has chosen to make a cheap version of a piece of weight-lifting equipment (with various levers, pulleys, etc.) will have to solve a large number of problems and take many decisions, though the project as a whole would not be seen as one where the problem was more open.

The third problem is that many schemes still leave a lot unassessed. For example, they do not actually assess capability in terms of the personal qualities, organization and planning abilities required. These may, of course, colour a teacher's view of the work of a pupil, but may not be taken into account formally; rather, they operate as 'hidden criteria'. If projects are centrally about capability, as is usually argued, then it is a curious omission. Aligned with this is the neglect of attitudes and values. You might also wonder about the lack of assessment of knowing and understanding.

There is also a lack of concern for other issues, such as the non-ethical values brought to bear in judging pupils' products; the ethical questions that could be asked about whether the choice of a project was one worth spending the time and effort on; and the value judgements involved in any technological solution arrived at by a pupil. Could pupils be asked to comment on any value issues relevant to their project? For example, in developing an electronic security system for a house, could a pupil comment upon this as a solution to burglary? Issues of energy, resources and environmental conservation, as well as safety, are obvious aspects which might be relevant to many projects.

Finally, group work is usually discounted in assessed project work because of the difficulties in identifying individual contributions.

Most of these problems can be put down to general inexperience in assessing technology project work and, perhaps in time, solutions will be found to them.

Problems with project work

It is here that I must acknowledge that technology project work is an inherently tricky business. In the primary school and the early years of secondary education the measure of risk can be kept to a minimum by skilful organization and direction by the teacher, but in trying to solve real problems chosen by pupils there is no guarantee of success, only degrees of risk. This is particularly true for pupils embarking on major technology projects that may take two or three terms to complete. Here I shall look at areas that are known to cause problems and offer some possible solutions.

Matching pupils' ability to project difficulty

If the projects tackled are to be technological there will be large areas of uncertainty, and pupils will almost certainly have to develop an understanding of areas of knowledge and practical skill that they have not previously encountered. It is part of the teacher's role to guide pupils so that they tackle projects of acceptable risk: that is, projects suited to their abilities and inclinations.

In giving this guidance there is no substitute for knowing the pupil well. This includes not only details of their previous technology experience, and performance in a wide variety of related subject areas across the curriculum, but also an awareness of the home background and the level of support a pupil is likely to receive.

In my experience, the most useful information is locked in colleagues' heads and the most effective way of realizing it is to hold a meeting where proposed projects for pupils are discussed. Any inappropriate or over-ambitious project will quickly be revealed and appropriate support strategies for weak pupils can be developed, or they can be redirected. In addition, such a meeting gives the teachers supervising technology project work an overall view of the projects being undertaken and allows them to start planning with this in mind.

Finance

Often the bulk of consumables used in a major project has to be paid for by pupils or their families. It is disappointing and frustrating for pupils to find a successful project halted because, 'I'm sorry, but we can't afford it.' This can lead to bitter and angry exchanges within the family, so a realistic assessment of the likely cost of materials should be shared with pupils and their families.

For pupils without significant financial support at home there are other support mechanisms available:

- tackling problems in conjunction with local industry, and both funding and expertise can be forthcoming in such ventures. This is particularly appropriate for pupils in the sixth form.
- tackling problems within the school, where negotiating with headteachers and school governors can lead to appropriate funding.

Expertise

One problem often encountered is that pupils need access to knowledge that is unfamiliar to both the teacher and the pupil. This should neither surprise nor daunt you: the very nature of the exercise should lead you to expect it. It is your response to this situation that is important. There are three well-tried avenues.

The first concerns utilizing the available teaching expertise. Clearly, each teacher will have particular strengths as well as all-round skills. It is important to make pupils aware of these, so that they can discuss their project with an appropriate teacher.

The second avenue is to use local industry. The availability of an education–industry liaison officer is a tremendous boon, but many useful contacts can be built up by using Yellow Pages and the local Chamber of Commerce.

The third avenue is to use local further and higher education establishments. My experience is that when approached properly they seldom fail to respond positively and often make equipment available for use, thereby enhancing the pupils' experience of project work considerably. Indeed, the very act of contacting outside experts and negotiating a convenient time for explaining the project and its problem is a venture with no guarantee of success but the possibility of considerable gain. Such opportunities are the very stuff of technology projects.

Class size

The complex role played by teachers in supervising project work requires energy, enthusiasm and determination. A technology project class supervised by one teacher should no consist of more than 20 pupils, preferably 15. In an over-large class, the teacher's energy and enthusiasm become diffused and quiet determination becomes grim crisis management. There is little to be done in the face of too-large classes, other than reduce risk to a minimum (and hence learning opportunities) by advising pupils to investigate standard problems in a way that leads to conventional, well worked-out solutions with little flair or innovation. In examination classes, results for such projects will be on the low side and the very reasons for tackling technology projects will have been denied.

Perhaps the most serious effect of a large class, other than seriously damaging the teacher's health and sanity, is the way it mitigates against consistent effort from the pupils. Strategies for supporting pupils through project work have been discussed; none is more important than regular, frequent consultation with the teacher. The larger the class, the less frequent the consultation; an over-large class and the situation becomes ragged and the regularity of the consultation disappears as well.

Ancillary support

One major factor influencing the success of technology project work is the presence of technicians who understand the nature of the enterprise. Without the support of technicians the organization of consumables and specialist facilities for individual projects becomes a major headache which detracts from the teacher's prime task of guiding pupils through project work.

The duties of a technician supporting major project work are significantly different from those of a technician servicing standard coursework. The technician will be dealing with individual pupils and their requirements from session to session. It is therefore important to organize a system for effective communication between pupils and the technician – notes at the end of a lesson listing the requirements for the next lesson, for example – and to avoid long queues 'waiting for the technician'. The clear corollary to this is that the technician must have time between lessons to meet the listed requirements. Lack of adequate technical support will have similar effects to large classes on the quality of pupils' experiences of technology project work, and their motivation.

Concluding remarks

You have seen that some of the problems associated with technology project work in schools can be solved by good organization and cooperation between those involved in the endeavour. The difficulties caused by other problems can be lessened, but not eradicated, by adopting less adventurous project work. Above all, it is important that technology project work should be a positive experience for those involved, both teachers and pupils. If this is not so, many of the educational advantages to be gained from such work will be lost and the considerable effort needed from both teachers and pupils to maintain the activity will not be forthcoming. It is difficult to capture the breath of spring that successful technology project work brings to a wintry curriculum. Perhaps it comes from the risk of failure and uncertainty with no right answers, only possible solutions.

The rage and disappointment when things don't go as planned can be hard to handle. The tug at the elbow and resulting conversations in the corridor have to be experienced to appreciate the immediacy of the learning. The cries of joy when something works must be heard. The 'standing tall' by pupils of all abilities when they have done something they thought beyond them has to be seen. Analysis, design and planning have their place, but the key is the teacher – the teacher who is prepared to let pupils tackle the unknown, and prepares them to do so.

References

Black, P. and Harrison, G. (1985) *In place of Confusion: Technology and Science in the School Curriculum*, London: Nuffield Chelsea Curriculum Trust.

Cross, A. and McCormick, R. (ed.) (1986) *Technology in Schools*, Milton Keynes: Open University Press.

Hargreaves, D. (2001) Speech made at the London Institute of Education. Reported in *Datanews*, January 2001: 1.

15 Design and Technology and pupils with special educational needs
Curriculum Council for Wales

This teacher support material was written by a group of practising teachers and advisory teachers as part of the CCW Teacher Support Programme.

Design and Technology tasks, whether written or practical, can be presented at different levels to pupils, according to their needs. This chapter considers some of the needs of pupils with 'special educational needs', and how these might be met when planning Design and Technology work for all pupils.

Who are the 'one in five'?

It is estimated that 20 per cent (one in five) of pupils will have special educational needs at some time during their school life.

Pupils are said to have special educational needs if they have significantly greater difficulty in coping with their schoolwork, compared with other pupils of a similar age range. They are in need of some form of extra help to try to raise their levels of achievement.

These pupils may have difficulties which are:

- of a physical or intellectual nature;
- connected with a sight, hearing or speech impairment;
- emotional or behavioural;
- specifically related to aspects of communication and language;
- more general, covering some or all aspects of school work.

The usual definition of special educational needs comes from the 1981 Act and refers to pupils with disabilities and learning difficulties. Some schools also include gifted pupils and those for whom English is not their first language; this chapter does not attempt to address the needs of these pupils.

As indicated above, the term 'special educational need' covers a wide range of learning difficulties. Many pupils have special needs which are only temporary and so the actual percentage of pupils with a special need at any one time is probably nearer 16 per cent than the 20 per cent quoted (figures taken from *Getting in on the Act,* DfE 1990). Of this number approximately 2 per cent have statements of special, educational need.

Aspects of design and technology specific to certain pupils with SEN

Many schools have established, within their curriculum development plan and subject policies, a coherent and detailed curriculum for pupils of all abilities. For some pupils with special educational needs this may mean that they are taught National Curriculum Programmes of Study from levels outside the range specified for their particular age and key stage.

In special cases there is provision within the Education Reform Act for temporary exemptions by headteachers, or more permanent disapplication by an LEA through an amendment to a statement of special educational need.

The following statements from the English National Curriculum (DfEE/QCA 1999) apply to certain pupils with special educational needs.

> In relation to including all pupils and 'overcoming potential barriers to learning', teachers should take specific action to provide access to learning for pupils with special educational needs by:
>
> (a) providing for pupils who need help with communication, language and literacy ...
> (c) planning for pupils' full participation in learning and in physical and practical activities ...
>
> (DfEE/QCA 1999: 36)

Examples are given of the provision that may be made, including using different formats for text, using ICT, signs or symbols to aid communication; and for practical activities, using specialist aids or equipment; adapting tasks or providing alternative activities. There are likely to be similar statements in the curriculum guidance offered in other countries.

What are the practical implications of these statements?

The first is about *communication difficulties,* and suggests alternatives to assist communication which could include the use of:

- computer programs and hardware such as concept keyboards;
- a scribe or mentor who is familiar with the difficulty;
- prepared cards containing symbols, phrases, messages or prompts;
- acquired alternative methods such as sign language, lip-reading or touch;
- audio/video tapes and recording to provide the pupil with appropriate information and to enable the pupil to record him- or herself.

The second statement is about *carrying out practical work* and could mean in practice that:

- a pupil unable to prepare hot food products using an electric or gas cooker, for safety or other reasons, could use a microwave oven, be helped by a friend or teacher or even work with cold ingredients;

- a pupil unable to coordinate or control certain tools or machines to cut, shape or form materials could use pre-cut or prepared pieces and/or be assisted considerably.

Structuring the depth of focus in a design and technology activity or task

When devising design and technology activities for pupils, teachers should consider the appropriateness and depth of focus, or level, at which the activity is pitched. For example, is it appropriate to introduce a design and technology task relating to 'transport' at the same depth of focus for all abilities and needs? In this case, could all the pupils begin successfully if the task asks them to 'design a model vehicle and devise a way of moving it using stored energy'? In many instances there is a scope or flexibility available for the teacher to structure different layers within the activity and guide particular pupils to an appropriate, achievable, yet challenging task.

The two examples in Figure 15.1 and Figure 15.2 show how this might be done. Both these examples help illustrate not only flexibility and opportunities for different abilities, but also how planning the task in this way can help the teacher to manage the activity and provide an element of progression as pupils take on more open tasks toward the top of the diagram.

Flexibility in design and technology processes

The … processes indicated by the statements in the National Curriculum Attainment Target do not always form a linear or mechanical route through a design and technology activity and should not be viewed or taught as rigid steps or stages.

Design and technology activities involve, in differing intensities and to different extents, a complex interplay of exploring and clarifying the task; generating, developing and communicating ideas; evaluating; planning; making … products; and testing.

In relation to these processes pupils with special educational needs will have particular gifts and abilities in particular types of work. Because these processes can, and will, vary from one design and technology activity to another, it is possible for teachers to devise activities for some pupils on the basis of their strengths and successes. When teaching pupils with SEN this will mean directing design and technology activities around *making* and letting the other important processes be incorporated through and around *making*.

Centring design and technology on making … products does not mean that other processes should be neglected. Indeed, pupils will need to have access to these other processes to provide balance in their programme over a whole Key Stage and, of course, to provide assessment opportunities. …

From time to time teachers will need to devise short design and technology activities which provide a particular emphasis and opportunity for pupils to achieve success in one or more processes.

For example, a focused task where pupils cut, shape, form and test strips of different materials provides excellent opportunities, through discussion and recording of comments, to assess aspects of evaluation, materials awareness and knowledge. This

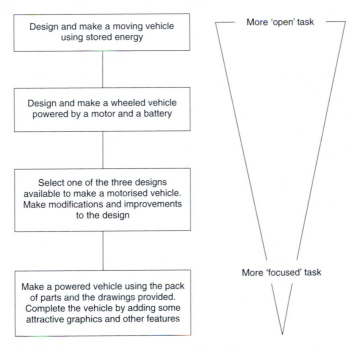

Figure 15.1 'Adjusting the depth of focus' in a control technology task

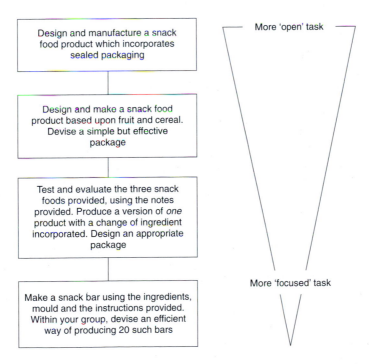

Figure 15.2 'Adjusting the depth of focus' in a food technology task

can also provide opportunities to identify uses and possible projects in which these materials could be used.

Likewise, by providing a range of outline ideas for solutions to a design-and-make activity, the teacher will be able to support the pupils and provide a good start for them to begin generating, developing and communicating their own ideas based around these beginnings. Again this would provide opportunities for assessing particular successes at particular levels of attainment.

Devising short 'extending tasks' in design and technology

For some pupils with special educational needs, the nature of their difficulty may not unduly affect their working and achievement in design and technology. For example, a pupil with a slight hearing impairment can probably cope well with most design and technology work, given appropriate aid and any necessary support.

For other pupils ... the nature of their learning difficulty can greatly affect success in Design and Technology. Many of these pupils can gain success and achieve progress by being involved in fairly short 'extending tasks'. Short time-span projects which are devised to promote and provide small elements of success are not only very rewarding for the pupil but also provide an opportunity for that success to be assessed.

The accumulation of success and achievement in this way can be structured so that a gradual move towards a ... level of attainment can be achieved. Without this structure a pupil may remain between two national curriculum levels of attainment for months or even years.

An example of a short 'extending task'

The example of a short extending task given below could be devised to support progress and achievement in, for example, a pupil's communication skills in drawing. The task might follow the pattern outlined below:

1   pupil uses a light-box, tracing paper or grid paper to produce a copied drawing of a shape;
2   pupil follows faint guidelines or dotted lines to produce a drawn shape;
3   pupil produces own drawing of a shape alongside printed version on page, with key lines provided dotted;
4   pupil produces own drawing alongside printed version;
5   pupil produces own drawing of shape from observation.

In this example it is possible to trace the pupil's progress from being able to communicate by drawing with considerable help through to communication with little or no help and with intention. It should be noted, however, that such structuring and the devising of short extending tasks requires a great deal of teacher time and planning.

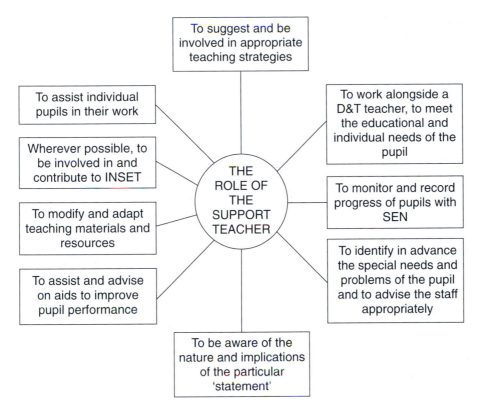

Figure 15.3 *The role of the support teacher*

The support teacher

In some instances pupils with SEN will have the assistance of a support teacher in the classroom, and for working in Design and Technology. Support teachers have the experience, patience and expertise, in coordination with the class teacher, to provide a range of valuable services for the pupil. Such support work requires close collaboration and agreement on roles and responsibilities between teacher and support teacher. For many teachers the presence of another colleague in a teaching situation is a new and often unsettling experience. Figure 15.3 indicates some of the roles of a support teacher and could be used by teachers and support teachers to help formulate and agree upon responsibilities.

Design and technology processes: some possible problems and solutions for some pupils with SEN

Depending on the nature of their special educational needs, pupils may experience problems relating to certain design and technology processes. ... The following provides guidance for teachers on some of the problems, and offers some possible solutions (see Tables 15.1, 15.2, 15.3). For convenience this guidance is presented under the three types or groups of 'learning difficulty', namely:

Table 15.1 Some possible problems and solutions for certain pupils with physical and sensory difficulties

Possible problems	Possible solutions
DEVELOPING, PLANNING AND COMMUNICATING IDEAS	
Certain project titles could be inappropriate	Consider project areas carefully and incorporate pupil interests and experiences if possible.
Difficulties may directly restrict access to resources and situations, e.g. a visit.	Plan for provision and access. Provide alternatives where necessary.
Speech or other impairment could limit ability to communicate and approach the task.	Provide alternatives for communication, such as scribe or concept keyboard.
Pupil lacks appreciation of likely problems their learning difficulty may bring to bear on later design and technology processes, for example, when making.	Highlight the positive and achievable aspects. Provide alternatives to assist situation, e.g. some pre-cut parts for making.
Clumsiness or difficulties in expressing ideas and in producing drawings.	Use a scribe to help record ideas and provide drawing aids.
Pupil has very limited range of ideas and experiences.	Provide plenty of appropriate resources, stimuli and ideas.
Difficulty in relating needs and concepts of task to ideas and solutions.	Provide a range of achievable though challenging ideas and solutions for pupils to develop.
Frustration and failure caused by restricted methods of communication imposed.	Teacher needs to value and make provision for a range of communication, e.g. talk or ideas communicated directly by working materials.
WORKING WITH TOOLS, EQUIPMENT, MATERIALS AND COMPONENTS	
Manipulation and coordination problems.	Direct practical support. Adapted tools and equipment. Use of jigs and devices.
Preparation and making lacks accuracy and quality.	Use of templates, jigs, some pre-cut parts. Tactful inputs by the teacher.
Unfair dependence on other pupils in the class or group.	Provide more support. Provide some additional time for pupils. Share support around class. Increase independence.
Lack of time to consolidate and practise skills and processes demotivates the pupil.	Provide extra time if possible. Less complex tasks. Shorter tasks.
Frustration and demotivation.	Reward all forms of progress. Devise short extending tasks. Relate activities to pupil interests.
EVALUATING PROCESSES AND PRODUCTS	
Expectations of failure if comparisons are made with high achievers.	Ensure comparisons with peers. Highlight progress as an individual.
Low levels of evaluation and testing, e.g. 'I like it' or 'It doesn't work'.	Provide checklists of considerations, questions, options.
Pupil has little interest in improving or modifying work done, wants to finish quickly.	Make the improvements with the pupil and highlight the increased value. Reward slower work.

Table 15.2 Some possible problems and solutions for certain pupils with intellectual difficulties

Possible problems	Possible solutions
DEVELOPING, PLANNING AND COMMUNICATING IDEAS	
Inability to see value or point of the design and technology task.	Is the task appropriate? Teacher leads and feeds ideas including the showing of some finished examples.
Lack of confidence and inability to grasp or start the activity. Task is too 'open' and demanding.	Lower the level of expectation. Focus the task to suit ability and provide clear boundaries and sub-tasks.
Ideas developed are impractical.	Highlight any positive part of ideas. Explain why other pupils cannot realize some ideas.
Pupil has very limited ideas and experience to draw upon.	Provide a range of appropriate stimuli and/or some possible ideas for pupil to develop.
Inability or low interest to connect designing with making. 'Why design?'	Use product examples to illustrate the importance and enjoyment of designing. Design directly with materials.
Ideas are stereotypic and narrow.	Provide plenty of ideas and stimuli. Develop ideas with pupil.
Pupil only wants to 'make' something.	Devise short 'making' tasks having small and compulsory elements of designing.
Lack of confidence and pride in design work.	Praise small achievements. Pair up pupil with helpful and sympathetic pupil.
WORKING WITH TOOLS, EQUIPMENT, MATERIALS AND COMPONENTS	
Inability to retain instructions and to listen at length.	Provide regular reminders and/or information cards. Use shorter tasks and instructions.
Low levels of coordination, accuracy and detailing.	Use of jigs, templates, patterns, pre-cut parts. Teacher contributions.
Health and safety problems. Low appreciation of potential dangers.	Take all reasonable precautions. Restrict access if necessary. Reward safe working. Provide clear rules.
Work is rushed and sloppy. Inability to transfer and repeat previous skills and knowledge.	Reward slower work. Provide short extending tasks. Repeat and practise skills. Teacher assists finishing.
Frustration and behavioural problems.	Set clear rules and expectations. Reward all progress. Short productive tasks. Build upon pupil interests.
EVALUATING PROCESSES AND PRODUCTS	
Low levels of expectation and appreciation of quality.	Use examples to show value of improvements. Illustrate good and bad design in products.
Limited vocabulary and understanding of concepts.	Provide checklists and plenty of group discussions. Help pupil to evaluate and discuss some favourite products.
Pupil sees little value in testing and evaluating. Wants to 'make it and take it home'.	Make testing and evaluating fun. Show how modifications can greatly improve product before taking it home.

Table 15.3 Some possible problems and solutions for certain pupils with emotional and behavioural difficulties.

Possible problems	Possible solutions
DEVELOPING, PLANNING AND COMMUNICATING IDEAS	
Low interest and concentration span.	Base activities around pupil interests and strengths. Short tasks. Provide choices.
Low standards of behaviour.	Provide clear and precise rules and methods of working.
Poor communication skills and low interest in forming own ideas.	Use of IT applications. Promote discussion of ideas. Reduce amount of writing and research.
Pupil withdraws and does not take part.	Trigger interest and involvement via pupil interests and previous successes in design and technology. Devise short tasks.
Ideas are unrealistic and do not match ability to 'make'.	Re-develop an idea generated by the pupil. Provide a range of ideas and solutions for pupil to adopt.
Pupil doesn't want to design and only wants to make.	Devise a 'make' task which will only work if some designing is done. Show importance of 'design' in pupil's favourite items.
Ideas are few and stereotypic.	Provide plenty of ideas, alternatives and stimuli.
Low level of communication.	Teacher acts as scribe for ideas. Plenty of discussion. Use of IT.
WORKING WITH TOOLS, EQUIPMENT, MATERIALS AND COMPONENTS	
Low level of patience. Wants to finish quickly.	Reward slow, steady progress. Short tasks.
Pupil destroys or hides poor work or mistakes.	Highlight mistakes in the work of others. Show how many mistakes can be corrected. Remove fear of making errors. Teacher makes intentional mistake during a demonstration.
Pupil loses interest over long period of time.	Use short achievable tasks. Work on two tasks to provide variety and rotation. Include pupil interests.
Pupil is moody and stops unexpectedly.	Use friends in class to assist. Teacher patience. Discussion.
EVALUATING PROCESSES AND PRODUCTS	
Processes regarded as irrelevant. Pupil wants to finish quickly.	Assist with some improvements to show value. Make testing and evaluating fun.
Pupil has fear of judging own work against higher achievers.	Discreet individual or peer group evaluation. Praise small amounts of success.
Pupil cannot associate these processes with the design and technology activity.	Explain reasons for testing, evaluating and modifying. Teacher undertakes processes to highlight the value.

- physical and sensory difficulties;
- intellectual difficulties;
- emotional and behavioural difficulties.

Within each of these types or groups ... the processes central to National Curriculum Design and Technology are also grouped. These processes, which are interwoven when pupils undertake designing and making, are described as:

- developing, planning and communicating ideas
- working with tools, equipment, materials and components
- evaluating processes and products.

Suggestions to assist pupils in practical classroom tasks

This section provides some practical suggestions to help certain pupils with SEN in the classroom and is based upon the experiences and ideas of teachers. The list is not exhaustive and teachers should also endeavour to consider other methods of supporting pupils. Some of the suggestions relate to particular types of learning difficulty and to particular areas of design and technology, but many of them could benefit all pupils, for example the suggestion relating to the use of cutting guides. The suggestions are grouped as follows:

- communication;
- safety;
- organization;
- tools, adaptations and alterations.

Communication

Using an audio tape or dictaphone

In many classes a tape recorder is used to record pupils' ideas, comments and evaluations. For many pupils this form of communication allows them to express their ideas and comments in a way that writing or drawing might not. A teacher can also use a recorder to store an explanation or the stages of a demonstration, so that some pupils can play back the information at their own pace and be reminded of ordering and detail.

Using a concept keyboard

A concept keyboard is a touch-sensitive electronic panel linked to a computer to provide pupils with an easy input facility. Overlay panels or sheets can be placed onto the concept keyboard to provide symbols or words which, when touched, trigger signals on the keyboard beneath, and thus to the computer. Plastic key-panels are also available which fit directly over the existing computer keyboard to simplify and enlarge the range and uses of keys. In design and technology activities a concept keyboard could be useful for some pupils as they undertake an evaluation exercise, for example.

Using grid papers

To assist pupils to draw particular shapes and forms on paper, a range of grid papers can be purchased. Some papers have lines at various angles to help pupils form 3D drawings. Used in conjunction with a light-box, grid paper can be a very useful aid. Grid-printed card is now available for helping with card modelling and in trials this has proved successful with pupils of all abilities.

Using patterns, templates and guides

The provision of commercial and classroom-made templates and guides is essential for speedy and accurate work in design and technology. Professional designers, craftworkers, chefs and fashion designers, for example, all rely on such aids. For many pupils the assistance given by a pattern or similar aid can make the difference between success and failure.

Braille and large-print rulers

For pupils having visual difficulties, a range of Braille and large-print rulers, measures and other devices are available from specialist suppliers.

Using coloured overlays

Research has shown advantages in using colour-tinted clear plastic overlay sheets (OHP sheets) with pupils who experience difficulties with reading and with remembering key words. This method could be used to highlight particular words, stages and instructions in design and technology work. For example, some key words or parts of a diagram, relating to safety or hygiene, could be overlaid in red when using an overhead projector.

Making storyboards

Although time-consuming to produce, storyboards can provide an excellent reminder and visual tutor for many pupils undertaking procedures and tasks in design and technology for the first and second time. A stage-by-stage description of an operation can be produced using suitable artwork, symbols, notes or signs.

Safety

Low-temperature electric glue-guns

Glue-guns are an excellent tool for the classroom, but can be quite dangerous due to the high temperatures of the glue and their tendency to suddenly spurt out quantities of hot glue. A number of suppliers now stock low-temperature glue-guns which are much safer and still provide the quick-joint facility.

A sewing-machine-foot needle guard

When using an electric sewing machine the curved front edge of the foot not only directs the fabric correctly towards the needle but can easily draw in fingers too. A small and low-cost simple-to-fit attachment is available, which is essentially designed to protect the needle during transportation, but can be used to reduce the hazards of machine use with some pupils.

Safety rulers and cutting guides

The use of modelling knives for design and technology activities and art work has increased in recent years. A traditional 'M' section finger-profile safety ruler is essential when a teacher allows craft knives to be used to cut straight lines.

One other version, and probable improvement on this design, is the home-made 'T-Shape' safety ruler. The inverted 'T' provides a good straight cutting edge and keeps the holding fingers behind a protective ledge. 'T' rulers can be made from old aluminium window-frame strips or from extruded 'T-shape' aluminium available in lengths from some DIY stores and builders' suppliers.

A 'safe-cut' electric modelling saw

Reasonably priced electric saws are available which cut using the principle of a vibrating rather than rotating or sliding blade. The fine cutting blade vibrates and hums, and will cut only rigid materials such as wood, plastic and card. If skin accidentally touches the small blade, it will vibrate at the same frequency as the blade and so no damage will occur.

Under supervision, these saws can be used by a wide age- and ability-range and are excellent for model-making and for the cutting out of curved profiles and templates.

Using low-voltage and rechargeable power tools

Many manufacturers supply low-voltage power tools and transformers for use in schools and industry, thus cutting down the risks of electrical injuries and accidents. A range of rechargeable power tools is also now available; these can be of excellent benefit for working in design and technology by cutting down the number of trailing electric leads and in some cases the potential power available within the tool.

Rotary guillotines for cutting sheets of paper, card and plastic

Although all guillotines of the pull-down type are now fitted with bladeguards, they can be difficult to use as vision is reduced by the protective shielding. A number of roller, wheel or rotary-cutting guillotines are available which provide easy action with safety, in situations where the teacher allows use of a guillotine. Very often the risks in using rotary guillotines can be far less than in letting some pupils use scissors.

Organization

Large labels on equipment, tools, racks and cupboards

Putting large and clear name labels on equipment, tools, racks and cupboards will greatly assist all pupils as they learn about equipment and its location. For pupils with severe visual impairment other strategies will need to be used, for example Braille and/or raised silhouettes.

The positioning of pupils

Through experience most teachers know the best places to position pupils with particular needs when undertaking a demonstration or lesson. It is easy to forget that many of the children are seeing and following the operation from an upside-down view. It takes little planning to ensure that pupils with learning difficulties are positioned on the same side as the teacher if that will help, or that the teacher adapts the explanation or demonstration to cater for particular pupils.

Tools, adaptations and alterations

Using sticky pads and tape

A range of tapes, sticky pads and rubber feet are available in stores and from suppliers. Products such as these, which help pupils to hold things still, are of great benefit in improving their coordination and manual control. As adults we often forget that our own strength and coordination overcome many of the problems that children experience when trying to hold something still.

A hand-drill stand

Using a hand-drill properly is quite a difficult operation for many pupils. When analysed it is apparent that there are five or six physical and mental actions involved in using a hand-drill. A stand or holding jig can be purchased or made which clamps the drill in a vertical position, thereby releasing the hands to assist the drilling and removing some of the complexity of use.

Adjusting work-table or chair heights

A range of school furniture is available which has height adjusters on the legs and feet. Attachments can also be purchased to fix to existing furniture so that height adjustments can be made. Adapting working heights is essential for many younger pupils and those requiring wheelchair access, for example.

Using a light-box

A light-box is a worktop or unit which has a clear or translucent top, under which is fitted a fluorescent light. The upward shining light will penetrate a few layers of paper and thus allow pupils to make successful tracings, copies and drawings.

A light-box can be made by replacing the lid of an old school desk with a clear plastic top, and mounting a neon striplight within the desk space. Aluminium foil can be used to line the inside of the desk to help reflect light upwards. *Warning: do not use a standard light bulb because of the heat generated. Have your unit checked by a qualified electrician and a safety officer.*

Modified handles and knobs

For pupils who have difficulties in gripping, holding and manipulating the smaller knobs and handles on some classroom equipment, one idea is to slit a tennis ball, or other suitable ball, and slip it over the problematic knob or handle. This provides a useful, temporary adaptation where necessary.

In some cases, the reshaping or enlarging of a handle can prove to be a valuable modification to a tool or appliance. One way of doing this is to surround the existing handle with car-body filler and then for the pupil to grip the soft filler whilst wearing a rubber glove or a covering of clingfilm. The filler will quickly set after the hand is removed. *Some fillers produce heat when hardening, so care is needed.*

A jig for sanding wheels and discs

Accurately making and shaping a model wheel or disc can be quite difficult. If a classroom is equipped with an electric rotating sander, then a simple jig can be made to fit onto the machine to help produce accurate discs.

The rough-cut disc or wheel is temporarily fixed by a nail or screw to rotate on a base-board, which is clamped in front of the sanding surface. Slight forward pressure into the sander is applied whilst the disc is rotated by hand on the nail or screw. Quick and accurate discs can be produced in this way, and this jig is especially useful when large quantities are required. *Use of such a jig by pupils is the responsibility of the teacher in charge.*

A measuring board and stick

There are many ways of helping pupils to measure and mark sizes onto materials. One such method is as follows. A stepped board is made with standard or required distances clearly marked or coded with colours. Different sections of material can be placed against the appropriate step and the length marked off at a common edge. Such a device can be incorporated into a sawing block or bench hook.

Similar assistance can be provided by using a stick or strip of card. A plain piece of wood-strip or card can be marked off with appropriate distances and/or symbols for a particular project. Pupils then only have to deal with a few marks on the stick, as opposed to the many on a standard ruler, and distances can be easily transferred onto the materials being used.

Such simple aids are also useful for all abilities, for example when pupils need to quickly check dimensions of products on a small production-line project.

A hint to help with nailing

Holding nails in position whilst hammering them in is often a difficult and painful experience no matter what one's age or ability. One useful tip is to first push the nail into the end of a strip of thin card or foam. The nailing is then started by sliding the card into position and hammering with the fingers well back. The card or foam can be pulled away as the nail is driven in. As well as saving the fingers, this tip is valuable when trying to hold and start a nail in a difficult corner or position.

An 'extra hand' when using scissors, cutters and snips

Mastering the use of a pair of scissors, snips or general-purpose cutters can be difficult for some pupils, especially for some of those with physical difficulties, when cutting complicated shapes from tougher materials. A hint is to carefully clamp one of the handles into a vice or fix it to the edge of an old worktable. This leaves just one handle to be operated and provides an easy-to-use fixed guillotine or shears.

Coordination and accuracy can improve quickly, and downward pressure on the one free handle increases cutting efficiency. Please note that scissors handles do not last long if over-tightened regularly in a vice. Also *remember to remove the tool or cover the blades when not in use.*

References

DES/WO (Department of Education and Science and the Welsh Office) (1990) *Technology in the National Curriculum*, London: HMSO.

DfE (Department for Education) (1990) *Getting in on the Act*, London, HMSO.

DfEE/QCA (1999) *The National Curriculum Handbook for Secondary Teachers in England*, London: HMSO.

16 Developing students' capability in Design and Technology through collaborative approaches with Mathematics and Science

Jim Sage

When designing and making, pupils can draw on knowledge from many areas, but there are particular links between Design and Technology and Science and Mathematics. This chapter explores what the links are and how they can be utilized effectively.

Introduction

There are many aspects of Design and Technology that relate to work in Mathematics and Science. Some of the more obvious 'content' links are included in the revised National Curriculum Programmes of Study. However, enabling students to effectively transfer and make use of knowledge, understanding and skills between subjects is a complex issue; but there is no doubt that helping students to make effective use of these relationships will lead to improved capability in Design and Technology.

This chapter covers:

- the issues to be addressed when planning collaborative working in schools
- the nature of the links between the subjects involved
- some strategies that can be used to address these issues
- common areas of content and developing understanding
- the benefits of collaborative working
- a process for planning collaborative work
- the implications for Design and Technology.

Collaborative working – the issues

There is a set of issues to be addressed when planning any collaborative work with colleagues. Failure to address these early in the planning phase has led to lack of success in many initiatives in the past. The issues can be conveniently grouped under the following headings.

Logistical issues

These include problems such as the timing and sequencing of the activities in each subject as well as timetabling and student grouping. These issues need to be carefully considered during the planning stage of the collaborative programme. Successful planning at this stage will usually involve key decision-makers in each of the departments as well as senior managers in the school.

Subject cultures and philosophical issues

Within each school curriculum subject there is an understanding of the philosophical background to its development, its place within the overall curriculum, its content and skills and the methods used to teach the subject. This gives each subject its own 'culture' which needs to be carefully considered during collaborative work. For example, the culture amongst many Science teachers is one of a need to deliver the content of the subject, whereas for Design and Technology the culture should be more about teaching processes. Often these cultures can lead to barriers and blocks that make planning collaborative working difficult. For example, many Science teachers will not understand the level of intellectual demand required by many design strategies used in Design and Technology and they may have an image of its culture as being about 'craft skills'. Mathematics teachers when involved in discussions about collaboration, are frequently less than impressed by the often-held image of Mathematics as being a 'service subject'. This is a view that is easy to reinforce when discussions revolve around the contributions that mathematical skills make to work in both Design and Technology and Science rather than recognizing the 'subject culture' of Mathematics.

Conceptual development issues

In many ways this is by far the most important set of issues to be addressed. Students cannot easily transfer understanding from one subject to another; this is not the fault of the students. For example, often the way a topic is taught in order to achieve conceptual understanding in Science does not lend itself to the development of an understanding of the concept that can be translated into the 'knowledge for practical action' that is useful in Design and Technology. Science teaching will try to establish students' understanding of the basic concepts of force multiplier systems, energy transfers and efficiency when teaching about machines. What is required in Design and Technology is the ability to *apply* the 'technological tools' of mechanical advantage and velocity ratio. An electric current or energy transfer approach to understanding electrical circuits does not help the student use a multimeter to measure potential differences when fault-finding an electronic circuit. Science teaching about diets, making use of Recommended Daily Allowances to provide relevance, does not help Food Technology teachers using Dietary Reference Values in the design of food products. Yet all of these are very rich areas for collaborative approaches!

Mathematical skills are developed to serve the purposes of mathematics; students need to be supported if these skills are to be effectively transferred so that they can be applied in another subject area.

The transfer of knowledge from one subject area to another is a complex process and often involves a de-construction and re-construction of the form of the knowledge before the transfer can take place effectively. It is absolutely vital that this is fully taken into account during the planning stage of any collaborative programme.

The nature of the links between the subjects

Science and Design and Technology

There are several ways in which the nature of the links between these two subjects can be viewed. From the point of view of Design and Technology the most useful view is that of *Science as a resource for Design and Technology tasks*. Science can provide:

- knowledge and understanding of appropriate concepts
- skills, techniques and procedures, such as procedures for experimentation, investigation and research
- focused practical activities related to a particular topic area.

Another view is that *Design and Technology can act as a context for work in Science*. For example, the area of 'evaluating processes and products' in Design and Technology includes the need for an understanding of the underlying scientific principles. This obviously requires the application of an understanding from Science. However, it also provides the opportunity to develop interesting and relevant contexts for the students' work in Science. Examples from the Design and Technology classroom include students studying familiar consumer products, such as personal stereos, sports equipment or fashion clothing, these provide opportunities for students to learn about product design, meeting the needs of the intended users of the product, the use of materials, quality control and assurance procedures and marketing. It can provide familiar contexts for students to sort out, refine, develop and apply their scientific understanding. This can also be applied to investigating mass-produced food products, food preparation and processing techniques, control systems and manufacturing systems. The use of anthropometric data in the design of products provides an excellent stimulus for work in Science on human variation, as well as enabling the students to learn some basic statistical techniques.

The reverse situation – *Science as a context for Design and Technology* – can also be exploited. For example, within the overall context of the need for more sustainable development, the Science curriculum contains a number of references to the use of energy and the need for energy conservation through more energy-efficient appliances, devices and processes. One useful starting point for this would be to consider energy management in the school, involving a series of science investigations to obtain the data and information needed to develop a range of strategies to reduce fuel bills and environmental impact. During these investigations students would encounter many opportunities for the design and making of energy-related products and devices, such as temperature and lighting monitoring and control devices, automatic timing devices, the small-scale use of renewable energy, door- and window-closing devices and so on. These can be exploited in Design and Technology as contextualized, referenced or specific tasks allowing for differentiation.

The role of Mathematics in Design and Technology and Science

The mapping of Mathematics onto the other subjects raises some difficulties; one area of mathematical knowledge or a particular mathematical skill will be useful in many areas in both Design and Technology and Science. One way of dealing with this is to develop a set of 'generic' Mathematics tasks that can be used to support a range of Design and Technology and Science activities. These can then be incorporated into the collaborative project at appropriate points. These generic tasks should be developed by a Mathematics teacher working with Design and Technology and Science specialists. They could cover areas such as:

- 2D and 3D modelling
- nets and developments
- using spreadsheets to develop mathematical models from investigative data
- calibration of devices and instruments
- analysing the relationship between two (or more) variables
- display and analysis of quantitative data, including some basic statistics (for example, in making use of anthropometric data or in understanding quality control)
- using and interpreting graphical information
- reading scales and making measurements
- making and using scale drawings
- the geometry of levers and linkages
- rations
- assessing accuracy and reliability
- making estimates.

This allows abstract mathematical concepts to be developed through linking them with practical activities in the other subjects and provides the context for the application of mathematical procedures and techniques (Ma1 Using and applying mathematics). It also encourages a more mathematical and rigorous approach to be adopted in Design and Technology and Science.

The role of ICT

Experience has shown that students develop more effective ICT skills when these are learnt through a relevant context where there is a clear need for, or advantage to, using ICT. Mathematics, Science and Design and Technology all offer excellent opportunities to develop these ICT skills, and collaborative work will lead to the development of more relevant and meaningful contexts. In particular, there is great potential for the use of spreadsheets and databases in all of these subjects and the use of computer and mathematical modelling has a place in all three. Design and Technology and Science can provide opportunities for developing the use of ICT in measuring, monitoring and control systems. CAD/CAM is also a key use of ICT in Design and Technology.

Every attempt should be made to incorporate ICT activities into the collaborative project, but the guiding principle should be that IT is the best and most effective way of carrying out the activity. Activities should not be contrived simply to provide an opportunity for ICT.

Problem-solving and investigation

'Problem-solving' as a teaching technique appears in the repertoire of almost every subject in the school curriculum and is now one of the key skills to be promoted across all subjects. Mathematics, Science and Design and Technology would all most certainly stake a claim in the use of the term. Similarly, 'investigations' are carried out in all three subjects and there is some similarity in the processes used to carry out these investigations. Table 16.1 shows one analysis of these processes.

In all three subjects the stages used follow the pattern:

- define the problem or situation
- plan how to proceed
- perform – the investigation, analysis, making the product, implementing the solution
- review and evaluation.

Table 16.1 Approaches to problem-solving

Mathematics	Science	Design and Technology
Identify a problem and plan an investigation	Raise a question, make a prediction or propose a hypothesis and plan an investigation	Identify a need and plan the development of a solution
Build a mathematical model and select the mathematics to use	Design a suitable investigation to test the prediction or collect evidence to test the validity of the hypothesis	Carry out research and generate a range of design solutions to meet the identified need
Analyse the model using mathematics	Carry out the investigation and collect the evidence	Implement the optimum solution
Interpretation and validation of the model	Interpret the data collected and check the validity of the prediction or hypothesis	Evaluate the effectiveness of the solution

This is not to suggest that the process used in these subjects is necessarily a linear one, as opposed to a cyclical or even an iterative one; it is recognized that investigative approaches and designing and making activities do not fit easily into this neat process. However, these stages can generally be recognized in these activities even though the ways of achieving them may be quite different. The analysis is included here to show that there are common areas of process as well as content between these subjects.

At first sight this appears to be an attractive area to use to develop collaborative work. However, in the planning stage of the activity it is vital to establish a common language and understanding between teachers of all the subjects terms such as 'problem-solving' and 'investigation'. Further confusion can also arise over the meaning of 'open-ended' and 'closed' investigations; for example, the meanings in Science and Mathematics may be quite different.

Some strategies for linking work in the three subjects

There is a variety of ways of developing collaborate strategies to link students' work in Mathematics, Science and Design and Technology in order to enhance capability in all subjects. These can be grouped into three broad areas.

Increasing *awareness* among teachers of the Programmes of Study for each subject, and taking these into account when planning schemes of work. This can be used to:

- make sure that particular concepts or skills are covered at an appropriate time in order that they can be used in the other subjects
- cross-refer from one subject to the other and draw students' attention to links that could be used to improve the quality of their work
- build progression into the development of conceptual and procedural understanding in all subjects.

The references included in the National Curriculum Programmes of Study are a starting point for identifying areas of common interest, but there are many more areas where there needs to be an enhanced awareness of links between the subjects (see the later section on common areas of content). The increased awareness can be further enhanced through the use of common contexts and stimuli for students' learning.

Cooperative programmes, using joint planning of a particular topic to provide a coherent and cohesive framework to develop activities. This can be used in two ways:

1   with separate but linked activities taking place in each subject area, but within a common framework, with students frequently reminded or asked to make links. For example, a series of activities to develop understanding in Science could also form focused practical activities to support design-and-make tasks in Design and Technology.
2   students given more responsibility for planning their work which is taken from one lesson to the next irrespective of the subject; they obviously need to plan the activities to make best use of specialist facilities and teacher expertise.

An *integrated programme* using a more holistic approach, where the activities are planned to make use of resources from all of the subject areas involved. The main focus will be an extended task with a range of resource activities to support this main task; these resource activities will cover all of the subjects involved. This type of activity can be carried out using a suspended timetable slot for 2–3 days or a whole week, or a planned timetable slot using a time allocation from each of the subjects involved. This approach can be used to take full advantage of industrial links, visiting 'experts' or local events.

One effective approach is to use a common context for all the activities, with one major activity to which all of the subjects involved will contribute. A series of '*structured inputs*' can then be developed in the individual subjects to support the 'core' activity. These structured inputs will:

- provide data and information
- act as resource activities and focused tasks to develop skills and understanding
- include individual and group activities
- be matched to the individual requirements of the National Curriculum in the subjects involved.

This method allows for flexibility in the curriculum model adopted to deliver the collaborative programme. The structured inputs can be used to develop either a coordinated or integrated programme. It also allows for differentiation and progression to be built into the activity.

Two examples of the use of structured inputs

1 Developing food products
2 Electronic products.

Developing food products

Developing a range of food products based on tofu made from soya: this provides a vegetarian diet with good protein quality as well as a wide range of possibilities for new food products. The development of any food product involves obvious links with science through work on nutrition. However, this needs to be developed in a complementary way as well as exploiting other contributing knowledge and skills from Science and Mathematics.

Examples of possible supporting focused tasks

Food technology:

- investigating the effects of different cooking methods on the texture of the tofu

- investigating different methods of flavouring tofu
- investigating commercial tofu products
- identifying target groups and product ideas using diet surveys.

Science:

- understanding the need for protein quality as well as quantity in a diet
- understanding the process of coagulating the protein in soya milk to make tofu
- increasing the scale of production – investigating the effects of a range of coagulants to understand the relationship between pH and yield and the effects of the coagulant on texture and flavour.

Mathematics:

- collecting and using data about the proportion of males and females with vegetarian diets in different population groups to identify possible food products based on tofu
- quantitative food product evaluation
- using database and spreadsheets to design food products with particular nutritional values to match identified product needs
- understanding RDAs and DRVs (Dietary Reference Values).

Electronic products

Most Design and Technology courses include the making of simple electronic products involving sensors and simple processing blocks such as transistors, 555 timers, etc. There are obvious links with Science through developing an understanding of electrical circuits and components. However, there is frequently a serious mis-match between the approaches used leading to, at best, a complete separation of the subjects and, at worst, confusion in students' minds. Some examples of the mis-match are:

- the notion of 'simple electronics' in a Year 7 programme in Design and Technology being taught at a conceptual level not covered until GCSE level in Science
- a 'current, flow of charge or energy transfer' model used in Science to establish a basic understanding of electrical concepts and the 'voltage' approach used in Design and Technology to explain the use of a potential divider in all sensing circuits (that is, if the concept is explained at all rather than students just following set procedures).

Some of this becomes apparent when observing both students and teachers struggling with fault-finding when the final product does not work!

Some examples of possible focused tasks to help with the transfer of understanding:

From Science:

- understanding of a potential divider – this requires a progressive approach to develop students' understanding of the relationship between potential difference and resistance before applying this to the potential divider
- investigating the characteristics of electronic components to help students understand how they can be used in a potential divider to provide a voltage signal for processing
- the skill of using electrical meters.

From Mathematics:

- an understanding of ratio using the practical example of a potential divider to give the numbers to add relevance to the mathematics
- the use of quantitative data to select appropriate sensors and other components
- understanding 'preferred values' for components.

Common areas of content across Mathematics, Science and Design and Technology

Identifying common areas of content between these subjects is not difficult. The following areas of Design and Technology all have clear links with Science:

- materials
- food technology
- energy transfers
- control systems
- electrics and electronics
- mechanical systems
- structures
- the science of fibres
- evaluating the environmental impact of products and processes
- making risk assessments
- ergonomics and anthropometrics.

Examples of areas linking Design and Technology with Mathematics are:

- developing spatial awareness
- nets and developments
- 2D and 3D modelling
- the use of spreadsheets as a design tool
- assessing accuracy and reliability
- display and analysis of data.

In many ways, more important than identifying common areas of content is the identification of strands of conceptual and procedural development to be built into a collaborative programme. As an example, the area of systems and control has been used to show how to develop common strands of conceptual understanding across Mathematics, Science and Design and Technology. The analysis shown in Table 16.2 can be used to develop a coherent approach, building in the development of conceptual understanding and allowing for both progression and differentiation. It describes parallel strands of progression in the three subjects. From this example a general process can be extracted which can then be applied to other topic areas.

If collaborative work is used to develop students' understanding then it is vital to establish at the planning stage what the concepts and procedures are and to develop the strands and steps that lead to progress in students' conceptual and procedural understanding.

Where these strands cross the subject boundaries there must be a coherent strategy for their development. If parts of the strand are covered in different subjects the other subjects need to build in activities to support and reinforce the understanding and to aid the transfer from one subject to the other.

Formative assessment strategies will need to be developed to collect the evidence needed to monitor students' progress and plan the next stage of their work.

The benefits of collaborative working in schools

The work of a number of projects with first-hand experience of working in schools with teachers and students highlights the clear benefits of collaborative work to both students and teachers. The key benefits to students are:

- enhanced learning through reduced confusion, greater coherence and linking abstract work in one subject with practical activities from another
- increased motivation through a greater perceived relevance and personal involvement
- a reduction in the assessment load where shared coursework assignments are used.

This leads to clear benefits for teachers through:

- more effective learning for students
- more effective use of teaching time through exploiting the links between subjects rather than duplicating teaching

Table 16.2 Links between Design and Technology, Science and Mathematics within the electrical and electronic aspects of Systems and Control

Design and Technology	Science	Mathematics
Understanding basic electrical circuits	Need for complete electrical circuit.	Understanding and using measuring instruments and units.
	Ways of controlling the current in electrical circuits.	Discrete and continuous measures.
	Use circuit diagrams.	Design and use data collection sheets.
	Measuring the current and potential difference (pd) in series and parallel circuits.	Use of letters to represent variables and formulae to represent the relationships between variables.
Use electrical switches to control devices.	Use switches to control electrical devices.	Manipulate algebraic expressions.
Use sensors in switching circuits. Simple feedback systems.	Investigating the characteristics of sensors. The principles of a potential divider.	Explore a variety of situations that lead to the expression of relationships.
Using electronics to control other subsystems: mechanical, electro-mechanical, and pneumatic subsystems.	Forces: types of force; forces can cause objects to turn about a pivot; the principle of moments; force, area and pressure.	Process and interpret data.
Analyse the performance of these systems	Measuring forces, movement, angles.	
	Measuring the 'energy' at stages of an energy transfer system. Sankey (energy flow) diagrams. Conservation of energy. Energy is always dissipated in energy transfers; the efficiency of energy transfers.	

- an improved understanding and awareness of other subjects
- better management of resources and the development of shared resources
- staff development, for example, through the discussion of teaching and learning approaches.

A process for planning collaborative work

Taking account of all of the above it is possible to outline a process for planning collaborative work in schools; this process has the following components:

Stage 1   Identify and agree a common broad area of content.

Stage 2   Identify the learning objectives – some of these may be common to the subjects involved; others might 'belong' to one subject but be dependent on the nature of the joint activity. This will also involve the identification of the knowledge, understanding and skills to be developed.

Stage 3   Identify strands of conceptual development that run through the subjects involved and employ strategies that support the effective transfer of understanding from one subject to another.

Stage 4   Discuss and agree the teaching methods and approaches that will enable the learning objectives to be achieved.
Different approaches to the same area of content or to a particular skill may be adopted in the different subjects. Each subject will bring to the collaborative project its own repertoire of teaching approaches. However, because they are part of a coherent and well-planned activity this will reinforce students' understanding and capability rather than raising conflicts and confusion in the minds of the students. Discussions about teaching and learning styles also provide extremely useful informal staff development.

Stage 5   Plan for coherence and progression.
A coherent structure and a coordinated approach to the topic need to be developed even though the activities may be covered in separate subject areas. At this stage it is also useful to identify the monitoring, review and evaluation procedures that will be used in order that the lessons learned can be transferred to other activities.

The implications for Design and Technology

The work carried out in school-based projects concerned with links between Design and Technology and other areas of the curriculum raises the question of whether there is a discrete body of knowledge and skills that is exclusive to Design and Technology. It is certainly true that developing skills in designing and making are at the heart of the subject. As Kimbell *et al.* put it:

> Process-centred capability, the ability effectively to pursue an activity from inception to completion, is the central requirement of Design and Technology capability. It requires the development of knowledge and skill, but that is not the point at all. The point is to be able creatively to make use of that knowledge and skill in tackling tasks in the made world.

> (APU 1996: 113)

Some of the knowledge required will come from the National Curriculum Programmes of Study for Design and Technology, but there is no doubt that some of the essential knowledge and understanding that contributes to Design and Technology activity will come from students' work in Science, or that mathematical skills are an essential tool for both designing and making. Of course, students will also draw upon their experience from other areas of the curriculum, as well as other aspects of their life, what David Layton refers to as 'eclectic pillaging' (Layton 1993). However, the knowledge and skills from Science and Mathematics are rarely capable of being used effectively without undergoing significant re-working to make them appropriate to the designing and making task – to turn them into 'knowledge for practical action'; in this sense, they become the property of Design and Technology. However, it is extremely unlikely that students can undertake this re-working without a great deal of support through structured activities (the problems of transfer of understanding have been raised earlier in the chapter). Specific activities to help the students make sense of the knowledge, understanding and skills they have in the context of the Design and Technology task and to then turn it into the 'knowledge for practical action' they need must be a key component of any Design and Technology programme.

This makes it imperative that a degree of coordination is established between these three departments in schools; the benefits to students' learning and development are clear.

References

APU (1991) *The Assessment of Performance in Design and Technology*, London: SEAC.

DfEE (1999) *Design and Technology in the National Curriculum*, London: DfEE.

DfEE (1999) *Mathematics in the National Curriculum*, London: DfEE.

DfEE (1999) *Science in the National Curriculum*, London: DfEE.

Kimbell R., Stables, K. and Green, R. (1996) *Understanding Practice in Design and Technology*, Buckingham: Open University Press.

Layton D. (1993) *Technology's Challenge to Science Education* (in the Developing Science and Technology Education series), Buckingham: Open University Press.

Owen-Jackson, G. (2000) *Learning to Teach Design and Technology in the Secondary School,* London: RoutledgeFalmer.

Sage, J. (1992) *Developing Relationships between Science and Technology in Secondary Schools,* Proceedings of IDATER 92 (International Conference on Design and Technology Educational Research and Curriculum Development), Loughborough: Loughborough University of Technology.

Sage, J. and Steeg, T. (1993) *Linking the Learning of Mathematics, Science and Technology within Key Stage 4 of the National Curriculum*, Proceedings of IDATER 93 (International Conference on Design and Technology Educational Research and Curriculum Development), Loughborough: Loughborough University of Technology.

Further resources

The ASE/DATA *Science with Technology Project*: The Association for Science Education and the Design and Technology Association.
The resources produced by this project are available from ASE Booksales, College Lane, Hatfield, Herts AL10 9AA.

The *Mechanics in Action Project*, Department of Education, University of Manchester, Oxford Road, Manchester.
Resources linking work in Mathematics with Science and Technology including:
McLachlan M. and Williams J. (1993) *Collaborative Work between Maths, Science and Technology in Stockport Schools*, Stockport LEA and the Mechanics in Action Project.
The above two projects were closely involved in the setting up of the Technology Enhancement Programme (TEP).

The leading Design and Technology curriculum projects such as the *Royal College of Art Schools Technology Project* and the *Nuffield Design and Technology Project* have also addressed the issues raised in this article.

17 Planning for capability and progression

Pat Doherty, John Huxtable, Jane Murray and
Ed Gillett

*This chapter was originally written by the Design and Technology advisory team from Somerset,
and has been updated for this collection by the editor. It considers how pupils progress in the various aspects of Design and Technology, and how they develop 'capability', and suggests ways of
planning work to encourage pupils' progression and development.*

National Curriculum Design and Technology – is there a missing link?

National Curriculum Design and Technology calls for the tackling of designing and
making activities to meet particular needs. Issues encountered whilst designing and
making are likely to demand the interaction of new and developing concepts that
take students beyond their previous personal and educationally provided experience.
They will be required to make increasingly more complex decisions and judgements
and to develop concepts related to design and technology. Students will build their
own platform of experience by drawing upon knowledge understood, skills developed and values formulated. Design and technology capability will enable students
to cope with, participate in and make informed decisions about the values and
purpose of technological change.

Education in design and technology should recognize this complex interaction
and develop learning opportunities accordingly. If this educational experience is to
be developmental then it must not be based on repetitive design process tasks or
specific practical skills alone. Fundamental to engaging in design and technology
activity is the relationship between the concepts drawn from specific knowledge,
skills and values. Design and technology capability is the management of the
complex inter-relationship between these concepts, in a way that facilitates the
positive procedures of designing and making to achieve outcomes in response to
human need.

The National Curriculum in England (those in Wales and Northern Ireland are
similar) requires that students be assessed against statements describing levels of
achievement. These 'level descriptions' outline the processes in Design and
Technology, but a holistic design and technology experience should offer more.
Such an approach calls for interaction between all of what we describe as the 'ground
rules'. This can also be the key to both assessment and progression.

The ground rules for Design and Technology in the statutory orders cover:

- setting the work in context
- the planned Programme of Study
- the range of materials pupils work with
- outcomes.

What does the National Curriculum omit?

The Programme of Study for Design and Technology makes no reference to:

- An understanding of children's conceptual development in design and technology;
- The relationship between the 'ground rules';
- How holistic design and technology will be taught.

This leaves teachers to address the following issues:

- How do children manage their design and technology experiences?
- What are the concepts handled in design and technology and how do they inter-relate?
- How can a student's grasp of the concepts of design and technology be ascertained; how can progression be planned for effectively?
- What does capability in design and technology really 'look' like and how does it develop?
- How can a student's capability be assessed?

How do children develop in design and technology?

The role of the teacher is to improve the learning of the child. Design and technology activity must enable students to engage in activities that continuously develop essential concepts whilst working towards tangible outcomes.

To be effective in the development of this learning, an understanding of the way in which children achieve progress in design and technology capability is essential.

In the past the focus for activity and learning in the 'practical' areas of the curriculum was very much on the practical activity and the product; the emphasis then swung almost entirely towards the requirements for students to record in detail much of their thinking, research, ideas and planning. It is vital that in design and technology both the reflective (thinking) and active (doing) aspects are given full consideration as they are inextricably linked parts of a dynamic, interactive, iterative process. …

Each activity/experience students undertake builds upon a platform of personal experience, and the level of capability they bring to each new activity is characterized by that platform of experience. How much the personal platform is extended will depend upon the degree to which capability is developed within each activity.

A model for understanding the development of design and technology capability

The following model of the conceptual development in design and technology capability can help when formulating schemes of work for children, by enhancing the opportunities provided through their learning experiences to develop capability in a planned and progressive way.

This model of conceptual development demonstrates a manner in which pupils will not only 'develop their attainments' but also develop holistic design and technology capability. It is critical that experiences in Design and Technology are not wholly 'driven' by the Attainment Target level descriptions and Programmes of Study. This would give a narrow experience and miss many opportunities for a 'full and rounded' design and technology experience. [...]

Knowledge, skills and values in Design and Technology

The knowledge and skills required for National Curriculum Design and Technology are laid out in the Programme of Study and Attainment Target. ... The values will determine the attitudes being taken by students when confronted with issues and constraints in design and technology activities.

Education in design and technology concerns the relationship between knowledge, skills, values and attitudes when producing outcomes in response to perceived human need. It would seem, therefore, that there must be some fundamental concepts that facilitate activity in design and technology.

Design and technology concepts

Concepts can be defined as organized but ever-changing groupings of thoughts or notions used to understand, classify and manage knowledge, skills and values.

Conceptual development in design and technology requires the assimilation of knowledge, practice of skills and the formation of values and attitudes (see Figure 17.1). Obviously the three are very much interlinked, but it is the identification of the concepts at the heart of design and technology that enables the relevant inter-relationships to be made.

Some concepts are simple, some more complex and they appear to have a hierarchy. When exploring some of the 'words' identified as describing design and technology 'concepts' it is apparent that they fall into 'categories'. It seemed that the categories could be further grouped as follows:

1   What resources go into a design and technology activity?
    (The human, physical, financial and technical resources that influence the procedures)
2   How is a design and technology activity handled?
    (Processes, techniques and methods employed in the generation and manufacture of outcomes)

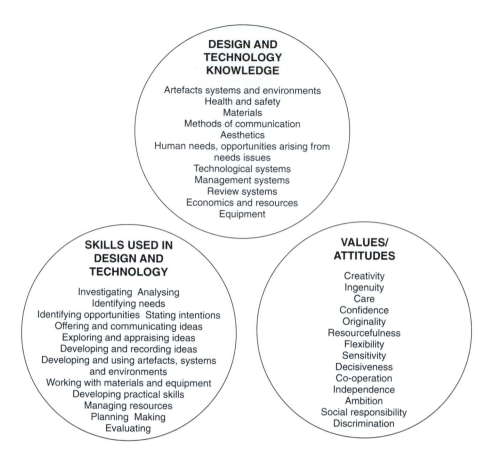

Figure 17.1 *Concepts in design and technology*

3 Why issues/actions need consideration?
(Human interaction and the way in which people are inextricably linked to the processes and resources)

Design and technology concept groupings

When considering a design and technology activity it seemed that these three broad concepts of *what* resources a design and technology activity, *how* a design and technology activity is handled and *why* issues and actions need reflection were those that needed to be handled and inter-related. These three broad concept groups take on relevance *when* set in contexts that determine *whatever* outcomes are realized to meet perceived human need.

It is only when an inter-relationship is established between the above elements of design and technology that capability is achieved (see Figure 17.2).

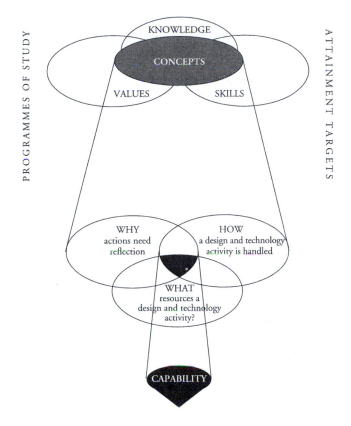

Figure 17.2 Inter-relating the concept groupings in design and technology capability

The difference between ability and capability

The following figures demonstrate one model of conceptual development in design and technology. The graphic description shows that if the concepts of *how*, *what*, and *why* are developed separately they foster *ability*. This ability can be to a very high level, but if the concepts are developed in such a way that inter-relation is enabled then *capability is* achieved.

The growth of an individual concept is shown in Figure 17.3. It uses the analogy of a 'window' into a concept determining the degree to which that concept is accommodated in the mind. As knowledge feeds that concept so the window opens, increasing the degree to which that concept is accommodated in the mind.

Managing and inter-relating the three individual concepts of *how, what* and *why* is shown in Figure 17.4. The 'window' analogy is used again to show the varying degree of assimilation, and the 'swivelling of the lamps' models the cognitive adjustments that need to be made to facilitate conceptual links. The three stages show an increasing accommodation of each concept with its associated increase in ability. However, though some inter-relationships are being made, as yet it is not with all three concepts.

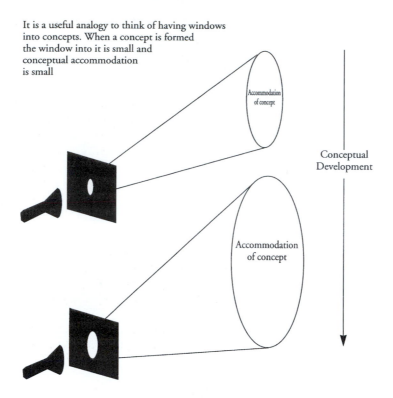

It is a useful analogy to think of having windows into concepts. When a concept is formed the window into it is small and conceptual accommodation is small

Accommodation of concept

Conceptual Development

Accommodation of concept

As knowledge feeds the concept its window opens further so increasing the degree to which the concept is accommodated in the mind

Figure 17.3 *The growth of an individual concept*

It is only when the concepts are managed to enable inter-relationships to be made between all three, as shown in Figure 17.5, that one can feel that design and technology *capability* is being developed.

Progression, then, in design and technology capability encompasses:

• the development of the ability of pupils to handle individual concepts of increasing breadth and depth;
• the ability to handle a larger number of increasingly complex concepts.

The matrix in Table 17.1 is an attempt to provide a holistic 'template' for design and technology activities, based on the three concepts described. … Teachers have found it useful when read vertically to give a 'holistic feel' for design and technology activities, which can tend to be lost if experiences are just national curriculum-driven. The matrix, when read horizontally, can begin to give indicators or pointers for structuring progression of capability. It is not implied that the progression spans 5–16; it is likely to be very different for individual children, groups and activities.

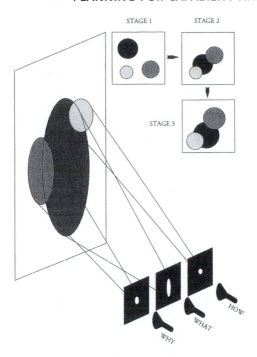

Figure 17.4 Managing and inter-relating individual concepts

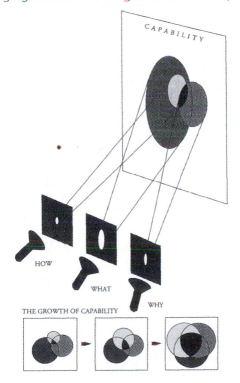

Figure 17.5 Managing concepts towards developing capability

Table 17.1 This matrix is an attempt to provide an holistic 'template' for design and technology activities

What resources a design and technology activity				
Human	from self and close peer group	working with others from extended peer group	working with others from outside school	working with increasing autonomy
Personal	working from personal experience	working to extend personal experience	continuing to establish and extend personal limits realistically	willingness and confidence to commit oneself
Energy	use, sources	control, transfer	release, conservation	generation
Materials	a selected range of materials, equipment and components	a wider range of materials, equipment and components	a greater breadth of sources	diverse operational characteristics
Finances	simple costings of materials	costing time, people, skills, budgets	cash forecasting, pricing, incomes	business systems, financial management
How a design and technology activity is handled				
Exploring	generation of ideas, creativity, information handling	developing ideas, innovation, investigative	design, prediction	transfer, hypothesis
Communication	imaging, expression of ideas, proposals, modelling	responding, plans, graphicacy, technological vocabulary, audience	specifying plans and methods, use of data	use of information technology, detail
Making	practicality, organization	techniques, prototypes, adjustments	management, production, procedures	specialist conventions
Evaluating	testing, choices	select, analyse, appraise, justify	review, set objectives, question, interpret	intuition, review, distinguish, determine
Why actions need reflections				
Constraints	competence, time, economics, properties	fitness for the purpose, environment, conservation, efficiency	ethics, market forces, external requirements, opportunity	capabilities, technologies, legality, conflicts
Human needs	of self, of others	opportunities, safety, health, protection, satisfaction	historical, cultural, social	human dimensions, ergonomics
Considerations	preference, improvement, aesthetics	value, conservation	finish, function	optimization, quality, efficacy

Implications for planning and assessment

As far as planning is concerned our experience has shown that it is critical to plan a structured range of progressive activities in advance for any Key Stage, giving careful consideration at the planning stage to the following points:

- The *how, what* and *why* of design and technology for each activity (as discussed in this chapter).
- Focusing on particular aspects of the Attainment Target and Programme of Study in an activity.
- The opportunity across a range of activities for specialist enrichment.

To make the task *manageable* teachers should be encouraged to focus on particular aspects of the Attainment Target to a high profile, whilst covering others to a lower profile. It makes teaching, and ultimately assessment, possible. Across a range of activities in a Key Stage it is possible to *structure* experiences that develop design and technology capability through integrating the diversity of specialist methods, techniques and materials and their related knowledge, skills and associated values.

Assessment of Design and Technology needs to be approached in two ways: first, that of 'holistic' assessment where an 'overview' method is adopted, looking globally at the way children engage in design and technology activities. Second, 'focused assessment' where aspects of activities are used for the basis of assessment over a Key Stage. A combination of the two methods will provide the desirable balance if built up progressively. […]

Summary

We must guard against giving children experiences that are narrow and prescriptive – a trap that we fall into if experiences are purely attainment target- and programme of study- driven. It is vital to ensure that children receive full and rounded experiences, and we believe the key to this is to take a holistic view of the provision. The way into this is to identify and understand the concepts that underpin the way in which children manage and develop that management of the design and technology procedures. The development of schemes of work that target a focus for activities which contribute individually to a collectively structured experience is the way to progressively develop capability.

References

DES (1990) *ERA 1988 Section 4 Order Technology; Design and Technology and Information Technology*, London: HMSO.

DfEE/QCA (1999) *The National Curriculum Handbook for Secondary Teachers in England*, London: HMSO.

Somerset (1990) *Somerset County Curriculum Statement*, Taunton: Somerset LEA.

18 Assessment in Design and Technology
Helen Wilson

This chapter begins by discussing the importance of considering assessment when planning schemes of work and individual lessons. This leads to a consideration of what is assessed and how. Finally, it presents an example of assessment procedures in the author's school.

Introduction

Assessment serves different purposes and takes different forms. This chapter begins by looking at how assessment requirements can be used to inform planning. When work has been planned with assessment in mind, I then consider the forms that assessment can take – formative and summative – and how pupils can be involved in the assessment process. In Design and Technology, there is assessment of process as well as content so I briefly consider what can be used as evidence when assessing pupils' achievement.

If assessment is to be fair to all pupils then it has to be consistent and reliable. There are two ways of trying to ensure this, one by 'standardizing' teachers judgements before they assess, the other by 'moderating' their assessments when they have been made, and both these processes are described.

Finally, I end the chapter with an outline of the Key Stage 3 assessment procedures in my own department, to show how these principles apply in practice.

Assessment and planning

Assessment is fundamental to good teaching and learning in Design and Technology, and it can form the basis for planning schemes of work and individual lessons. Systematic planning, ensuring (with reference to any National Curriculum or examination requirements) that each unit of work identifies appropriate knowledge and skills, together with appropriate learning objectives, will:

- enable pupils to develop their design and technology capability
- help in developing continuity and progression across a Key Stage, and across the different material areas
- allow for planned opportunities for the formative and summative assessment of each pupil's learning during the unit of work.

Table 18.1 A long-term curriculum map for Years 7–9.

	Food technology	Electronics	Resistant materials	Textiles technology
Year 7	Fruits and vegetables	Torch project	Boat project	Wall hanging

	Electronics	Resistant materials	Textiles technology	Food technology
Year 8	Buzzer toy	Clocks	Hat project	Pastry product

	Resistant materials	Textiles technology	Food technology	Electronics
Year 9	Chairs	Charity project	Batch production	Door sign

Table 18.2 National Curriculum requirements that might be met in a Year 7 Food Technology project.

	1								2					3			4				5							6		
	a	b	c	d	e	f	g	h	a	b	c	d	e	a	b	c	a	b	c	d	a	b	c	d	e	f	g	a	b	c
F T	*	*	*	*	*	*			*			*			*	*			*	*	*									

Using assessment criteria as a planning tool

When planning the teaching and learning of Design and Technology, how it should be taught and subsequently assessed, it helps to have a thorough understanding of the criteria against which judgements will be made about pupils' performance. Knowing where you are going enables you to plan how you will get there and how you will recognize that you have arrived!

There are three stages to planning work, each stage more detailed than the previous one. The first is long-term planning, in which units of work are 'mapped' across the year or Key Stage and against the National Curriculum. This is particularly important in Design and Technology. The whole department should work together on long-term planning, as account needs to be taken of pupils' work in different material areas and unnecessary repetition needs to be avoided. A long-term planning 'map' might look like the chart shown in Table 18.1.

This chart contains little detail, but merely shows which material areas pupils will work in and the units of work that they will undertake. There should be documentation accompanying it which shows how each unit of work meets the requirements of the National Curriculum. For example, the first project in Food Technology might meet the requirements shown in Table 18.2 (based on the National Curriculum 2000 for England, DfEE/QCA 1999: 136–8).

There are gaps here, which could be met in other units of work or in later years. This, then, identifies which aspects of the curriculum are to be met in the unit of

Table 18.3 Progress by level across the attainment target (QCA, 2000)

	LEVEL 1	LEVEL 2	LEVEL 3	LEVEL 4
Developing ideas	Pupils generate ideas and recognise characteristics of familiar products	Pupils generate ideas and plan what to do next, based on their experience of working with materials and components	Pupils generate ideas and recognise that their designs have to meet a range of different needs	Pupils generate ideas by collecting and using information. They take users' views into account ...
Planning	Their plans show that, with help, they can put their ideas into practice	They select appropriate tools, techniques and materials, explaining their choices	They make realistic plans for achieving their aims. ... They think ahead about the order of their work, choosing appropriate tools, equipment, materials, components and techniques	They ... produce step-by-step plans
Communicating ideas	They use pictures and words to describe what they want to do	They use models, pictures and words to describe their designs	They clarify ideas when asked and use words, labelled sketches and models to communicate the details of their designs	They communicate alternative ideas using words, labelled sketches and models, showing that they are aware of constraints
Producing quality products	They explain what they are making and which tools they are using. They use tools and materials with help, where needed	They use tools and assemble, join and combine materials and components in a variety of ways	They use tools and equipment with some accuracy to cut and shape materials and to put together components	They work with a variety of materials and components with some accuracy, paying attention to quality of finish and to function. They select and work with a range of tools and equipment
Evaluating process and products	They talk about their own and other people's work in simple terms and describe how a product works	They recognise what they have done well as their work progresses, and suggest things they could do better in the future	They identify where evaluation of the design-and-make process and their products has led to improvements	They reflect on their designs as they develop, bearing in mind the way the product will be used. They identify what is working well and what could be improved

	LEVEL 5	LEVEL 6	LEVEL 7	LEVEL 8
Developing ideas	Pupils draw on and use various sources of information. They use their understanding of the characteristics of familiar products when developing … their own ideas	Pupils draw on and use a range of sources of information, and show that they understand the form and function of familiar products … and develop detailed criteria for their designs and use these to explore design proposals	Pupils use a wide range of appropriate sources of information to develop ideas. They investigate form, function and production processes. … They recognise the different needs of a range of users and develop fully realistic designs	Pupils use a range of strategies to develop appropriate ideas …
Planning	They work from their own detailed plans, modifying them where appropriate	They produce plans that outline alternative methods of progressing	They produce plans that predict the time needed to carry out the main stages of making products	When planning they make decisions on materials and techniques based on their understanding of the physical properties and working characteristics of materials
Communicating ideas	They clarify their ideas through discussion, drawing and modelling … communicating their own ideas	They make models and drawings to explore and test their design thinking, discussing their ideas with users	They … communicate ideas, using a variety of media	Pupils … respond to information they have identified. … They identify conflicting demands on their design, explain how their ideas address these demands and use this analysis to produce proposals
Producing quality products	They work with a range of tools, materials, equipment, components and processes with some precision. They check their work as it develops and modify their approach in the light of progress	They work with a range of tools, materials, equipment, components and processes and show that they understand their characteristics. They check their work as it develops and modify their approach in the light of progress	They work with a range of tools, materials, equipment, components and processes, taking full account of their characteristics. They adapt their methods of manufacture to changing circumstances, providing a sound explanation for any change from the design proposal	They organise their work so that they can carry out processes accurately and consistently, and use tools, equipment, materials and components with precision
Evaluating process and products	They test and evaluate their products, showing that they understand situations in which their designs will have no function, and are aware of resources as a constraint. They evaluate their products and their use of information sources.	They evaluate how effectively they have used information sources, using the results of their research to inform their judgements when designing and making. They evaluate their products as they are being used, and identify ways of improving them	They select appropriate techniques to evaluate how their products would perform when used and modify their products in the light of the evaluation improve their performance	They identify a broad range of criteria for evaluating their products, clearly relating their findings to the purpose for which the products were designed and the appropriate use of resources

work which, in turn, will indicate the assessment criteria to be met. This first stage of planning, identifying the assessment criteria to be met, allows the second stage to continue.

A note of importance here for the long-term planning of Design and Technology work: if possible, account should be taken of pupils' previous experiences – for example, if you teach a resistant materials unit of work to a Year 7 group in September you need to consider how to teach the same unit to a Year 7 group in May, when they, unlike the first group, will have already worked in, say, food technology and electronics.

The second stage – medium-term planning – is usually done by a specialist teacher or group of teachers. A unit of work is planned in more detail, and considers what will be covered each week, the activities pupils will be engaged in, and teaching and assessment strategies.

Finally comes short-term planning, the planning of individual lessons, which usually specify in detail the lesson content, pupil activities, assessment and resources.

It is possible for each individual teacher to plan work and develop her/his own criteria for assessment but this is not helpful to other teachers, and would make comparison of pupils' performance difficult. The National Curriculum gives assessment criteria (in the Attainment Target level descriptions, DfEE/QCA 1999) which, if used by all teachers, ensure that all pupils across the country are being judged against the same criteria (the reliability of the judgements is a different issue). In Design and Technology it also ensures that pupils working in different material areas are judged against the same criteria.

The statements in the level descriptions are set out holistically. However, for the purposes of planning, it is helpful to identify the different elements (strands) involved with designing and making contained in each descriptor. The Teacher Guide produced by the Qualifications and Curriculum Authority (QCA) as part of the Key Stage 3 schemes of work for Design and Technology (QCA 2000) contains a valuable chart which clearly shows the progression through the levels, and in the different strands (Table 18.3).

At the departmental planning stage it is valuable to identify which aspects (strands) should be the focus for assessment within each of the different design-and-make tasks undertaken by each year group. This long-term planning will help to provide a structured Key Stage programme, which offers continuity and progression. It also helps to make assessment manageable. In some projects it may be more appropriate to focus on one or more strands in order to develop specific aspects of capability. As well as determining the strands to be addressed, planning at this level should also consider the appropriate range of levels on which to focus the teaching, in different units of work. At the end of a year or Key Stage a project that is assessed against all the strands can be used to identify holistic capability.

Using the chart in Table 18.3, or something similar, helps those teachers planning activities or tasks to identify the expected outcomes for each level. This, in turn, helps them to plan appropriate opportunities within each unit of work for pupils to acquire the necessary skills (through focused practical tasks, product analysis or design-and-make activities) in order to demonstrate their ability. Time spent on planning the assessment alongside the scheme of work will ensure that the tasks remain focused, and ultimately make individual pupil assessment considerably more reliable.

When teaching the planned work, it is essential that the assessment criteria are shared with pupils so that they understand the relevance of the work they are doing, the requirements for achieving success and how they can demonstrate and develop their capability. This can be done through providing:

- a 'pupil speak' version of the assessment criteria strands at different levels, that is, a chart in language appropriate to the age and ability of the pupils
- reminders to pupils each lesson
- 'I can' checklists as part of the evaluation at the end of a unit of work.

Teacher assessment

But what is it that is assessed in Design and Technology? National Curriculum documents (DENI 1996; DfEE/QCA 1999; ACCAC 2000) set out the knowledge, skills and understanding that teachers are required to teach, so attention must be paid to pupils' learning of these. However, these statements are quite broad, for example:

2 Pupils should be taught:
  e about the working characteristics and applications of a range of modern materials, including smart materials
4 Pupils should be taught:
  d how multiple copies can be made of the same product
(DfEE/QCA 1999: 136–7)

Teachers therefore need to think carefully about how these broad statements relate to each material areas and the specific activities and tasks to be planned. There does need to be some assessment of individual elements. You will want to know, for example, if a pupil can thread up and use a sewing machine, has the knowledge to select an appropriate type of wood for a practical task or knows how to write a specification. You will also want to know if they can engage in the processes of Design and Technology: do they know how to research, plan, evaluate? But assessment in Design and Technology is not just about assessing individual pieces of knowledge or individual skills; pupils need to be able to use the knowledge and skills at the right time and in the right way, in order to demonstrate their capability.

Pupils display their Design and Technology capability when designing and making products through applying the knowledge and skills they have acquired through focused activities. Teacher assessment involves making ongoing judgements about pupils' progress towards capability (formative assessment) and overall judgements on the level each pupil has achieved, in relation to the assessment criteria outlined in the level descriptions (summative assessment).

Formative assessment

Formative assessment enables the teacher to evaluate what pupils have learned and provides pupils with information about their strengths, weaknesses and significant achievements.

During individual lessons, formative assessment could occur through:

- observing pupils whilst they are working
- individual discussions with pupils about their work
- group or class discussion or question and answer sessions
- reviewing homework
- marking design work and practical work
- setting short written or practical tests
- marking homework.

Marking and recording

Marking pupils' work is a well-known and often-used form of formative assessment, and is part of everyday teaching and learning. Pupils need to know how well they have performed, and records of this need to be kept in order to monitor their progress. Pupils' progress from one National Curriculum level of attainment to another may appear to be slow, as each level covers approximately two years of teaching. It is important, therefore, for pupils to receive regular feedback on their progress, as this provides them with encouragement and motivation to develop their capability.

Formative marking of pupils' work should be constructive and provide specific guidance. For example, comments might read:

> Good. This shows that you have based your ideas on your research. To improve your work to the next level you will need to use more information in your research, for example by looking at websites and by talking to a wider range of people.

or

> This is good work. You have shown that you can evaluate your own work. To improve your work, in your next evaluation remember to refer back to the criteria in the specification when doing your evaluation.

How work is marked will depend on the type of task, and the departmental policy. Tests or activities to determine the extent of factual knowledge, or the ability to carry out specific practical skills, could still be marked traditionally, i.e. as a mark out of 10, against clearly defined criteria. Other tasks, such as research or design work, could be graded, with criteria being more descriptive: for example, a design task could be graded:

A several *appropriate* solutions proposed
   designs well-annotated
   one design chosen, based on appropriate evaluation
   good design skills demonstrated (appropriate to the task)

    B   several solutions proposed
          few annotations
          one design chosen, some evaluation evident
          some design skills demonstrated

    C   few solutions proposed
          no annotation
          one design chosen, no evaluation of proposals
          few design skills evident

    D   one or two solutions only
          no annotation
          one design chosen
          poor design skills

Sharing these grading criteria with pupils will allow them to see what they need to do in order to achieve higher grades.

Marking can also be used to acknowledge the effort a pupil has made when carrying out a piece of work. Again, schools usually have their own policy and system on this. Acknowledging the effort a pupil has made in relation to his/her individual ability is important, particularly if less able pupils are not to become disillusioned with their progress. It can also be used to show more able pupils when they are 'coasting' and not working to their full capability.

Design and Technology departments usually have an agreed marking policy, which takes account of the whole school policy. Teachers should ensure they are familiar with, and use, the system operated within their department. An agreed, consistent approach to marking will be helpful to the pupils, particularly where they are taught by more than one teacher.

Summative assessment

On its own, however, formative assessment cannot provide sufficient evidence to make an assessment of pupils' overall design and technology capability. Using formative assessment from a number of focused activities, together with summative assessments from a number of design-and-make tasks, gives a clearer picture for the end of Key Stage assessment.

At the end of a unit of work, year or Key Stage, summative assessment could include:

- assessing completed design work, including notes
- assessing completed practical work, including notes
- setting written or practical tests.

Teachers' summative assessment of pupils' capability is based on their understanding and interpretation of the level descriptions for Design and Technology set out in the National Curriculum documentation. These descriptions are clusters of criteria statements that describe pupil attainment, in holistic capability terms, at a particular level. They provide a framework to enable teachers to make a summative (final) assessment about a pupil's performance. The descriptions are designed to be used on a 'best-fit' basis: this means that teachers use their professional judgement, alongside the evidence provided by the pupil, to judge the level at which the pupil is performing. The level descriptions then provide a checking mechanism for this judgement, providing they meet the majority of the criteria in the descriptor the level is awarded. Teachers may, however, decide that a pupil needs to move up or down a level, if criteria at a higher or lower level provide a better fit against the pupil's performance. This assessment, and its subsequent reporting, is a statutory requirement at the end of each Key Stage, although teachers often use level descriptions when producing end-of-year assessments.

Assessing work against the level descriptions requires a different approach from that used when marking. Using the variety of evidence that they have gathered, teachers need to identify and record to what extent each pupil has demonstrated capability, as described in the cluster of statements for each level. Reference to the 'strand chart' noted earlier (Table 18.3) can be helpful here as progress in specific elements, such as developing ideas or producing quality products, from within the level description can be monitored, for example by identifying whether a pupil is working towards the level identified; achieving the level or working beyond the level identified (in which case, the pupils' work or performance would be assessed against the criteria at the next level). Progress can also be monitored by reference to the extent to which teacher help is required for the pupil to achieve the level identified: is it with help; with limited help; or without help?

Involving pupils

As mentioned earlier, sharing assessment criteria with pupils enables them to recognize what they need to do to demonstrate their capability. Involving them in their assessment can also help them determine whether they have demonstrated their capability, enabling them to recognize what they have achieved.

Pupils could be involved in assessment through:

- assessing their own work, with reference to the assessment criteria
- recording their achievements on a checklist
- discussing problems with their practical work and suggesting possible solutions, for example carrying out quality control checks to determine how well they have carried out specific practical tasks
- evaluating the design and manufacture of products they have made
- evaluating the way they have worked during a task.

In reviewing their work pupils can also be involved in setting themselves targets by identifying ways they can improve different aspects of their work in future activities and tasks. Many Design and Technology departments use an 'evaluation sheet' which pupils complete at the end of a unit of work; this often includes consideration not only of the finished item but also of how the pupil has worked.

Self-assessment provides pupils with a sense of ownership which can encourage and motivate them and in turn can help them develop more individual responsibility for their progress.

Assessment evidence

In addition to planning units of work that provide pupils with opportunities to demonstrate their abilities, it is also necessary to consider how evidence of ability will be recognized, assessed and recorded.

Design and Technology is not just about knowing and understanding, it is about *doing*. Assessment should, therefore, take account of how pupils *apply* their knowledge and skills during a task. It might be necessary for teachers to take account of ephemeral evidence, gained through observations and discussions during designing and making, if this shows how pupils are thinking or applying knowledge and skills.

Evidence of pupils' achievement might be seen through:

- a product
- a piece of written work
- an annotated design, or designs
- a presentation
- their, or your, notes of a discussion or conversation
- your notes of pupils' questions, answers or comments
- your observations of pupils.

The first four of these are quite straightforward: you have an article, a piece of written work or you see a presentation which you can assess against the criteria. The other three forms of evidence are less obvious, and so may be missed. In a lesson, you may have a conversation with a pupil which shows an understanding of the need to take account of user needs when designing, or how batch/mass production would influence the design. It is important that this does not go unrecognized or unassessed. Teachers should be prepared to make a note of any relevant comments, which need only be brief – and dated – to show that the conversation took place. Alternatively, the pupil could be encouraged to note it down in the design folder or logbook. In a practical lesson you may observe a pupil measuring accurately or selecting an appropriate piece of equipment and using it correctly. Again, observations such as these need to be noted so that their achievement can be rewarded.

The production of a design folder, often used in design-and-make activities, can provide evidence of achievement, which might otherwise be lost. (See Chapter 14 for a further discussion on the use of the design folder in project work and Chapter 10 for collecting evidence when pupils use ICT in their work.)

Evidence of achievement needs to be kept to support teacher assessment; however, it is not practicable or necessary to keep everything that every pupil produces. Nor is it realistic to keep pupils' practical work (in Food Technology it is impossible), since usually they will want to take home what they have made, but objects can be photographed for the purpose of keeping records. Digital cameras make this much more manageable as work can be stored on disk. A sample of pupils' design folders could be kept, however, and used as reference materials for staff and exemplars for other pupils.

There are no guidelines on what should be kept as evidence, nor on how this should be organized, and each department will develop its own preferred system. There is no point in collecting vast amounts of pupil work that is not referred to, and any item of work should be kept for a clear purpose. Stored work should also be updated at regular intervals with better, or more recent, examples.

Standardization and moderation

Building up a portfolio of pupils' work for the purposes of standardzation can be valuable in maintaining consistent standards of assessment across the different material areas within the department. The portfolio should contain examples of assessed design folders and practical work, for different units of work, in different materials and at different levels, to act as benchmarks for future assessment. These should be updated on a regular basis.

It is important that the different members of the Design and Technology department have an agreed standard of what constitutes achievement at each of the levels. This is particularly important between teachers specializing in different material areas. It is, therefore, advisable for departments to hold standardization meetings, at which they discuss samples of pupils' work in order to establish and agree the criteria required for each level.

At a standardization meeting, there should be work from the different material areas at different levels of achievement. Each teacher from the different areas is then required to assess the work and make a judgement as to the level they think each piece of work has demonstrated. Their judgements are then revealed so that similarities and differences can be discussed, until agreement is reached. This is not an easy process and can be time-consuming, but it is important that teachers assess consistently and reliably across the different areas within Design and Technology.

There are guidance materials produced by QCA, Local Education Authorities, the National Association for Advisers and Inspectors of Design and Technology (NAAIDT) and the Design and Technology Association (DATA) which can be used to assist in the standardization process.

Examples of design folders and practical work, together with their assessed levels, could also be displayed within the department, to assist pupils in relating their own work to the requirements for each level of attainment.

Standardization occurs *before* the formal assessing of pupils' work takes place, to help ensure that all teachers work to the same standard. *Moderation* is a similar process which takes place *after* assessment. During moderation, a sample of work marked by one teacher is marked by another teacher against the same assessment criteria; the second teacher is usually a more experienced teacher and, in Design and Technology, usually from the same specialist area. If the marks, or levels, awarded are similar then the teacher's assessment is judged to be satisfactory; if the marks are too high or too low then they are adjusted accordingly, to maintain the standard. It is a requirement of examination boards that moderation should be carried out within departments when GCSE examination work has been marked, to ensure consistent marking across the department and between different teachers. Moderation is always carried out by examination boards, both for teacher-assessed coursework and for written examinations, to ensure that assessment of pupils' work is consistent across the country.

Assessment, recording and reporting policies

Assessment also serves the purpose of allowing for the monitoring of progress of groups and individual pupils, and reporting on this. Assessment outcomes can be used to inform:

- pupils – of their achievements during as well as at the end of a unit of work and to suggest how they can improve
- parents – of their child's progression individually, in relation to the class and to national expectations and to suggest how they can help with their child's progress
- teachers planning subsequent modules of work – to identify what has been learnt, what aspects need to be reinforced and which pupils are ready to develop new skills
- senior management and governors – of the progress of individuals and groups within the school, in relation to their targets and in comparison with other similar schools. This helps to identify success and where aspects of the curriculum may need strengthening.

Schools are required to keep annually-updated records of pupils' achievements and capability in Design and Technology. Deciding what should be assessed, how it should be recorded and what should be kept as evidence is the responsibility of each individual school. The Design and Technology department needs to be aware of the school's assessment, recording and reporting policy and develop a system that satisfies both this and national requirements.

The policy and system adopted by the department should try to ensure that the collecting and recording of assessment evidence does not become too onerous or time-consuming. Evidence needs to be judged for its reliability and usefulness. The recording of assessment should also be simple to use, and provide clear information for others. Assessment records are used as the basis for reports, both written and verbal (parents' evenings), so should be compiled with the requirements of these in mind.

Formal reporting requirements are defined by government regulations. These usually form the basis of schools' policies, although some will go further, and departments will be required to produce informative reports which meet the policy guidelines.

Assessment in practice

The Design and Technology curriculum is structured in numerous different ways in schools across the country, each with its own system for assessing, marking and recording achievement. The system currently being used at my school is just one example of how this is being done at Key Stage 3. It is not put forward as a model that is necessarily appropriate for all schools, but it is probably similar to many other systems currently being used successfully, and may offer ideas that could be developed to suit the needs of different schools and different Key Stages. The system was developed with the introduction of the first revised National Curriculum orders in

1995 and has evolved over the years, in the light of experience and to take account of the changes in Curriculum 2000.

The system of marking and recording assessment we use was developed in an attempt to address the issues discussed earlier, the need to:

- use assessment criteria at the planning stage of a unit of work
- share assessment criteria and requirements with pupils
- provide formative feedback to pupils
- provide summative assessment of achievements
- involve pupils
- provide information on pupils' performance to other teachers, to pupils and to parents.

In Years 7 and 8, across all the material areas, we use a similar format. The example given here (Figure 18.1) is for a Year 8 textiles technology module.

The sheet is designed at the planning stage and forms the front page of a pupil work-booklet containing worksheets related to the topics listed on the sheet. The tasks are divided into two types:

1 focused resource tasks, called here 'resource tasks' – at the top of the sheet – structured activities that are formatively assessed. These are a mixture of short written tests and practical tasks. Each has clearly defined criteria against which the outcomes are marked.
2 design-and-make tasks – these relate to activities designed to provide evidence based on the level descriptions in the National Curriculum. They show the separate strands, and sub-processes within those. These sub-processes are each assessed separately against the criteria and an indicative National Curriculum level awarded. This allows teachers, and pupils, to identify specific areas in which there may be strengths or weaknesses.

In order to make pupils aware of the relationship between the worksheets in their booklet and the assessment criteria, the latter are outlined in the design-and-make section of the assessment chart. The statements are taken from the criteria in the level descriptions.[1]

The letters on the chart (E–A) relate to effort marks based on the school assessment policy. The work in the pupil booklet is marked on a regular basis during the module, with an effort grade and formative comments as appropriate. The marks are transferred to the assessment sheet by the pupils when their booklet is returned to them, and in this way it provides feedback as their work progresses. The marks awarded are also recorded in the teacher's mark-book.

At the bottom of the sheet there is space for the teacher to add comments and set targets for the pupil. There is also space to record grades for attitude, behaviour, 'responsibility' and homework (these also appear on the pupil's school report). The Attainment and Effort spaces are for recording internal grades, in line with the school assessment and recording policy. There is also a space to record the number of commendations (merit marks) a pupil has earned during the module.

YEAR 8 – MARK RECORD AND ASSESSMENT

Name: .... Tutor Group: ....D&T Group: ....

RESOURCE TASKS			MARKS
Written and practical tasks to develop the knowledge and skills to help you with your design-and-make task	Manufacturing textile products		/10
	Stitch settings		/10
	Curved seams 1		/10
	Curved seams 2		/10
	Pattern making		/10
	Looking at garment labels 1		/15
	Looking at garment labels 2		/10

DESIGN-AND-MAKE TASK – LEVELS 4 / 5 / 6		E	D	C	B	A	NC
RESEARCH Collect and use information about how existing products are made and take account of user needs.	Product analysis						
	Existing products						
	Customer needs						
DESIGN DEVELOPMENT Clarify and communicate your ideas through discussion, drawing and modelling showing you have used what you know about existing products.	Design specification						
	Design ideas						
	Evaluation of design ideas						
	Final design proposal						
	Swing tag designs						
PLANNING Work from your own detailed plans, modifying them as you need to.	Production planning						
	Production schedule						
	Organisation in lessons						
MAKING Select and use textiles, tools and equipment safely. Complete your product accurately and to a good standard.	Using tools and equipment						
	Quality of finished hat						
	Finished swing tag						
	Magazine advertisement						
EVALUATING Test and evaluate your product.	Testing						
	Evaluating						

TEACHER COMMENTS/TARGETS:

Attitude to work:	E	D	C	B	A
Behaviour:	E	D	C	B	A
Bringing correct equipment:	E	D	C	B	A
Homework:	E	D	C	B	A

Design folder work: Attainment .... Effort ....

Practical work: Attainment .... Effort ....

Signed: Commendations awarded: ....

©H.M. Wilson 2000

Figure 18.1 An example of a Year 8 mark record and assessment sheet

ASSESSMENT CHECKLIST – RESEARCH

Name: .... Tutor Group: ....D&T Group: ....

Level	IN MY FOLDER THERE IS EVIDENCE THAT I HAVE …	P	T
3	Shown I understand the function of one or more bags.		
	Written a design brief with help.		
4	Shown I understand the function of more than one bag.		
	Written my own design brief.		
	Collected pictures of existing bags and described each one.		
	Used a survey to collect information about customer needs and opinions.		
5	Shown I understand the function of more than one bag.		
	Written my own design brief.		
	Collected pictures of existing bags and described each one in some detail.		
	Evaluated an existing bag showing I understand its function.		
	Produced a survey to collect relevant information about customer needs and opinions.		
	Produced a few conclusions from my research.		
6	Shown I understand the function of more than one bag.		
	Written my own design brief.		
	Collected pictures of existing bags and described each one in good detail.		
	Evaluated an existing bag showing I understand its function and structure.		
	Produced a survey to collect relevant information about customer needs and opinions.		
	Presented the results of my survey in charts.		
	Produced some relevant conclusions from my research.		
7	Shown I understand the function of more than one bag.		
	Written my own design brief.		
	Collected pictures of existing bags and described each one in excellent detail.		
	Evaluated an existing bag showing I understand its function, structure and construction.		
	Produced a survey to collect relevant information about customer needs and opinions.		
	Presented the results of my survey in charts.		
	Produced several relevant conclusions from my research.		

TEACHER COMMENTS

Attainment ....

Effort ....

Commendations awarded ....

Signed ....

©H.M. Wilson 2001

Figure 18.2 An example of a Year 9 assessment checklist

For Year 9 pupils a different format is used, as they undertake a major project that is assessed holistically. Pupils are given a separate assessment recording sheet for each of the 'strands' within the design-and-make process, which outlines the requirements for several levels of achievement within that strand and provides guidance as to what is required. Figure 18.2 shows an example of the assessment sheet for the 'research strand'.

Over the past few years the department has tried several different formats for providing pupils with guidance materials for their major project. The format shown here has proved most successful as it enables pupils to see clearly what is expected for the different levels, they can select their own target level and can monitor their own progress as their work progresses. The checksheets for each strand mean that, at each stage in the development of pupils' work, formative assessment can take place and comments made to help them to achieve their target level.

Conclusion

The assessment of Design and Technology work is not easy. It requires careful planning to ensure that focused activities provide opportunities for the development of knowledge and skills, and design-and-make tasks allow pupils to demonstrate capability. Teachers need to be aware of assessment opportunities, and build these into activities and tasks. However, assessment evidence can be generated by written work, practical work or through discussion or observation at any point in a pupil's work, so teachers – and pupils – need to be vigilant.

Note

1   The strands used here, and those used for the other assessment record sheets produced for September 2000, were developed before receiving the QCA Exemplar Schemes of Work for Design and Technology. Appendix 1 in the Teachers' Guide of this document sets out strands showing progression by level across the attainment target. In producing future assessment sheets it is intended that we use the headings suggested by QCA.

References

ACCAC (2000) *The School Curriculum in Wales*, Cardiff ACCAC.

DENI (1996) *Circular 1996/21*, Belfast DENI.

DfEE/QCA (1999) *The National Curriculum Handbook for Secondary Teachers in England*, London: HMSO.

QCA (2000) *Design and Technology, A Scheme of Work for Key Stage 3, Teachers' Guide*, London: QCA.

3 Design and Technology and wider school issues

19 Design and Technology's contribution to the development of the use of language, numeracy, key skills, creativity and innovation and thinking skills

Louise Davies

This chapter identifies the teaching and learning in Design and Technology which contributes to other aspects of pupils' learning and development. It is adapted from the Qualifications and Curriculum Authority Design and Technology scheme of work for Key Stage 3 Teachers' Guide.

Use of language across the curriculum

The *use of language across the curriculum* requirement in the National Curriculum in England indicates areas of language to be included in all subject teaching. This aims to encourage pupils to use language, both spoken and written, to think, learn, express ideas and to use information and evidence to support their analysis, ideas and views. Pupils also need to be able to read texts with understanding, evaluating their usefulness and reliability.

The National Literacy Strategy in primary schools in England is an ambitious programme designed to equip the vast majority of pupils with the literacy skills they need to be successful in secondary school. These skills need to be reinforced and built on in order to maintain and improve these standards. Helping pupils with the language demands enhances their learning in design and technology and supports the development of literacy skills.

Pupils are likely to be more successful if there are consistent approaches to writing, speaking, listening and reading across the curriculum. This should be part of whole-school policies, to promote effective and coherent approaches to the teaching and learning of language. To assist schools in this process, QCA has developed a set of expectations in language and learning for each of Years 7, 8 and 9. These language objectives have been built into the schemes of work for all subjects, and are highlighted in the Language for Learning box on the back page of each unit, along with specialist vocabulary.

In Design and Technology, general accuracy in using language includes:

- the use of technical terms, oral or written, whilst communicating design intentions to teachers and peers
- clarity in recording specifications and planning manufacture

- clear summaries of attitudes and reasons for them, in expressing evaluative judgements.

Technical terms and concepts for design and technology abound and are essential to effective participation in the subject. They include:

- the expression of ideas (terms such as *concept model*, *design specification*, *texture*, *harmony*, *balance* and *proportion*)
- those relating to materials and making processes (terms such as *malleable*, *components*, *ingredients*, *solder*, *vacuum form* or *whisk*)
- description (such *as hard*, *workable*, *lightly cooked* or *well done*)
- the language of evaluation (such as *better because ...*, *more suitable to ...*, *compromise* and *optimize*).

Patterns of language associated with design and technology include:

- annotation of visual material
- oral expression combined with gestures and the physical presentation of samples
- extended text in expressing plans, purposes and intentions
- reasoned explanations in communicating evaluative summaries.

Accuracy in using language in Design and Technology is rigorous and exacting. Written and spoken language must be accurate. Its accuracy has a real purpose and can be tested; for example, if a written set of instructions is inaccurate, poorly laid out and confusing, the product will not be made to the quality required. Note, however, that it is important for you to listen carefully and sympathetically when pupils are to articulate a new, and for them, difficult idea. You can ask questions that help them express their views more clearly. Or, if a pupil is having particular difficulty, you can explain their ideas back to them and ask if your explanation makes sense.

Numeracy

Clear links can be made between Design and Technology and the National Curriculum requirements for Mathematics including *number and algebra*, *shape, space and measures* and *handling data*. During planning and realization and when they evaluate processes and products in Design and Technology, there will be opportunities for pupils to collect, sort, represent and analyse data in lists, diagrams and graphs, make estimates, measure lengths and angles to an appropriate degree of accuracy and to calculate, when they draw to scale or work out the effects of loads on a structure as examples. [...]

Key skills

The QCA Key Stage 3 schemes of work provide a foundation for the common areas of learning defined as Key Skills, namely:

Communication

Pupils will find this skill essential in Design and Technology: in oral work (listening, describing effects or observations, discussing, interchanging ideas with other pupils and teachers); in reading to extract information; in written reports or recording of ideas in presentation, both formal and informal; in design folios; in drawing throughout the design process; in flow charts showing production schedules, using images and making displays.

Application of number

These skills are inherently important in Design and Technology and can also be exploited beyond that which is merely necessary to the task in hand to play a major part in developing concepts and skills. Being numerate is a product of success in learning mathematics and pupils benefit from applying their skills across the curriculum, particularly in the context of real needs. Numeracy demands practical understanding of ways in which information is gathered by counting and measuring, and is presented in graphs, diagrams, charts and tables. Some aspects of design and technology, such as *food technology* and *electronics,* intrinsically require accuracy and precision and are self-fulfilling in this respect – resulting in patent failure or success. Some of the units are designed to exploit this potential. The units, as a whole, include opportunities for the calculating of nutritional content; costing possible products; communicating data and concepts; framing arguments in a reasoned numerically supported fashion; the numerical control of machines and the production of scale drawings.

Information technology

These rapidly changing technologies naturally enhance almost all aspects of design and technology, from information and communications technology (ICT) to help research, through computer-aided design (including visual presentation and analysis tools) and computer-controlled systems to computer-aided manufacture (including sewing, milling, cutting, engraving). Increased access to electronic and communications technology, including the internet and national and local grids for learning, offers particular value to Design and Technology due to its eclectic nature, releasing pupils from the limits of information and other resources held in the school. Other significant uses of ICT skills in the subject include interpreting, exploring and analysing information; developing and displaying data, using computer models; and evaluating the role of software and ICT itself. New computer applications will continue to emerge to support the subject at Key Stage 3 in ways not yet exploited, such as *virtual reality imaging*. (The use of ICT in teaching Design and Technology is discussed in detail in Chapter 10.)

Working with others

Key Stage 3 offers particular opportunities for both group projects and peer support for individual work for specific tasks, stages or whole units, including the sharing of ideas; effective group planning; group investigating; allocating roles and tasks in the group; keeping a log of responsibilities; and respecting the well-being of others. The QCA Schemes of Work, Unit 7E – 'Activity week' (optional), Unit 8D – 'Using control for security', Unit 9D – 'Using control for electronic monitoring', each provide a framework for team-working. (Group work is also covered in Chapters 8 and 13.)

Improving own learning and performance

Pupils will make good use of these skills in the design-and-make assignments, particularly in the planning aspects of assignments. Specific examples in individual units include pupils keeping a log of their work; planning particular activities or a sequence of tasks; adapting work methods to changing circumstances; planning independent ways of working; organizing the workload; practising and improving techniques; and prioritizing decisions on timing stages of production.

If focused practical tasks are presented as teacher support, to resource pupils in making decisions, then a significant aspect will be evaluating the process and the product, as well as negotiating future targets at the end of a design-and-make assignment (DMA).

Problem-solving

In Design and Technology, problem-solving can range from *ad hoc* ingenuity in making to strategic project planning and the consideration of significant alternatives in designing. Particular ways in which pupils can develop their problem-solving skills in this subject include the sorting, comparing and analysing of data or information; researching; understanding patterns or seeing connections; preventing hazards; recognizing issues; sequencing; recognizing different factors; explaining the workings of a system or design features; formulating and testing ideas; suggesting approaches; selecting options; predicting or making judgements and decisions and justifying their reasons and arguments; applying their ideas in a creative way, both in innovative designing and in ingenious making; developing criteria for product success, and refining ideas and evaluating their products.

If your pupils know where they are learning important key skills during the Key Stage 3 design and technology course they will understand the wider contribution this subject is making to their education. …

Creativity and innovation

Creativity and innovation are mentioned specifically in the 'Importance of design and technology' statement at the beginning of the new Programme of Study for Design and Technology in England (DfEE/QCA 1999). You can enable your pupils to be creative by providing lessons in which the class has the time to use different strategies to generate a wide range of design ideas. Your pupils can become innovative by taking some of these ideas and turning them into useful applications relevant to the designing and making assignment in hand. Design and Technology is about the practical application of knowledge, skills and understanding – it shifts the focus away from what pupils know and places it on what they are able to do with that knowledge. The creative and innovative problem-solver can be helped to develop the ability to formulate new solutions when designing, to transfer general knowledge and understanding to a relevant designing and making context and to focus attention in pursuit of a goal within that process. In order to 'create', pupils need confidence to learn in areas that are unfamiliar. The design and technology process of developing, planning and communicating ideas supports them as they formulate design questions then suggest design solutions which lead them to discovering ways forward and hopefully to invention.

Thinking skills

The QCA scheme of work for Key Stage 3 includes activities that enable pupils to reflect on their own thinking processes, and to clarify and reflect on their problem-solving strategies when working collaboratively or alone. Designing and making assignments require pupils to use the full range of thinking skills.

Information processing skills

These enable pupils to locate and collect relevant information, to sort, classify, sequence, compare and contrast, and to analyse part/whole relationships.

Some examples of activities that develop these skills are:

Unit 7C   Using ICT to support researching and designing

Show pupils how to use ICT to search for source material to help then when designing, and how they can become more discriminating in the way they seek information, e.g. how to access existing computer databases to seek information on materials and processes, how to go on-line for a virtual visit to see how others design and manufacture products.

Unit 9B   Designing for markets

Discuss with the pupils how to identify who the user is and research what the user wants, through product research and user research, e.g. how they can go about finding out what products other businesses are producing, comparing existing products, asking potential customers to test products, providing questionnaires for the potential users.

Reasoning skills

These enable pupils to give reasons for opinions and actions, to draw inferences and to make judgements, to use precise language to explain what they think, and to make judgements and decisions informed by reasons or evidence. Some examples of activities that develop these skills are:

Unit 7A   Materials

Discuss values issues relating to sources of materials, e.g. organically produced foods, finite resources, recognizing that when answering the question 'Am I using the best material for the job?' it may not be a simple decision about choosing the material most appropriate to meet the functional needs of the design. For example, what happens to this product after it has been used? What effect will it have on the built and natural environment? How does the existence of this product have a social, cultural or economic effect?

Unit 9A   Selecting materials

Explore how the development of new materials and technologies has allowed designers to achieve things that were not possible before. For example, we now have sufficient understanding of the chemistry of materials so that we can tailor-make materials to have the properties we want – and in future we are likely to see materials made to measure for a huge range of applications. Ask the pupils – what areas of research should we focus on? What products might be made? Who will benefit?

Enquiry skills

These enable pupils to ask relevant questions, to pose and define problems, to plan what to do and how to research, to predict outcomes and anticipate consequences, and to test conclusions and improve ideas. Some examples of activities that develop these skills are:

Unit 8D   Using control for security

Ask pupils to survey security systems in local or city shops. Make a list of all of the various systems, e.g. security tags, security guards, in-store video surveillance, street video surveillance, staff bag searches. Try to establish who the winners and losers might be.

Unit 9E   Ensuring quality production

Discuss how items are produced cheaply and in quality so that they all come out the same. What kinds of materials, equipment and processes are most suitable when many identical products have to be made? How serious would it be if one product was below standard? Discuss how to investigate the best method for producing an item and how to collect data when testing to help make a choice between two methods.

Creative thinking skills

These enable pupils to generate and extend ideas, to suggest hypotheses, to apply imagination and to look for alternative innovative outcomes. Some examples of activities that develop these skills are:

Unit 8B   Designing for clients

Have a class debate – where do new ideas come from? If possible use examples from designers and older pupils about how their ideas emerged. Discuss and allow pupils to try out strategies for generating new ideas e.g. brainstorming, word extension, analysing products, using part of a visual image, taking everyday objects and thinking up new uses for them, visiting places, talking to people, using the work of a design movement, other times and cultures, instant modelling with a variety of materials, experimenting with materials and processes, observing changes as a result of fashion trends and lifestyle shifts, collecting images that inspire, reviewing films, going to exhibitions and galleries.

Unit 8F   The world of professional designers

Design-and-make assignment – in the style of Ettore Sottsass: the famous Italian designer and his contemporaries established a design group known as Memphis. They decided to follow just one rule in their designing – the outcome must be fun. Design an unusual gift for a friend or relative. Investigate the work of modern designers and use their ideas as a source of inspiration.

Evaluation skills

These enable pupils to evaluate information, to judge the value of what they read, hear or do, to develop criteria for judging the value of their own work and others' work or ideas, and to have confidence in their judgements. Some examples of activities that develop these skills are:

Unit 7   Building on learning from Key Stage 2

Ask the pupils to bring in a piece of design and technology work from their primary school to show to the class. Discuss the work with the pupils, pointing out particular skills and knowledge that they already have and how these will be used in the coming months. Ask them to make a list called 'What can I do already?' focusing on their strengths.

Unit 9F   Moving onto Key Stage 4

Show pupils how they might analyse and record their progress during the project and reflect back over the Key Stage 3 course: for example:

- Self-assessment of skills.
- Thinking about or discussing the criteria for good work and reflecting on what aspects of their work meet those criteria.
- Reflecting on their own experience of their learning and becoming more aware of their preferred learning styles.
- Reflecting on their enjoyment and effort.
- Target setting and ideas for improving their products, the process and their learning. Planning their own progress: for example writing targets and discussing them for the next project with prompt questions such as: What did

you do best? What do you need to work at? What advice and help have you been given? What is the most useful thing that you have learned? What will you do differently next time?

Undertaking tasks to develop thinking skills

Research has identified three major phases in undertaking tasks which offer significant opportunities for developing pupils' understanding of, and skills in, thinking: framing; doing a challenging task and plenary or debriefing. These can be interpreted in Design and Technology as shown in Table 19.1.

The strategies for achieving closer attention to thinking skills in the design and technology context include:

- teacher reflection on, and modelling of, thinking skills
- pair problem-solving
- cooperative learning
- group discussion.

Table 19.1 Phases in tasks where students' thinking skills can be developed

Framing	Getting pupils interested.	Launching the brief for a DMA enthusiastically and thoroughly.
	Indicating purposes	Including stating why the task is worth doing.
		Showing how prior experience and FPTs will help them.
	Giving confidence	Looking ahead to the stages a DMA will go through.
	Clarifying procedures.	
Doing a challenging task	Increasing challenge (perhaps for some not all)	Giving open-ended briefs. Questioning pupils' intentions; providing conflicting information; reducing instructions and making pupils sort difficulties themselves. Using extension tasks.
Plenary or de-briefing	Reviewing with individuals, in groups or as a whole class.	Evaluating pupils' approaches to their designing and making. Using their products to reveal the weaknesses in their designing and making processes. Revealing equally worthwhile alternatives. Preparing them for future DMAs.

References

DfEE/QCA (1999) *The National Curriculum Handbook for Secondary Teachers in England*, London: HMSO.

20 Value judgements
Evaluating design
Susan V. McLaren

The aim of this chapter is to review the place of value judgements within Design and Technology education, to assess the potential impact of curriculum guidelines and teaching approaches on pupils' learning experiences.

Introduction: The case for teaching evaluation of design outcomes

Bertram, in 1938, argued that, as with every other capacity, there must be training in order to be able to judge design: 'Without some knowledge and directed practice, it is no more likely that a man (*sic*) would make an accurate judgement of this matter, than he would in law or medicine' (Bertram 1979: 59). He stated the case for the training of children on matters of 'good' design through a sufficient knowledge of technical processes, aesthetics, historical and cultural values as presented by 'experts'.

Is *training* an appropriate or feasible approach to achieving a society of individuals who are each aware of their own likes and dislikes of design and able to articulate the reasons for their personal response? Who should be educating for the increased awareness of both design and media manipulation; for the greater understanding of, and deeper reflection on, the marketing strategies employed? What experts should be called upon? The world of design has become ever more complex and involves a wide range of parties each with specialisms that contribute to the whole. The most contentious of values can be revealed by exploring the relationship of a consumer to the market-place and manufacturing industries and by delving into the cultural context of design and technology. This requires an understanding of design cultures and systems as a whole. Therefore, who can be defined as the 'experts' on 'good' design?

There is a difference between design for human need and design for a market driven by the economic demands of a capitalist culture. This difference often results in conflicts between the values of various interested and affected parties. Pacey (1983) explores these conflicts, drawing on his fieldwork in Asia and Africa. He advocates the need to balance the specialist's view of what a situation seems to require – for example, that of an engineer, hydraulics expert, architect, or geologist, etc. – against broader insights from the wider community. Technology is not only about technical facts. It involves a people-centred approach which integrates emotions of the user(s), function, environmental concerns and potential of locale. Pacey promotes dialogue and interaction, between the experts and the user groups, which aim for an appropriate technology. A common language enables the interaction to be mutually beneficial.

The need for a broader understanding of design is generally recognized. Kingsland (1969) observed that:

> [western] children now grow up in a world of sealed boxes and mysterious goings on in factories and buildings guarded by security officers. Even buildings arriving in pre-fabricated units are assembled behind a screen of shuttering, while the family car disappears for servicing into workshops behind the garage forecourt to be operated on in secret.
>
> (1969: 20)

Alienating children from the involvement in technology, which is an integral part of the culture in which they live, does nothing to help them think carefully about what the needs, problems and opportunities for design really are. If they are to have the confidence to devise new ideas to resolve these, or at least gain some knowledge to assess the success with which a designer has done so, they must be provided with the critical skills necessary to carry out an assessment of the existing world and to develop informed attitudes. In turn, informed attitudes produce a more discriminating buyer, one who can demand a better environment in which to live and more appropriate application of the technologies we have available to enhance the quality of life.

Much has been written on the need to raise awareness of values in design and technology in the global context at school level (Conway 1994; Budgett-Meakin 1993; Jenkins 1993; Layton 1992; Prime 1993).

Curriculum guidance

In Scotland, the theme of an informed consumer and user appears in the rationale of a range of current Design and Technology school syllabuses. *Technology Education in Scottish Schools, A Statement of Position* (Scottish CCC 1996) provides the basis for all curriculum development with regard to technology education and supports and enhances the concept of existing guidelines through the promotion of technological capability.

Technological capability is described as comprising four interconnected and mutually supportive aspects: technological perspective, technological confidence, technological sensitivity and technological creativity.

The aspect of technological perspective is concerned with

> ways of seeing and thinking about the world (past, present and future), of reflecting on the effects of human interaction with the environment and of thinking imaginatively about better ways of doing things. It also involves being able to appreciate the complexity of decisions which may involve the resolution of tensions between aesthetic, cultural, economic, ethical and functional aspects of product design.
>
> (Scottish CCC 1996: 8)

Technological sensitivity means

> a caring and responsible disposition; a habit of mind which asks and reflects on questions about social, moral, aesthetic and environmental – as well as technical and economic – aspects of technological activity undertaken by oneself and others in a variety of contexts.
>
> (1996: 9)

The importance of appreciating the non-neutrality of design and technological activity is developed throughout the curriculum documentation for Scottish education. For example, included in the aims of the Higher Arrangements[1] in Craft and Design is the following: 'to increase awareness of economic considerations and the social implications of design and manufacture' (SQA 1999: 3).

The recently revised Scottish guidelines for Technology – *Environmental Studies; Society, Science and Technology* – are permeated by a strand entitled 'Developing informed attitudes'. This advises that, through technology, pupils should be encouraged to appreciate that ideas and solutions that might satisfy some might be unacceptable to others. They should begin to understand 'the way products come into existence, are bought, sold, used, discarded and the effects upon social systems and environmental quality' (Learning and Teaching Scotland 2000: 76). Also, the guidance suggests that pupils should develop an understanding of 'the interplay between meeting needs through the use of materials, money, time and conserving and improving the quality of the natural environment through minimising harmful effects of actions'. However, there is little written on the methodologies or strategies for the teaching of product appraisal, or the development of the evaluative skills required to foster an understanding of such a complex process, subject to so many influences and often conflicting values.

The comfort factor in teaching value-based appraisal

Teachers themselves may not feel particularly comfortable in the arena of values. Indeed, they may not have had reason to examine their own value base and may feel ill-prepared to help their pupils do so.

As Ruth Conway, Coordinator of the Special Interest Group, Values in Design and Technology Education (Validate), urged in her opening address to the Values in Design and Technology Conference:

> We need to dig deeper than simply judging how well a product is made and performs, how attractive it looks and its value for money ... We need to ask on what basis have the choices been made? What has inspired and motivated the decision makers? What is the range and knowledge and what are the interests and concerns that have guided the value judgements? ... There are two sets of criteria involved: the criteria in the mind of those whose value judgements have led to this particular product and the criteria in the mind as we come to investigate, analyse and evaluate it.
>
> (Conway 1995)

It is the personal involvement through emotional response to design, the searching of one's own values, that many find avoidable. The value base and issues that are integral to each of these aspects should not be ignored in favour of maintaining a 'neutral teacher'-centred education programme, which causes no 'discomfort' but which denies the individual the opportunity to develop thoughts, express feelings, make connections, or offer opinions.

Criteria with which design can be evaluated

Since thinking and reflecting critically about everyday design and technology can reveal so much beyond the locale of the product, its fitness for purpose and how well it meets the performance specification, evaluation has a central educational role within the Design and Technology curriculum. However, the process of evaluation is complex. To begin with, we have the problem of interpreting the question of what constitutes good design. This question is one that many international educators and authors in design and technology have struggled with for many years, and continue to debate. No general definition of good quality design exists. Are we to consider the quality of the doing or the done?

Although the quality of thought and action demanded by the *process* of designing is recognized as important, greater emphasis is placed on the more tangible aspect of design activity, i.e. the quality of the *product* or *outcome*. Initially, this would appear to be easier to quantify and, of course, to assess.

However, in order to determine quality, the criteria against which it will be judged must be specified. The evaluator then uses evaluative skills and understanding to conduct a meaningful audit. The question of which criteria are chosen to evaluate design outcomes often differentiates design from objective, technical, problem-solving activity.

In attempting to evaluate design outcomes, we should appreciate that products are not conceived or bought to fulfil one purpose only. There are many factors which influence and manipulate purchasers, such as social or cultural associations, status or prestige symbolism. Therefore, as Meikle (1988) implied, identifying the criteria by which designs can be evaluated can also reveal the marketing research, and consequent approaches to design and promotion, that lead to 'differentiating products, segmenting markets and adding emotional value to products' (1988: 45). If we are to attempt to understand beyond 'likes' and dislikes' and begin to define quality in design we must consider the historical, social, economic and political context, which will help us to understand the value system within which the design evolved. We cannot merely evaluate objectively, against a static, universally accepted specification.

Considering the uses of technology determines whether 'real world' technology is neutral, or 'value free' (Layton 1992: 9). Design activity and applications of technologies can reshape people's values and call new ones into play. New actions are made possible, and people have the choice to exercise the action or not. These decisions are made by value judgements. Furthermore, technological innovations have altered the circumstances in which choices are made. Papanek (1985) and Whiteley (1993) explore the social and environmental responsibility of the designer, and the role of the consumer, in a rapidly changing society and increasingly multicultural context with shifting values.

Questions, rather than criteria, can be posed and explored to stimulate evaluations which require value judgements to be made. Suggestions from the special interest group, Values in Design and Technology Education, include the questions:

> To what extent does the idea meet people's need? What is a 'real' need? Is the product well enough made to carry out its purpose as well as in principle? Is meeting the need a worthwhile investment of time and resources? Does the proposed solution have other consequences which should be taken into consideration?
>
> (DATA 1997: 3)

Effective teaching and learning of value judgements

The value of product appraisal, evaluation and case studies is underrated as a teaching and learning approach in Design and Technology education. It is through the combined experience of evaluation *and* design that designers gain confidence in their tacit knowledge, an essential component of the skills and qualitative decision-making processes of design activity (Schon 1987).

At school, the teaching of design evaluation and product appraisal is often over-simplified and seen as a final 'stage' within a 'process'. For example, a teacher-devised pro forma is sometimes used to lead pupils through a series of questions intended to help them evaluate their design outcome. These pro forma questions are usually as follows:

- Does it perform its intended function?
- Is it attractive?
- Is it well made?
- Are there any changes you would make?

Many schools seem preoccupied with evaluating products in terms of finish, accuracy of manufacture and aesthetic 'appeal'. The question of 'for whom is the product aesthetically pleasing?' and the issue of 'for whom is the product acceptable?' are rarely evaluated. The consequences and potential impact, in a wider economic, societal or environmental sense, of what the pupil has designed or proposed are rarely examined. The results of the pupil's labours become the object for his/her own criticism. The pupil answers the questions posed, knowing that this part of 'the process' must be completed before she or he is permitted to move on to the next project. If the experience of evaluation is to be meaningful, there must be a strategy to ensure more is achieved.

An alternative approach would be to give a greater degree of importance to the processes of evaluation and research throughout the learning experience. This demands extended time: for deep thinking, for discussion and for sharing individual value judgements on the work of others as well as the pupil's own. To facilitate the process the teacher could provide key questions which would enable pupils to explore and reflect on the consequences of their decisions and actions, and those of other designers. For example:

- How necessary is this product? Who has decided it is needed?
- What is the need that is being addressed? How was it addressed in the past?
- Who would want to own or buy this product? Who do you think it is intended for?
- How is it to be used? What alternative uses could it be put to?
- What effect will it have on people's lives and relationships?
- What effect will it have on the built and natural environment?
- What will happen to it after its use?
- What factors lengthen or limit its life-span?
- Is there an alternative method of achieving the same function?

The evaluation could encompass activities which explore the perceptions and assumptions that initiated the process of designing. This could be tackled through an activity of collecting research data on the product, followed by a role-play scenario, through which the research findings are interpreted and personal statements are included, to explore the possible issues, influences and factors. The characters involved in role play may come from the target user group, indirect users, manufacturers, patrons and designers. Cost effectiveness, in relation to environmental impact, time, raw materials and manufacturing processes, etc., could be studied through product life-cycle research activities. Investigations and evaluations could explore beyond the materials and manufacturing processes to include the consequences of using a specific resource in a particular way, and the impact this has on both users and workers. Evaluating the relationships between the supposed target user group and those involved at each stage of design and manufacture can provide greater understanding about those who are indirectly affected by design decisions or by-products of the manufacturing process. Pupils could identify 'winners' and 'losers' in the development of a product or the application of technology. The Nuffield Key Stage 3 Design and Technology Project includes a task for use with pupils for this purpose. The pupils discuss the product or system under scrutiny, considering the people who are directly affected by it and those who are indirectly affected. An illustration of this is for pupils to examine who constitutes 'winners and losers' in the context of Athenian car drivers, who participate in the destruction of their own heritage and health but still perceive their need to drive in the city as paramount. Each affected group is colour-coded and the balance of colour helps the pupils to decide whether the product is a 'good' one or not, and prepare their justification. This leads to the examination of the ethical and moral choices to be considered and the factors that enabled or influenced the critical design decisions.

Evaluation as an educational experience – can it be taught?

Criticism is perceived as a relatively easy process. It is often a fairly straightforward procedure to find something to criticize about a system, a product or environment, especially if one has cause to experience it at first hand. Critical thinking conjures negative connotations and is perceived to be a form of attack. This perception arises from the notion that when asked to react about something it is easier to respond with a negative comment than with a positive one. It is easier to see what one considers to be 'wrong' than what is 'right'; we recognize the norm and attack anything that wavers from the expectations we hold. Therefore, when asking a group of pupils to conduct an evaluation of a product, the most readily offered opinions will tend to be negative and often unsupported. As de Bono observes, 'criticism is very emotionally attractive and satisfying. Attacking an idea instantly makes you seem superior to that idea' (de Bono 1994: 27). The curriculum offers opportunities to create debate and discussion between pupils that demands more than '… just because I do' as justification for their criticism.

Observations of children evaluating artefacts and environments illustrate the immediate obstacles they face. Pupils may be frustrated, initially, by their lack of vocabulary to satisfactorily express their opinions and communicate their value judgements. We can enhance their language skills, to better equip them for discussions of this nature, through sensory and emotional awareness-raising techniques. These include strategies such as blindfold description 'games', 'best-fit' word prompts, analogies and creative writing activities.

Pupils may also feel inhibited. Therefore, the climate for a values-based critique needs to be comfortable and unthreatening in order to encourage the communication of personal value judgements. Peer group pressure will inevitably have an adverse effect on any critique which demands individual and independent thinking.

Presented and taught as a stand-alone component, the potential of evaluation is undermined. However, within a holistic process and as educational tools, critical thinking and the exploration of value judgements have enormous potential.

Barriers to identifying values

In order to develop teaching approaches we require ways of uncovering the values in technological products and of reviewing how the value conflicts have been handled or resolved.

Design opportunities, perceived needs and wants from which the resultant products arise, do not present themselves to designers in neat packages. They must be determined from ambiguous, unstructured scenarios and formulated in such a way as to allow the problem to be 'solved'. Many considerations will be difficult to define. Influential factors and constraints will have to be identified. It is through this initial 'framing' process (Schon 1987) that a designer begins to perceive the context and the extent of the task. This inevitably results in a wide range of interpretations of any one problem, due to the diversity of personal perspectives and values.

Therefore, the subject of the evaluation is only one reconciliation, a selection of specific choices and/or an integration of the various selected perspectives; it is not simply a *physical* product or environment. The resultant outcome is, in turn, evaluated against the design requirements, decisions and values of the initial problem, as framed not by the actual designer, whose thought and opinions and briefing may not be accessible by the evaluator, but as perceived by the evaluator him/herself.

Examination of artefacts, systems and environments through an analytical, systematic, scientific methodology and product autopsy may not reveal the initial complexity of such problem framing. We cannot critique using the mechanisms of ergonomics, user trials and 'expert' objective analysis only. There is an inherent difficulty in evaluating a static product from a 'concluded' viewpoint. Access to the conceptual insights of the designer in the process of designing is not always possible. Therefore, the evaluator may miss the implicit ideology, the implications and the wider effects on society. Within design there are many things which are implicit, remaining under the surface and not discussed to any great extent, if at all. Perhaps it is because design itself is based on implicit responses and intuitive rationalization of complexities that, even if communication is attempted, there may not necessarily be universal convergence of meaning. The ambiguity of design should encourage us to evaluate from a number of perspectives, and against a wide range of criteria, which includes value judgements.

Using product design case studies

There is growing interest in developing well-researched and -resourced design case studies. These are preferably built up from a variety of sources, including input from the initial designer/design team or client, and they should offer more opportunities than simply analysing what others do. The case study should describe the initial scenario and dialogue and tell the story of the design activity and decision-making, from conception through to marketplace, using graphics, transcripts, manufacturing and performance data, user tests and other aspects relevant to the particular case.

To 'present' a case study to pupils can result in passive storytelling. Case studies offer us the potential to explore and hypothesize on the initial problem framing from which the design emerged. Pupils must be actively involved in the process of evaluation for the experience to have any meaning or impact on their own design capabilities and understanding.

Multi-media methods of capturing discussions with designers and design teams, and the processes and discussions involved in their work, should be sought so that pupils can be privy to illustrations of decision-making processes. Case studies, prepared in collaboration with designers, manufacturers and clients, in CD-ROM format or on-line, enable pupils, for example, to:

- explore the consequences of various decisions and routes that were available
- observe animation and illustrations of the design as it evolved
- be introduced to the industrial process utilized and the scientific principles or design concepts on which the design was based.

The pupils could reflect on the question, 'Would the designer have done the same if she/he knew then what we now know?'

The teaching and learning approach suggested by *Technology Education in Scottish Schools: A Statement of Position* (Scottish CCC 1996) provides the pupils with experiences of 'proficiency tasks', which develop:

- *skills*   for example, recording research, media manipulation, design of fair user tests

- *knowledge bases* for example, the history of technological developments and their relationship to societal events and changes; calculation of forces; material properties
- *understanding of processes* for example, industrial manufacturing of plastic products; school-based forming and construction of plastic products.

'Creative practical tasks' are devised to provide pupils with a degree of autonomy in the application of the skills and understanding they have gained, and to challenge pupils to extend their skills and understanding. They also engage pupils in the identification of needs and exploration of opportunities for technological activity, through appraisal and evaluation of environments, societies, technological artefacts and systems. Integral to these tasks are the 'case study tasks' in which pupils study technology in the wider world and its interactions with society and the environment. It is envisaged that these case studies will involve pupils in fieldwork to local industries, interviews with adults other than teachers, and that they will begin to 'make informed judgements about the appropriateness of the technological products created by others' (1996: 12). The activities are intended to encourage pupils to 're-flect critically and constructively on the interplay between technology, society and the environment – now and in the past – locally, nationally and globally and in various cultural settings' (1996: 13).

The following description of a classroom project, 'For Want of Water', illustrates how such technological learning activities can construct an integrated experience. Pupils were asked to monitor, and reflect on their own attitude towards, the consumption of water in their own domestic situation. They were initially engaged in a simulation game, 'The Day the Water Stopped' (adapted from Save the Children), which encouraged them to explore their own emotional responses to water shortages. This involved them, as a group, in decision-making about actions to survive a water shortage in their home town, due to industrial contamination of the supply, and following the consequences of their decisions.

Further stimulus included an interactive case study approach which examined water scarcity and supply in Malawi, Tanzania and Bangladesh. A video, *For Want of Water* (adapted from Shell), illustrated hand-dug and tube wells, gravity-supplied water, community involvement in sanitation projects and women health workers and maintenance engineers. The importance of education and cooperative team-work towards the new appropriate technologies was also explored. The pupils simulated some of the principles of the various wells, guided by the teacher, and attempted, independently, to devise strategies for overcoming some of the problems illustrated, which were due to lack of mechanical equipment. The case study also offered opportunities for the pupils to design latrines and to explore the use of graphics and 'advertising jingles' to convey health messages and education.

Fieldwork at Kielder reservoir, the largest in the UK, helped pupils to appreciate the ways in which water was treated and brought to their house. The construction of the dam, and the environmental impact this had on the area, was described to them from geographical and historical perspectives. A variety of creative practical tasks resulted. These ranged from the design of methods of raising water from underground sources (exploring suction and displacement pumps, valves, low maintenance and accessible local materials, pulley mechanisms, gravity feed, etc.) to the construction of a working system to demonstrate hot and cold water pressured domestic supply. The teams considered comfort and appearance equally with efficiency and ease of maintenance of the design, aware of the difficulties in encouraging the use of new technologies, if not appropriate. All designs were modelled and tested to modify and refine them in readiness for demonstration, presentation and critique. Outcomes were evaluated so that pupils were encouraged to reflect upon the interplay between technology, society and the environment in a specific context and culture different from their own.

Throughout the project the pupils were fully involved and tackled their creative practical task with sustained motivation, and they displayed perseverance with emergent problems along the way. The project provided a balance between 'authenticity'[2] and other learning objectives, of procedural and conceptual knowledge, and allowed them opportunities to make significant decisions throughout their designing.

Through various forms of empathy, the 'personalization' of a case study can help pupils learn to apply their own knowledge and explore their own values. Personalization can be achieved by encouraging pupils to conjecture about the initial scenario which may have determined the boundaries within which the designer worked. This involves the pupils in reasoning and identifying the issues and principles that they perceive to be central to the case. They will inquire or hypothesize. How has this thing come into being? What variables were involved? What constraints? What discoveries? What conflicts and values? How did the designer deal with these conflicts? They can collect facts and research information to provide background to their personal construct of how the designer designed and made decisions. It is important that all suggestions, opinions and differentiated responses are appreciated by others. The individual interpretation of the complex processes that are explored through 'role play' should be acknowledged as valid offerings.

A range of learning opportunities evolves from the experience of evaluating the work of another through case studies, and consequently increased awareness and greater understanding of design values are achieved.

Pupils can be involved in creating their own 'case study', through collecting and collating factual data, evidence from fair ergonomic testing and hypothesis, and personal opinion. This investigation and exploration may highlight a particular issue, or unsatisfactory resolution, and pupils can reframe the initial problem as perceived or re-design the product to rectify the weaknesses identified. For example, a case study on lawnmowers, compiled by a student teacher, involved research of a timeline relating technological invention, social events and lifestyles; user tests of a particular manufacturer's model; principle and mode of function; details on materials and manufacture processes, etc. The case study resulted in the student concluding that the design met almost all requirements of a lawnmower. However, he identified a related problem. The lifestyle of many small garden owners may mean that the lawn cuttings are not placed on a compost heap but put into bags for collection by the garbage collectors. The procedure of tipping the 'cuttings collector bucket' into a loose bag was very difficult for an individual. The problem was resolved by a handheld simple hoop structure which gripped the top of the bag in an open position, allowing the cuttings to fall from the 'collector bucket' into the garbage bag. This design in turn can be evaluated against the values of another – should people be encouraged to dispose of grass cuttings in this way?

I suggest that we should be aiming to develop pupils' ability to transfer the type of reflection involved in the process of evaluation of design or decision-making. Each idea should be evaluated in terms of the effects, impact or consequences it may have on other aspects, or earlier decisions, and whether the impact is one of greater potential or creates the possibility of further problems. The ability to reflect critically on one's own work and the work of others is essential.

In theory, an education – and, in particular, a design and technological education – which recognizes evaluative and reflective 'skills' and encourages the exploration of value judgements, with all the 'difficulties in assessment' that entails, will enhance pupils' understanding of design.

As Bernard Aylward commented, the Programmes of Study we devise must help each of our pupils to:

> look afresh at materials, to think carefully what the problem really is, before he (*sic*) attempts to solve it, to be bold in trying quite new ideas and finally to produce something that is practical and sound, yet pleasing and fresh. If he (*sic*) cannot quite do that, he (*sic*) may at least gain some knowledge whereby he (*sic*) can assess soundly the success with which a designer has done so. He (*sic*) will be a more discriminating buyer and one who demands a better environment in which to live.
>
> (1969: 30)

Making connections – research and practice

If pupils are to develop their design understanding and capability it is crucial that they are given the opportunity to reflect on their explorations of a value-based appraisal of technology in society, and allow their reflections to influence their approach to design. The holistic approach to design and technology should be stressed. We must avoid perpetuating the myth, created by existing teaching approaches, that there is a separation of evaluation and design activity.

The Programmes of Work that are devised by educators should allow pupils to build up a bank of informed attitudes, images, understandings and actions. This could be achieved through progressive context-based design projects which are stimulated by appraisals, case studies, investigations into collections of related designs, role plays or explorations of documented approaches used by designers. A range of strategies and approaches is required to meet the individual needs of pupils. These should include those which encourage debate, topical discussion and commentary expanding the pupils' vocabulary, intertwining cultural and historical issues, and involve pupils in a voyage of self-discovery through the articulation of previously unvoiced opinions. Programmes that embrace the concept of resource-based learning, make the time for fieldwork and for pupil-centred activities, from short, structured, focused projects to long-term, open briefs, will require a committed, well-organized teaching team, who are themselves aware of the values and are confident in confronting the issues. Such programmes should enable a pupil to perceive new situations and scenarios through similarities and differences of previous situations experienced or studied.

It is not the intention, as Horrocks (1969) cautioned, that we study endless examples of design which have been classed as good or bad by some external body, but rather to 'defend and encourage the individual's freedom of choice and criticism based on reasoned understanding' (1996: 36).

Ways forward for curriculum development

The potential of the Design and Technology curriculum lies in the contextualizing and structuring of learning experiences. These should be devised to increase awareness, stimulate curiosity and encourage appraisal of the applications of technology, and provide challenging, open-ended, problem-solving opportunities.

If we are to encourage pupils to make connections and develop informed attitudes then there ought to be a strategy to ensure the development of critical thinking skills. Objective evaluation *and* exploration of the subjective responses, inclusive of value judgements, should be included in this strategy. It is through the connections of scientific concepts, technological applications, the impact on the global environment and the effect on society as a whole, that pupils can be encouraged to engage in constructive action thinking. This develops an appreciation, from a people-centred perspective, of the complexities of decisions, interests, values and influences that contribute to the world in which the pupils live. There is the potential to develop a design technology education where, as Finney (1993) urges, an audit of values, environmental impact and sustainability takes a central role.

Through the existing and proposed provision of the curriculum, there exists a framework within which design and technology can be developed as a broad process, through real-life contexts with concern for social and environmental implications. We must avoid reducing the curriculum to learned sequences of procedures, the mechanical application of acquired skills, and instead ensure that life skills developed by design and technology activity remain central. This will demand creative pedagogy, planning and presentation which allow greater flexibility and sensitivity than was required with the previous approach of quantifiable, objective, value-free 'reports'.

I suggest that, in order for teachers to be in a position to develop approaches to teaching evaluation, they require the confidence to explore their own values and to question the beliefs and perceptions they hold.

Conclusion

We have the rationale and the literature to support the philosophy outlined in this chapter. Our attention must turn to the development of the methodologies, strategies and approaches to support the educators. We require ways of uncovering the values within technological activity through which we can review how value conflicts have been resolved, or not, and methodologies for reflection on our response, from both an informative, objective view and from a subjective, emotional view.

Notes

1   The Scottish 5–14 curriculum is followed by an individually selected curriculum of Standard grades, two-year certificated courses (Scottish Examination Board, SEB) taken, normally, over the period of Secondary 3 and Secondary 4. Students progress on to the Higher Still courses of Intermediate 2, Higher, Advanced Higher, one-year certificated courses (SQA)

2   Authentic in the sense that it was personally meaningful to the pupils and purposeful within a social framework; as described in many conference papers by McCormick, R., Murphy, P., Hennessy, S., including 'Problem-solving in design and technology: a case of situated learning' (1994)

References

Aylward, B. (1969), ' Design education in practice', in K. Baynes (ed.), *Attitudes in Design Education*, London: Lund Humphries.

Bertram, A. (1979) 'De gustibus non est disputandum (You can't argue about taste)', in S. Bayley (ed.), *In Good Shape – Style in Industrial Products 1900–1960*, Collected Essays, London: Design Council. Essay first published 1938.

Budgett-Meakin, C. (ed.) (1992) *Make the Future Work: Appropriate Technology, A Teachers' Guide*, Harlow: Longman.

Conway, R. (1995) Introductory Address, Products and Applications – Exploring Value Judgements in Design and Technology Conference, Selly Oak Colleges, Birmingham, 11 February.

Conway, R. (1994) 'Values in Design and Technology education', in *International Journal of Technology and Design Education* 4: 109–16.

DATA (1997) *Exploring Value Judgements in Design and Technology, Guidance Notes 3.1*, Wellesbourne: Design and Technology Association.

de Bono, E. (1994) *Parallel Thinking – From Socratic to de Bono Thinking*, London: Penguin Books Ltd.

Finney, D. (1993) 'What are we trying to do to our children? What are we doing to our children?', in *Design and Technology Teaching* 26(1).

Horrocks, A. (1969) 'Art rooms', in K. Baynes (ed.) *Attitudes in Design Education*, London: Lund Humphries.

Jenkins, E.W. (ed.) (1993) *School Science and Technology: Some Issues and Perspectives*, Centre for Studies in Science and Mathematics, University of Leeds.

Kingsland, J.C. (1969) 'In search of an alternative road', in K. Baynes (ed.) *Attitudes in Design Education*, London: Lund Humphries.

Layton, D. (1992) *Values and Design and Technology*, Loughborough: Loughborough University of Technology.

Learning and Teaching Scotland (2000) *Environmental Studies: Society, Science and Technology, 5–14 National Guidelines*, Dundee: Learning and Teaching, Scotland.

McCormick, R., Murphy, P., and Hennessy, S. (1994). 'Problem solving in Design and Technology: a case of situated learning?', paper presented at Annual Meeting of American Education Research Association, New Orleans, Louisiana, April.

Meikle, J. (1988) 'Design in the contemporary world', a paper presented from the proceedings of Stanford Design Forum.

Nuffield Design and Technology Project (1995) *Resource Task File KS3*, Harlow: Longman Group.

Pacey, A. (1983) *The Culture of Technology*, Oxford: Basil Blackwell Publishers Ltd.

Papanek, V.(1985) *Design for The Real World: Human Ecology and Social Change*, London: Thames and Hudson Ltd.

Prime, G. (1993) 'Values in technology: approaches to learning', in J. Eggleston (ed.) *Design and Technology Teaching* 2(1).

Schon, D. (1987) *The Reflective Practitioner: How Professions Think In Action*, San Francisco: Basic Books Inc.

Scottish CCC (1996) *Technology Education In Scottish Schools: A Statement of Position*, Dundee: Scottish Consultative Council on the Curriculum.

SQA (1999) *National Course Specification in Higher Grade Craft and Design*, Scottish Qualifications Authority.

Whiteley, N. (1993) *Design for Society*, London: Reaktion Books Ltd.

21 Social, moral, spiritual and cultural issues in Design and Technology

David Coates and Nick Rose

A consideration of social, moral, spiritual and cultural issues is integral to Design and Technology, because of the effects these issues have on people's needs and expectations. This chapter considers how these issues might be made explicit in the teaching of Design and Technology, in order to make pupils more aware of them.

Values are an intrinsic part of Design and Technology because the nature of the subject deals with people's spiritual, moral, social and cultural needs and differences. 'What is needed for the future? What do people want? By what means could it be achieved and at what cost? How will what has been planned affect people, their environment, now and in the future? Values and value judgements always emerge when striving for the best balance or proposing the most inclusive and potentially enhancing range of possibilities' (Standen 1992: 83). These feelings are expressed through the design and manufacture of products ... from around the world, by designers with different agendas, resources and manufacturing capabilities.

Design and technology education is concerned with pupils designing and making quality products, reflecting what happens in the wider world. It provides excellent opportunities for pupils to apply value judgements of an aesthetic, economic, moral, social and technical nature in two contexts: when evaluating their own work; and when examining existing processes and products through product analysis activities (DfEE/QCA 1999). Through Design and Technology pupils can learn about the inter-relationship of the technical, scientific, environmental, aesthetic, economic, social and moral aspects of society in a practical manner. ...

Technology is seen as essentially a human activity. Since our earliest times we have been using technology to solve problems, to meet our needs and wants. It has developed our capability to grow food, build shelters and travel from place to place at great speed, for example. It would be easy to limit our definition of technology to simple examination of the finished product in terms of technicality and cost effectiveness, but pupils need to explore decisions that influence what we design and make, which come from balancing technical and cost factors with aesthetic, environmental and moral criteria (DfEE 1995b). The restricted idea of technology by itself ignores the human dimension. 'We create things that we value, the things we think beautiful or useful. We devise tools, machines and systems to accomplish the ends we value' (Prime 1993: 30). Consideration of values has the power to soften some perceptions of technology. When pupils design and make products to solve problems they express their creativity, inventiveness, imagination and sense of worth (that is, their spirituality), from which they develop products which meet precise specifications.

Values are central to 'quality' and 'purpose', and to the development of products in response to needs, desires or opportunities. ... What we design and make may have implications for developers and users, and there may be resource issues or side effects. Take the motor car. Is it a quality product? It clearly meets one purpose, to move people at speed, in comfort and safety. The design has been constantly improved over the years, in terms of speed, safety, reliability and economy. Most cars, however, use petrol which is manufactured from oil, a scarce resource. They produce pollution which has serious environmental and health effects. There is a potentially contradictory idea of the car as a 'quality product' which is 'fit for its purpose'. We weigh one value judgement against another in our decision to drive. The technology is not value free: value judgements are influenced by personal, social and cultural priorities. This balance between conflicting values can shape the community in which we live. An alternative view sees technology as increasingly pervasive, with harmful impact at a natural and a social level. For example, medical technologies have reduced death rates in developing countries, but have contributed to population growth. Progress has been viewed in technological terms, ... but technology can be shaped by the values and beliefs of a community. There is more research now into electrical cars, which pollute less, in response to environmental and social values which our society has begun to regard more highly. Values in the technology must match those of its users. When they do not, technological obsolescence occurs. An example of this would be the Sinclair C5 whose concept few people wanted.

Design and Technology in school should be transformative and offer a critique of current values. It involves head, hand and heart. The heart comes through feelings and value judgements which should be considered alongside the cognitive (head) and the manipulative (hand) (Ritchie 1995). Value judgements about technological activities are a significant feature of debate in the real world and schools should reflect this. Pupils will be faced with value judgements of many kinds: what is worthwhile? What is feasible? What might the consequence be? There is never any 'right answer' to a design and technology problem. If technology is about fulfilling human needs, we must define and evaluate need. Needs may be life sustaining (e.g. water, food and shelter) or be luxuries. Design and technology in schools includes food and textiles through which we can begin to understand these essential human needs and their provision.

Successful teaching respects pupils' contributions, and creates opportunities for them to evaluate their ideas against criteria of their own, of the class and externally set. Pupils need the opportunity to communicate their ideas in a non-threatening environment where everyone's ideas are valued. If they see that their ideas are valued they will be more prepared to listen to others and begin to appreciate other people's points of view, to realize that questions of values are important in the development of technologies. This way values are born.

Spiritual aspects

Design and technology can be an expression of creativity and imagination that promotes inner growth. There is a sense of wonder at a pupil's own achievements, and in studying the work of talented designers and makers. Personal reflection is a fundamental part of evaluation. Pupils are encouraged to express their feelings about products they are designing and making, and to understand the expression of other designers' products. The DfEE has described evaluating products and applications as: 'The aim here is to promote careful thinking, respect for others, concern for the Earth's limited resources, and a readiness to wrestle with conflicting values, including ethical dilemmas' (DfEE 1995a: 2). As pupils progress they will be challenged to develop their evaluative thinking from the analysis of 'simple features of familiar products' at Level 1 through to 'recognising the different needs of a variety of users, and use appropriate evaluation techniques to find ways forward' at Level 7 (DfEE 1995a: 14–16).

Does the outcome of a pupil's design and technological activity express that pupil's feelings? Pupils who have been given a task to design for others, such as a toy for a three- to seven-year-old, should question themselves to see how much their own childhood and interests have affected their designs. Pupils will often start projects with an evaluation of a familiar product: what was your favourite toy when you were a young child? Why was it special to you? When pupils enjoy designing and making, it expresses their own identities.

The primary school teacher might ask pupils to bring in greeting cards. Pupils would examine these and disassemble the component parts into title, graphics and message. The pupils would be asked to comment on:

- why they like or dislike the card?
- who gave it to them?
- what messages does it send?
- who is it for?
- how does the graphic image convey a message?

After this, pupils could design and produce a greeting card for their own celebration using their own lettering, images and message.

Studying textiles in secondary school, pupils might create mood boards, with images pasted on them, that show their views on designers' creations and interpretations, and provide motivation for design ideas. Given a South American theme they might investigate textiles in terms of colour, texture, pattern and materials. They would use material swatches, colour samples, pasted images and possibly use text to describe the feelings provoked by the textiles. The pupils would then undertake a design-and-make task to produce a bag, drawing inspiration from the images and materials that they had collected. This approach could be applied to other topics.

'Wonder' at the beauty of a designer object can motivate pupils when undertaking a new task. Wonder can be seen in the excitement of experiencing a new technology, for example a laptop computer. There is a joy to be had when encountering a well-designed product. The aesthetic beauty of Starck's juicer, the Ferrari motor car or the Forth Bridge can be studied to understand designers' outlooks and perceptions. Pupils using electrical circuits in the primary school, or electronics in a secondary school, for the first time are often in awe at their own ability to perform a seemingly magical task using components whose inner workings they do not fully appreciate.

They can explore how designers use beautiful forms found in nature and design artefacts that reflect these.

Designing and making artefacts can benefit a pupil's self-worth, but insensitive handling can have the opposite effect. A sense of achievement might come at a time of little success in academic subjects. Pupils are able to risk failure and yet still be rewarded by a teacher for innovation, empathy and experimentation. A teacher can differentiate project tasks to allow a pupil success. Some pupils will require greater teacher input and others might be encouraged towards self-expression through colour, shape, or through developing their interests. A project that involves a group of pupils with separate responsibilities will enable them to develop sensitivity to other pupils' ideas and respect for the opinions of others. Key Stage 1 pupils might be designing and building a model house from recycled materials. Key Stage 2 pupils could extend this idea by incorporating simple circuits into their model houses. Key Stage 3 or 4 pupils might design 'a car for the future'. Each pupil could be responsible for one aspect of the design, body styling, interior, energy source, materials and components. Throughout these projects pupils would need to be given time to combine ideas, accommodate other pupils' points of view and develop their role within the group. The social skills of working as a team in design and technology could benefit all pupils' work on group tasks. Pupils learn to value others' views in working towards a collective design and to work together in the manufacture of a large product.

Moral aspects

Technology should be set in contexts that are real to the pupils and not abstract. Contexts should develop from those with which pupils are familiar (for example, their own home) to the wider world. A technology curriculum which takes seriously the process of reviewing and evaluating should be one in which the values and beliefs in technologies are made objects of study (Barnett 1994). As the previous National Curriculum Orders stated, 'Evaluation is part of design and technology capability. In addition to considering the effectiveness and impact of a product, pupils will need to think about the appropriateness of the underlying values … The evaluation can then refer to the intended purpose and consider not only performance and cost effectiveness, but also implications for the people who develop and use them and the problems associated with resource utilisation and side effects' (DfEE 1995: 2).

There are clear moral dilemmas associated with the evaluation of some products of technology. Land-mines clearly do what the designer wishes (fit for purpose) in a very effective manner (quality design), but is it morally right to use them, considering the suffering they cause? One of the moral values that we should consider in schools is the worth associated with the sanctity of life. Secondary pupils might consider the consequences of technology; for example, nuclear power produces cheap electricity but also hydrogen bombs. In a primary school you might consider the design and technology of other times, giving children the opportunity to consider people's real needs and the issues of the past as well as the values they considered important in technological development. The pyramids are considered to be one of the greatest wonders of the world but were built at great personal sacrifice by large numbers of slaves. …

Consideration of value judgements enables pupils to harness their creative abilities towards goals they have chosen, with growing sensitivity to the needs of others. Pupils should be taught that there are alternative points of view, that the values of other people are not necessarily the same as their own. Their values may be about personal likes and dislikes and it is up to the teacher to help pupils to recognize the basis for preferences and encourage them to be more open-minded. As pupils get older they can deal with more sophisticated questions that involve value judgements concerned with economic, aesthetic, environmental, technical, social and moral issues, for example on the use of recycled products, e.g. fleece jackets made from plastic bottles.

Social aspects

Products made by pupils, as in industry, are designed to overcome problems and to satisfy needs. Design and technology can help pupils to understand the social influences on their own lives and how systems and products can affect us all. The critical evaluation of existing products might involve pupils asking whether we buy products that reflect our status in society and social values. The use of logos on designer clothing, labels on food products, and their advertising are an enormous influence on young people and projects that explore this would question their views. Key Stage 1 and 2 pupils might examine fizzy drinks cans from various manufacturers, exploring preferences for brandnames before blind tasting. Children might then design and make their own 'healthy' drink and design a package for it. Key Stage 3 or 4 pupils might be asked to look at a number of similar garments with logos on and analyse them for quality and worth. Pupils might be asked to design a garment and logo for a company that was targeting a particular audience. Pupils could explore issues of 'image' and 'peer pressure' alongside the practical activities.

Problem-solving activities could lead to a deeper understanding of human needs. A brainstorming session to 'design a pedestrianized shopping area' could, if well facilitated, lead to an understanding of the needs of shoppers, the disabled, young families, the elderly, the business environment, the emergency services and tourists.

If asked to design aids for people with special needs, primary school pupils could investigate their school for ease of access for disabled people. They could carry out an audit of suitability for wheelchair users by using wheelchairs to get around school. Someone who is wheelchair bound might come in and talk to the pupils about the problems they have. After identifying problems the pupils would then undertake a design-and-make task to overcome one of these problems using models and graphics to plan routes around the school for disabled people. This should raise social awareness in pupils.

At secondary school, pupils could investigate the problems people with special needs have when pouring hot water from the kettle into a cup. They could examine familiar products to develop their own designs. The teacher may invite a guest speaker into the classroom to convey first-hand the problems encountered by the disabled doing everyday tasks, and ask them back to evaluate the pupils' work. Pupils would then design and make a product from resistant materials that would try to overcome the problems.

Case studies that feature particular designers might be used as a basis for questioning the work of that designer. Designers of armaments, the means of producing nuclear energy, and motor vehicles could be discussed using the opinions of opposing organizations or pressure groups: e.g. arms manufacturers and Amnesty International; or motor vehicle designers and Friends of the Earth.

Modern advances in communications technology have helped human interactions, and possibly hindered them. Correspondence by letter was affected by the invention of the telephone yet email has rejuvenated the written word. How might future technologies, like video conferencing, change these interactions? The initial motivation for Trevor Bayliss when inventing the clockwork radio was to help communicate sex education to the African people, to prevent the spread of the Aids virus; now that the product has been developed to power an electric light and a laptop computer how might this be used in other societies around the world? The development of 'low tech' technology, using simple resources, is an interesting area to explore with pupils.

Changes in manufacturing industry, with mechanization and robotics, has had far-reaching effects on society. For example, to explore this pupils could visit a local factory or car plant and see robots in action, giving them some understanding of modern technology and the efficient use of the workforce. Pupils could then model a production line in school, for example by making up model Lego cars. They could first make models on their own, joining all parts together. This would be followed by the pupils working in a production line performing only one task. The time for the manufacture of ten cars could be taken in each case. The pupils could be asked to reflect on the benefits of automation in cost terms and how they might feel working as part of a production line, that is, the social implications. They could also consider the implications for mobility on the increased number of cheaper cars.

There are many social influences and pressures on designers, and pupils could research their effects and consider them in their own work. Key Stage 3 and 4 pupils involved in food technology could devise a questionnaire that investigates the social pressures surrounding dieting, the image of a supermodel having the ideal figure, the reasons for anorexia, fitness and acceptability of vegetarianism. In resistant materials pupils should be aware of why we restrict the use of hardwoods, how deforestation is motivated by local need, and yet there are far-reaching global needs. Mahogany and teak are used to make furniture, which has led to deforestation in South America. We need the furniture, the South Americans need the money and the environment needs the trees.

Pupils will encounter a range of monitoring organizations in their studies: health and safety is prevalent in all areas of design and technology and this will help students to take responsibility for their actions, and become aware of how they might affect other pupils and those for whom they design. …

On equal opportunity, design and technology has been perceived as traditionally a male domain, although this is beginning to change. Women's and girls' skills in a wide range of technologies, including food and textiles, have not been valued. Less effective lessons can often value and build on boys' interests and experiences more than those of girls. Girls' and boys' attitudes to technology are developed from an early age, therefore primary schools have an important role to play in ensuring all pupils participate and experience success in design and technology. Girls generally develop skills of cooperation and like working in groups where they support each other through sharing their ideas, skills and expertise. Design-and-make assignments might be set which allow pupils to work in cooperative groups even though they will be producing an individual final product. Girls react positively when they see the personal and social relevance of what is being taught. Including questions such as 'How does technology affect you, your family, your friends?' and activities which investigate, disassemble and evaluate products, can help to stimulate girls' interest in technology. Equal opportunities for different racial groups can also be explored: pupils could undertake a graphics project on stopping racism in football.

Cultural aspects

Europeans have had a tendency to be rather chauvinistic about technology, to look down on anything that does not come from our culture. Pupils need to become aware that technological advance is not the monopoly of a single culture, but that developments over the centuries have taken place in many countries and cultures. A study of the technology during the Crusades shows that the Islamic culture was far in advance of western Europe. They had systems for moving water around using one-way valves to stop back flow, complex water clocks, horizontal windmills, gas masks for miners, medicines and astronomical instruments, to name but a few developments. An important aspect of technology is therefore the recognition that there is nothing inevitable about technological developments. Different cultures have found alternative solutions to the same problem. Some ancient technologies, such as early porcelain glazes, cannot be copied, even with modern resources. … Controversies over the ozone layer and the greenhouse effect, and the use of embryo tissue present ethical issues for discussion. Technology is fully embedded within culture and reflects its values and norms. Some technological developments are created to celebrate a culture, to show to the world the values that the society has. This is a symbolic use of technology to produce prestigious buildings. The Sydney Opera House is designed to reflect the sails of the (invading, in Aboriginal eyes) ships entering the harbour. It represents the beginnings of modern-day Australia and a society with 'western' values. Products of technology can be status objects (e.g. a Rolls Royce) which signify wealth, power and grandeur.

The inherent values in a product cannot be discerned by simply examining a technological product. It needs to become meaningful. In a primary school the study of festivals, for example Diwali, could lead to the children designing and making sweetmeats and diva lamps for the celebration to help them to understand inner meaning. Pupils might design and make hats suitable for different climates, for example sun-hats. This would follow an evaluation of hats from different cultures designed to protect the wearer from sun, cold or rain. In a secondary school pupils might study Indian or Caribbean food, musical instruments, toys or cooking utensils from other cultures as product analysis activities to explore the technology of other cultures, and any implications this might have for ourselves. Pupils might then design and make an ecologically-friendly food product that could provide one third of the daily nutritional requirements of a teenager (Runnymede Trust 1993).

We must take care when identifying the contexts for design and technology to avoid reinforcing negative images of people in developing countries. Pupils might study houses from different cultures, or 'primitive' societies. The mud huts from some rural areas of Zimbabwe are a good example of technology that is relevant today. Architects study these to find out more about heating and cooling effects, air flow and solar power to use in their building designs (Mulberg 1992). The Mongol yurt, a tent-like structure made from felt, is designed to be easily transportable, but is also effective in keeping the people warm through very harsh winters. Design and technology work can help pupils to understand and appreciate the multicultural society in which we live without being patronizing. Pupils bring different values and beliefs into the classroom and teachers will need to approach these with sensitivity. This variety of cultural backgrounds can broaden the insight pupils have into the range of solutions to a problem. It can be a very effective way to show that one culture is not better than another in its design and technology achievements.

The cultural aspects of technology are linked to the idea of *appropriate* technology, which suggests … that things are not necessarily transferable from one culture to another. *Appropriate* technology is often specifically local, needs-orientated, resource-efficient and flexible. Western intensive farming techniques were tried in India and found to decrease, not increase, yields. Direct drilling of food crops interspersed with ground covering fodder crops was found to increase yields because it restricted the growth of weeds and stopped soil erosion during the rainy season. Technologies transferred from one culture to another can often be radically transformed by the society, but can also transform the recipient culture, not always beneficially. Alongside technology, pupils need also to examine potential consequences.

References

Barnett, M. (1994) 'Designing the future? Technology, values and choice', *International Journal of Technology and Design Education* 4, 51–63.

DfEE (1995a) *Design and Technology: Characteristics of Good Practice in Secondary Schools*, London: HMSO.

DfEE (1995b) *Looking at Values Through Products and Applications*, London: HMSO.

Midland Examining Group (1998) *Design and Technology: Syllabus D, Resistant Materials*, Cambridge: Midlands Examining Group.

Mulberg, C. (1992) 'Beyond the Looking Glass: technological myths in education', in C. Budgett-Meakin (ed.) *Make the Future Work: Appropriate Technology: a Teachers' Guide*, Harlow: Longman.

NCC (1995) *Design and Technology in the National Curriculum*, London: HMSO.

Prime, G.M. (1993) 'Values in technology: approaches to learning', *Design and Technology Teaching* 25(3), 30–36.

Ritchie, R. (1995) *Primary Design and Technology: A Process for Learning*, London: David Fulton Publishers.

Runnymede Trust (1993) *Equality Assurance in Schools: Quality, Identity, Society*, Stoke-on-Trent: Trentham Books.

Standen, R. (1992) 'The design dimension of the curriculum', in Budgett-Meakin C. (ed.) *Make the Future Work: Appropriate Technology: a Teachers' Guide*, Harlow: Longman.

Further reading

Budgett-Meakin, C. (ed.) (1992) *Make the Future Work: Appropriate Technology: a Teachers' Guide*, Harlow: Longman.
This is an important book that puts technology into a world-wide perspective. Contributors provide a range of perspectives in examining values and appropriate technology.

DfEE (1995) *Looking at Values Through Products and Applications*, London: HMSO.
This book provides guidelines for the discussion of various products, to reveal the values embedded in them, e.g. a collection of dolls.

4 Design and Technology and the community

22 Sustainability and Design and Technology in schools

Pip Goggin and Tony Lawler

This chapter considers some of the major issues in relation to sustainability, and the role that Design and Technology can play in helping to make pupils aware of these issues and how they can make a difference. Suggestions are given for how existing schemes of work may be adapted to give pupils a greater degree of involvement and understanding of the issues.

Introduction

The Earth seen from space gave the environmental movement its most powerful icon: a vibrant jewel in a black cosmos. It also serves to reminds us that we cannot escape the effects of our industrial activities. We are all sustained by the same biosphere. Manufacturing may be shifting to the low-waged developing economies but resource depletion and pollution affect us all: rich or poor – north or south. The evidence is overwhelming: global population is expected to double some time this century and the market for material goods is likely to increase eightfold, with the less developed countries rushing to adopt western material lifestyles. This could lead to global warming, with average temperatures rising by 2–5 degrees, resulting in widespread desertification levels. Ozone depletion may increase skin cancer and alter ecosystems with uncertain effects. Deforestation and loss of biodiversity are occurring at an unprecedented rate. More worrying is the rate of change: in just a few decades we have begun to threaten evolution spanning nearly 4 billion years (Myers 1994).

These problems are acknowledged at the highest levels in governments, organizations and business. Today, international as well as national and local initiatives find a unifying theme in the concept of 'sustainable development', first defined in the seminal report of the World Commission of Environment and Development (1987), *Our Common Future*. In it, the authors describe sustainable development as: 'development that meets the needs of the present without compromising the ability of future generations to meet their own needs'. However, like many environmental concerns, these are complex issues and do little to empower the individual in making informed environmental decisions on a day-to-day basis. The major question for many is: what can I do to reduce my impact on the environment? It is this question that this paper attempts to address by presenting a range of environmental approaches that can be readily adapted and used in the teaching of Design and Technology.

Environmental space

One of the more useful concepts to have evolved in recent years is the idea that each of us takes up 'environmental space' in terms of the amount of materials and energy we consume, and the amount of pollution and waste we create (FoE 1997). The Earth has finite overall environmental space because there are limits to the amount of resources we can extract and limits to the ability of ecosystems to tolerate pollution. In developed countries, each person's 'environmental space' is widely considered unsustainable (WCED 1987). Although only 20 per cent of the population live in the industrialized north, it (we) currently consumes over 80 per cent of the world's resources. Such inequities are not only unethical but also unsustainable.

But by how much do we need to reduce our 'environmental space' in order to achieve sustainability and a more just and equitable distribution of resources? A staggeringly simple but profound equation was proposed by biologists Anne and Paul Ehrlich (1990) to indicate the scale of the problem. They propose that environmental impact (E) equates to population (P), multiplied by material consumption per capita, or affluence (A), multiplied by the environmental impact of the technology used to produce goods (T). This relationship is expressed as: $E = P \times A \times T$. As a benchmark our present situation can be shown as $1 = 1 \times 1 \times 1$.

A call for a 60 per cent reduction in releases of greenhouse gases, to cite the most pressing environmental problem, has been made by the United Nations International Panel on Climatic Change; which means environmental impact becomes 0.4, not 1. Population will double in the next forty years and consumption per capita is expected to increase fourfold over a similar period.

Thus: 0.4 (**E**nvironmental impact) = 2 (**P**opulation) $\times$ 4 (**A**ffluence) $\times$? (**T**echnological impact).

To balance the equation, the environmental impact of the technologies we use to produce goods (in other words, design) needs to be 0.05, not 1, a reduction of 95 per cent, or a *twentieth of current levels*. Clearly sustainability cannot be achieved through design alone and in the absence of draconian population control, we are left with affluence. So it appears from the arguments so far that a dual approach is required to attain sustainable 'environmental space', firstly by reducing the environmental impact of the goods we produce; and secondly, by consuming less.

Design response

Problems of such magnitude leave many feeling helpless. Well-meaning behaviour, like recycling newspapers and bottles, probably does more to massage our conscience than save the planet. There is a need to empower people (children as well as adults) with the knowledge, ideas and tools that not only address current needs but also those of future generations (United Nations 1992 *et al.*).

Life-cycle thinking

Designers have begun to recognize that reducing the environmental impact of products requires a life-cycle approach. What this means is that at every stage in a product's life-cycle materials and energy are used and waste and pollution is created – from the

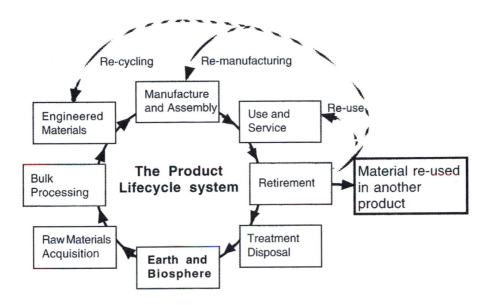

Figure 22.1 Modified from the 'Lifecycle Design Guidance Manual: US Environmental Protection Agency 1994'

extraction of raw materials from the ground – including all the stages in between: materials processing; product production; distribution; product use – to retirement and disposal. A typical product life-cycle is shown in Figure 22.1 and shows various inputs and outputs.

With an understanding of the many environmental impacts of a product during its life-cycle – from cradle to grave – it is possible to target design effort to reduce impact. What this kind of approach highlights is that although materials recycling, for example, can reduce environmental impact, it is by no means the whole picture and, in many instances, is a relatively minor factor. This life-cycle thinking was first developed by scientists to address the environmental impact of large industrial processes.

Ecodesign

Building on life-cycle analysis described above, ecodesign is a design approach that aims to: 'address all environmental impacts of a product throughout the complete life-cycle of the product, whilst aiming to enhance other criteria like function, quality, and appearance' (Eco2 1994). In order to facilitate such aims a matrix was devised to relate life-cycle phases to environmental costs, as shown in Table 22.1. Within each cell of the matrix a number of guidelines is included which can help designers reduce the environmental impact of goods. Such a life-cycle approach also prevents narrow environmental thinking and promotes an holistic design view.

Table 22.1 Ecodesign matrix

Life-cycle of the product

	Production	Use	Disposal	Distribution
Energy	Design to reduce energy in production	Design to reduce energy in use	Design to reduce energy in disposal	Design to reduce energy in distribution
Material	Design to reduce material in production	Design to reduce additional materials in use	Design to reduce material waste in disposal	Design to reduce materials in distribution
Pollution	Design to reduce pollution in production	Design to reduce pollution in use	Design to reduce pollution in disposal	Design to reduce pollution in distribution

(Row group label, left side vertical: Environmental impact)

This way of presenting ecodesign shows a range of relationships between recyclability, energy efficiency and use of non-toxic materials etc. This means that design for energy efficiency or low waste – or designing products that use recycled, non-toxic or fewer materials – cannot be regarded as ecodesign alone, but rather as constituents of ecodesign. Many companies now acknowledge the value of ecodesign in reducing their overall environmental impact and as part of future product strategies. In this respect it is likely that ecodesign concepts will become as commonplace as cost constraints are today.

However, although using ecodesign principles can reduce environmental impact, it does not necessarily mean that a product is sustainable in the longer term. In some instances certain product groups will be considered so polluting that they are simply not produced. Equally, others will be thought too frivolous and short-lived to use up scarce resources required for more pressing needs. Sustainability requires a much broader and global vision which places people's needs and access to resources in the context of environmental limits. As the Ehrlich equation suggests, the volume of goods consumed also needs to be significantly curtailed, and goods consumed need to be more fairly distributed between the developed North and developing South.

Sustainable design

The concept of sustainability refocuses design concerns towards social conditions, environment, development and ethics (Dewberry and Goggin 1996). Ideas such as: questioning the need for a product; achieving 'more from less'; a concern for quality of life instead of material standard of living; a focus on causes of environmental problems rather than their symptoms; and an onus on 'service' as opposed to 'ownership', all raise the question of how design will change to accommodate such 'radical thinking' (see Figure 22.2).

	Present position	Towards sustainability
Nature	Design for corrective action	Sustainable design
Design target	Symptoms	Causes
Focus	Product/micro view	Systems/macro view
Perspective	Intensive information Short term Linear	Extensive information Long term Cyclical
Characteristics	Standard of living End of pipe solutions Growing market	Quality of life Questions needs Ethics – equality
Design response	Technological fix Clean up problems Hardware Resource intensive More products	Dematerialisation Leasing/services Software/sharing People intensive 20 factor

Figure 22.2 *Ecodesign in the context of sustainability*

Ultimately the ability to follow through this degree of change will depend on human behaviour and value systems, and whether designers – as part of the current economic paradigm – can influence a shift in attitudes towards this goal. But designers make the link between people and production in the form of products, and in many ways shape the way people respond to designed goods. In this context, it is possible to imagine how designers and Design and Technology teachers can begin to promote a sense of reverence and respect for our material surroundings, and encourage a more environmentally harmonious existence.

The role of Design and Technology

As an area in the curriculum which always causes pupils to look into the future and produce answers to needs by practical application, Design and Technology is uniquely placed both to consider the issues of sustainability and to deliver understanding via practical project-work. The critical thing in all of this is that pupils are aware of their ability to choose, or design, a certain course of action; and, having done it, are made aware of the consequences of their decisions and endeavours. We are suggesting that this fundamental aspect of the subject has the ability that no other curriculum area has, to equip pupils for their futures.

A Key Stage 3 project was chosen deliberately from the DATA *Guidance Materials* pack as a typical piece of project-work where the planning and National Curriculum (1995 version) coverage are well documented. The chosen project is called 'The Bubble and the Market' and it involves an examination of product packaging and the production of a vacuum formed bubble pack to package a chosen object. The approach to pupils understanding the issues of sustainability takes three forms: eco-logging, eco-choice points and life-cycle design. We are well aware of the pressures on teachers to produce more from less in all aspects of their work, and so have made the examples deliberately limited, yet, we feel, sufficient to illustrate our approach.

Eco-logging

This approach can be applied to any existing piece of project-work, and involves the pupils, as part of their evaluations, listing the processes and materials that have been used in the project and then making a log of the amount of material and energy that has been used and also a view as to how much has been wasted, or how difficult is it to recycle what remains. Figure 22.3 shows an example of a log, and gives some rules of thumb to make the scope of the evaluation manageable.

Eco-choice points

Logging of materials and energy usage is only the first step, and only sets the agenda for further work. The pupils' understanding must involve deliberate choices and an analysis of the consequences of having chosen certain options. Using the same project we have indicated a range of constrained choices that pupils can make, in order that they can evaluate these choices in terms of materials and energy usage. This can therefore be used in conjunction with the eco-logging, or as a discussion point within the project. Figure 22.4 shows a deliberately small range of choice points that could be used in this project.

Designing for extended life-cycle

Traditionally the bubble pack has a very short life and serves to contain the product from the producer into the shop and then be thrown away when the consumer gets the product home. As such it reinforces the 'throw-away society' and comes into direct conflict with the issues of sustainability. The use of 'new' materials at all stages of a school project is how we, as teachers, give it value to the pupils. If, however, we are seeking to question this value system from a wider perspective, then the ability to reuse or modify once-used materials should take on a different value in the eyes of the pupils: by designing the package in such a way that the next stage in its life-cycle is not to be thrown away. The object could either be used again for the same function, or could become worth something in its own right. Thus the time before it becomes 'rubbish' is extended. The pupil-designer can affect what was initially a short-life package by the way that they design it. Once the basic concept is established then all that is required is that the brief for the project is modified. Pupils will come to terms not only with the immediate gratification of what they are designing

Sustainable design in design and technology
Eco-Log

1

Basic principles
Don't try to go any further back than this project
Keep the limits of the evaluations to the areas that the pupils have actually used – don't consider the wear and tear of equipment, or the on costs to support the activities

Basic costs and environmental costs
There is a strong correlation between the raw material costs and the costs to the environment for producing that material. Your own experience and raw material costs will give a representative starting point

Energy costs
Relating electrical power wattage and time used will give a fair starting point
Electricity, we have said, can be charged at Xp for 1000 watts of 1 minute (it is cheap)

Recycling/environmental costs
This gives a chance to have a value for the cost of recycling waste materials, and to add something for the impact on the environment. We have used a high cost of Yp and a low cost of Zp

Stages in the project	Material cost (p)	Energy costs (p)	Recycling costs (p)	Total (p)

Construct mould
  cut to shape (coping saw/jig saw)
  smooth and correct shape				

Vacuum form 'bubble'				
Trim bubble to shape (jig saw/scissors/ stanley knife)				

Backing sheet
  cut to shape
  apply graphics
  fix to bubble				

				Overall total

Possible savings and eco-evaluations
Using hand processes except for the vacuum forming would have saved
Being able to choose different materials for the mould and the backing board (like clay and card) could have made the mould reusable, and easier to shape, but in the end may not have looked as good
The vacuum forming wasted a lot of material each time. Could there be some way of only forming as much plastic as you need?

Figure 22.3 Example of an eco-log

Sustainable design in design and technology
Eco-Choice points

2

Basic principles
Limit the number of materials and energy choice points to 3 or 4
Make sure that the pupils are aware of the reasons and consequences of the choices
that they are making
Use the idea of choice points in conjunction with the idea of logging energy use

Stages in the project	Choice points	Reasons for choice
		Advantages/disadvantages
Construct mould	Choice of possible mould	Choices evaluated based
cut to shape (coping	materials	on
saw/jig saw)	softwood	cost of materials
smooth and correct	MDF	ability to recycle
shape	clay	materials
		energy used in their
Vacuum form 'bubble'	Choice of backing sheets	processing
	plastic sheet	quality of end product
Trim bubble to shape	high quality card	
(jig saw/scissors/	recycled board	
stanley knife)		
	Choice of fixing methods	
Backing sheet	of bubble to board	
cut to shape	glue gun	
apply graphics	snap fit moulded in place	
	adhesive tape	
Fix backing board to		
bubble		

Figure 22.4 Eco-choice points

and making now, but also what it was before and what it will be next. Figure 22.5
shows how such thinking could be applied to this project.

Designing for sustainability: an A level case study

The concepts of sustainability were introduced to a group of A level pupils (it would
seem to be just as applicable to GCSE) and then they were asked to design an eco-
torch, capable of being sold as an emergency torch by Friends of the Earth, which
would show some of the principles of sustainability. The results demonstrated very
clearly the breadth of understanding of the pupils in a unique way. What they produced, and the materials and means of production chosen, indicated whether their
concept of reuse of materials in the design went further than a crude definition.
Some showed a limited view based on simply buying the materials that were needed,
whereas others demonstrated a greater understanding and actively attempted to reuse
existing items as containers or components. Similarly, the concept of extending the

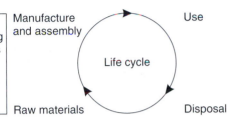

Considering and extending the life-cycle of the components and materials

Basic principles
View the design and making of this object as part of a much larger scheme, which recognises the cyclic nature of materials, and the need to extend the time before the object is no longer useful

Can we design some way of using recycled materials to prevent having to use raw materials?

Can we design some way of making the materials easy to recycle, or to give the object another use?

Manufacture and assembly — Use — Disposal — Raw materials — Life cycle

Can we use materials that have already been recycled like card or paper or plastics?
Can we reuse and remodel materials that have been used for other projects or are about to be thrown away?
Can we use materials that can be easily recycled for use in this context like clay from mould making?

Can we make it so that when this object has been used as packaging it can become something else?
(Can it be designed to be a valuable object in its own right e.g. door number, plaster mould, storage container?)
Can the materials be easily recycled/remoulded etc?
Can this object be used as a part of the next project (Project 7 working as designer makers)?

Figure 22.5 *Considering and extending the life-cycle of the components and materials*

life-cycle showed whether their understanding went beyond the notion that one could recycle plastic to actually saying what it could be used as, without elaborate and expensive recycling. …

In conclusion

Young people today are under enormous pressure to conform and to consume all manner of products. They would seem to be at a particularly vulnerable stage in their lives and have been, in most cases, successfully convinced by manufacturers that the solution to their insecurities about themselves is to surround themselves with icons to support their frail egos. We do not underestimate the power of young people's culture on their views of the world, neither do we assume that this work will change that culture overnight. We do believe that only by giving them an awareness of the issues and the capability to intervene in their situation will they be able to judge for themselves the choices that they have. And we must remember that the changes that we spoke of at the beginning of this article will be happening in their lifetimes, but maybe not ours. It is therefore more important that they have a defensible concept of sustainability than that we do.

The aim of this work is to illustrate the possibilities of the approach and to begin to collate work of a similar type. If this work is interesting to you or you have your own examples to share then please contact us on: email p.goggin @gold.ac.uk; t.lawler@gold.ac.uk; or Design Studies Goldsmiths London University, New Cross, London SE14 6NW.

References

DATA (1995) *Guidance Materials for Design and Technology Key Stage 3*, Wellesbourne: DATA

Dewberry, E. and Goggin, P. (1996) *Spaceship Ecodesign: The Next Generation*, Co-Design Partnership, Milton Keynes; *Green Issue* 5/6: 12-17.

Ehrlich P., and Ehrlich A., (1990) *The Population Explosion*, New York: Simon and Schuster.

Eco2 (1994) Eco2-IRN (Ecologically and Economically Sound Design and Manufacture – Interdisciplinary Research Network), Workshop on defining 'ecodesign' November 1994.

Friends of the Earth (1996) 'Earth Matters', *Environmental Space*, Winter 1996.

Myers, N. (ed.) (1994) *The Gaia Atlas of Planet Management*, New York: Anchor Press.

United Nations Conference on Environment Development (1992) Agenda 21, *Promoting Environmental Awareness* (Section IV, Chapter 36) and Bridging the Data Gap (Section IV, Chapter 40).

World Commission on Environment and Development (1987) *Our Common Future*.

23 Design and Technology and the challenge of refugee children

Susan MacPhee

This chapter describes the development of a learning resource designed to introduce pupils with English as a second language to Design and Technology. The resource may be used in any of the material areas, by pupils in Year 7 to Year 9.

The school context

The school in which this learning resource will be used is a multicultural secondary school situated in the London Borough of Hounslow. With its close proximity to Heathrow airport, the school has a large transient population of pupils who have recently arrived in the country from all over the world. Many of these pupils are refugees. The previous amount of schooling these pupils will have received varies considerably. At one extreme the pupils may have no previous school experience and at the other, they may have been well educated in their home country.

The school has a strong English as an Additional Language (EAL) department, which provides various levels of support for pupils, ranging from full withdrawal from the mainstream curriculum to in-class support. The school policy on EAL pupils is to gradually return them to mainstream lessons, starting as soon as possible following their arrival at the school. As Design and Technology is perceived as an 'easy' subject, because it is 'practical' in nature, this is one of the first subjects pupils are taught in the mainstream. Clearly this perception does not represent a true picture of the subject, as the range of activities in which pupils are involved varies enormously, and it is difficult, if not impossible, to equip a pupil with the appropriate theory to support their work if they do not have access to the language. Added to this problem is the fact that the pupils do not all arrive at the school on the first day of term, but rather in any week of the year at fairly frequent intervals. As most of the work in Design and Technology is taught through projects, which last for a number of weeks, pupils could be arriving at any stage of the 'design process', from researching the task to carrying out practical work and evaluating their ideas.

The present situation

At present, pupils arrive in the classroom and are given the same task that the remainder of the class are working on, but with a reduced requirement for written work. For example, if the rest of the class was designing, the EAL pupil would be shown another pupil's work and asked to produce some of their own ideas. This work would differ from the rest of the class because they would not be expected to add detailed descriptive or evaluative notes to their work. Alternatively, if the class was making their projects, the pupil would be shown how to use some basic equipment, asked to produce a quick design and then they would start practical work. The success of this approach has varied considerably, but even in the best-case scenario, pupils are left with a very limited understanding of what they are doing and it is often difficult to give them enough attention to help them to keep up with the rest of the class. It is also difficult in this situation to make an accurate assessment of the pupil's ability, due to the limited range of activities in which they have participated.

Typical problems arising for EAL pupils during designing are:

- they don't understand the task and simply copy whatever their neighbour has drawn
- it is more difficult for them to draw on theoretical support for their designs
- they may understand the task, but probably not the materials we have to work with
- they are frequently unable to develop their ideas beyond an initial sketch.

During making activities, many of the EAL pupils achieve more once they have seen what other pupils are doing and have grasped what they are expected to do. At this stage, however, if the pupils still do not understand what is expected of them it can be very frustrating and they may give up and try to simply help another pupil instead of producing their own product.

Whilst not wishing to return pupils to their withdrawal groups, it is clearly necessary to find a more satisfactory solution to these problems: ideally, one which will allow pupils to develop some key skills for design and technology and also develop some subject-specific vocabulary at the same time.

Issues arising from the refugee status of many of the pupils

When developing a resource of this nature, it is essential to take into account the fact that many of the pupils who will be using it are refugees. It must be carefully planned to work to the pupils' strengths and avoid issues which they may find upsetting, either for cultural reasons or as a result of the experiences which led to them becoming a refugee.

The way in which the resource is constructed needs to acknowledge the fact that the level of previous education the pupils have received will vary considerably:

> The first experience of school for any child can be daunting, bewildering and at times overtaxing. How much more difficult and stressful for a Somali child with no previous formal education, little or no English and limited experience of urban life to be suddenly exposed to the life of a British school?
>
> (Kahin 1997: 72)

Whilst this example refers to Somali children, it is likely to be true of many of the pupils by whom the resource will be used.

In cases where pupils did attend school in their own country, the system would have been very different. Most lessons would have been tightly controlled and teacher-led and the teacher/pupil relationship would have been considerably more formal. As a result, pupils may feel confused and intimidated by lessons in design and technology where pupils are expected to move around and make use of a wide range of equipment.

They may feel lost or insecure in a class where the teacher does not direct or monitor every stage of the lesson. The range and profusion of equipment in the school may seem overwhelming and intimidating.

(Kahin 1997: 73)

With this in mind the resource should probably allow the pupil to stay in one place throughout the lesson. In addition, it should not involve the use of a large range of equipment. This will hopefully allow the pupil to feel more confident and secure when tackling the task.

Cultural transition

In addition to the differences in the pupils' previous school experience, they are also being faced with large differences in culture between their own country and England. The way in which they deal with this varies. In some cases pupils may wish to integrate with the new culture so that they 'fit in', and in others they might become more traditional and hold on tightly to their cultural identity:

They may become more traditional or they may become aggressively British. The best adaptation involves being able to keep links with both the new and the old culture and making a bridge between the two.

(Melzak 1992: 3)

In order to help the pupils to make this bridge between the two cultures, the project could have a cultural emphasis. This would also serve to tell the pupils that we value them and their past, an issue which was found to be important to Eritrean refugees in Swedish schools. They said they liked teachers who asked them about themselves because the acknowledgement of their differences made them feel 'valued':

This made them feel their past was valued and they were recognised as being different from Swedish pupils. They liked initial questions about 'safe' areas such as their school in Eritrea, language, food.

(Melzak 1992: 5)

Similar 'safe' aspects of the pupil's former life could form the focus of the task. They could be asked to produce something which represents their home or school, or tells us something about their culture: for example, what they eat, or their language.

In writing about the integration of refugee children into the classroom, Jill Rutter, education officer at the Refugee Council, supports the view that it is helpful for refugee children to tell us about themselves. She suggests that the creation of autobiographical work is very useful to help refugee children deal with their circumstances. […]

Clearly issues of home will have to be approached carefully and sensitively, but the use of such techniques may provide a useful introduction to the school, whilst also helping the children to come to terms with their situation.

The use of graphics as an introduction to design and technology

Whilst research has shown that autobiographical writings and scrapbooks are a useful technique to use with refugee children, this would not be a typical design and technology activity. However, a similar type of exercise could be achieved through the use of graphics. This would be a useful approach in terms of making the resource equally accessible to pupils of all nationalities and is also appropriate with regard to the development of basic skills in design and technology. … As such, skills developed in this introduction to the subject would be of great use at later stages in the pupils' work in Design and Technology.

Graphic language

To allow for easy communication of the task, the resource itself should be presented to the pupils in largely graphic form. The pupils should then be required to create a graphic product. One reason why this would be a suitable format for all EAL pupils, regardless of previous educational experience, is that research has shown that children acquire graphical ability before the ability to write or use numbers (Cross 1986).

Therefore, most pupils would be able to respond to the task at some level and at the same time develop some valuable skills and understanding which would be of use to them in future work in design and technology. Indeed, research into the field of 'graphicacy', or the use of graphic language, has shown that the use of graphic communication can often lead to increased understanding about a subject (Cross 1986). […]

In addition to the use of graphic symbols and drawings, pupils could be encouraged to develop a wider range of modelling skills:

> Modelling of thoughts, ideas or images is essential for developing, clarifying, expressing and communicating ideas with oneself and with other people. Taking the images that have been modelled inside the head to a point outside the head makes them more accessible for oneself and others to predict, to test, to confront, to transform and to appraise. What is expressed by modelling is a result of images in the mind, these are influenced by what can be expressed by modelling outside the mind.
>
> (Murray 1994: 85)

The development of modelling and design skills would therefore be of use to the pupil, both in the completion of the current task and for future tasks in design and technology. When designing the task which the pupils will complete, there should therefore be a requirement for the pupil to demonstrate a range of different modelling techniques and not simply graphic symbols. This will allow the pupil to develop the widest range of possible skills and the teacher to develop a more complete picture of the pupil's abilities.

The project

In addition to the requirement for the resource to be representative of the type of work carried out in design and technology, and the need to be sensitive to the experience of refugee children, there are three central issues to be considered when planning the content of a resource of this nature:

1   the task must be fairly simple to explain to the pupils, given their limited access to the language
2   the resource must be easy to store and readily accessed if an EAL pupil joins a lesson
3   the project must be suitable for use in any material specialist room.

Taking into consideration the recommendations of those who have worked closely with refugee children, the project will be largely autobiographical in nature. It will provide pupils with the opportunity to express those aspects of both their past and present life which are important to them.

In addition to the use of simple drawn images, the pupils will be asked to model some of their ideas in three dimensions. This will allow for the development of the more complex skills which will be of use to them throughout their work in design and technology. It will also give the pupils an opportunity to express themselves in a variety of ways, making the task both more interesting and challenging.

The task will be as follows:

Produce a picture or model, which tells me about you and your life.

In order to support the pupils in carrying out this task, they will have access to a resource file which will contain a wide range of visual imagery, including drawings, maps, photographs of people and places, samples of fabrics etc., which are representative of a wide range of countries and cultures. It is hoped that with these visual stimuli the pupils will recognize something which is familiar to them and it will thus provide them with a starting point. It is very important that the images are carefully selected and do not represent anything which may be upsetting to the pupils but, rather, emphasize the positive aspects of life in countries around the world. ...

Also included in the resource file will be a simple explanation of the task in writing, with visual cues, to aid explanation. ...

To accompany this explanation, there will be examples of possible outcomes. This will take the form of a series of design proposals which show the development of a design through four stages. Each design will have simple annotation, identifying good and bad points of the idea. It is hoped that this will encourage pupils to try out a number of alternative designs and to produce their project using a range of graphic media.

To further aid explanation, the designs will be graded using a system of smiling faces, indicating the progressive improvement of the ideas. This use of graphical symbols should again simplify the explanation process.

The chosen subject matter for the example designs is a typical British house. This will allow the teacher to describe the project to the pupil by identifying the design as their home. They can then ask the pupil to describe their home in their country of origin, as a starting point for ideas for the project.

The first design is a simple two-dimensional drawing of a house which is made using different colours of paper. The picture gives very little information about the house or its inhabitants and would not take long to produce. This design therefore achieves a low grading with an unsmiling face (Figure 23.1).

In the second design, the house is drawn again but this time in three dimensions, allowing the inclusion of some detail about the surroundings. Whilst some use of mixed media is made, there are areas where the drawing is untidy because the background is showing through whereas in reality it would be hidden. This design achieves a better grade with one smiling face (Figure 23.2).

In the third design the picture is very similar to the second design, but more detail has been added and better use has been made of coloured paper to mask areas which should not be seen. As a result, this design achieves two smiling faces.

By the fourth design a large jump has been made to the creation of a full three-dimensional model of the house and its garden. Whilst this would not necessarily be the next step in terms of complexity, it opens up new possibilities to the pupils. In this design considerably more detail is included and a national flag appears on the side of the house, telling us a little more about its inhabitants. This design scores four smiling faces to indicate clearly to the pupils that a three-dimensional modelling approach to the project is highly valued (Figure 23.3).

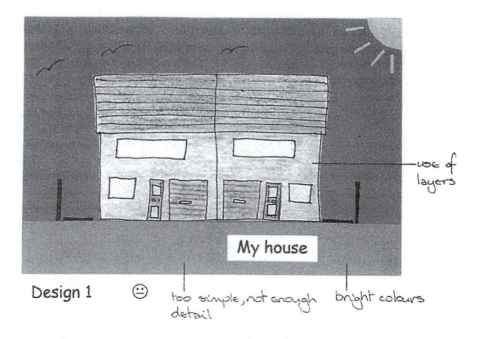

Figure 23.1 Design 1

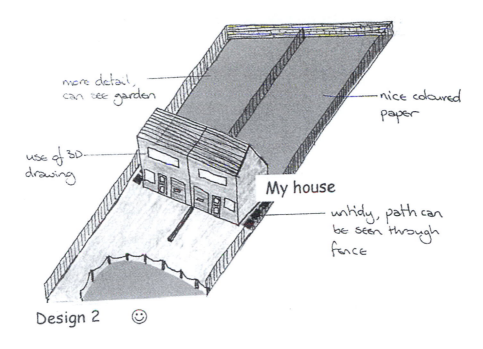

Figure 23.2 Design 2

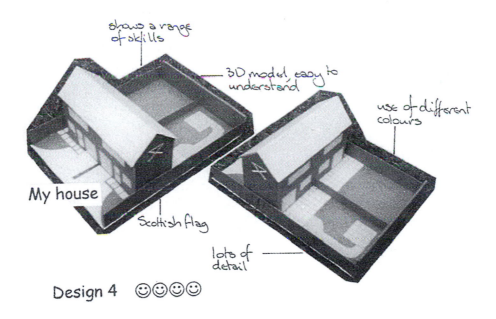

Figure 23.3 Design 4

By talking the pupils through each stage of the design and pointing out the smiling-face grading each has been awarded, they will hopefully understand what they have to do and be able to make a start on the project. Whilst they are carrying out their work, the smiling-face grading system should be used to indicate to the pupils how well they are doing.

Once the project has been used a number of times, photographs of previous pupils' work will also be included in the resource file, to provide additional inspiration for the pupils and to make the explanation of the task easier. In addition to the resource file, the pupils will be provided with a set of materials and equipment with which to produce their project. The set of materials should be kept in a box or folder, to make storage of the resource easy. The set will include: a range of types and colours of card and paper, string, paper fasteners, elastic bands. pipe cleaners, coloured pens and pencils, glue, sellotape, scissors and a ruler. It is important to provide each pupil with their own set of equipment which they are not expected to share with others. This will both allow them to concentrate on the task and remove any anxiety about having to ask other pupils to borrow equipment.

Anticipated outcomes

Easier transition into the curriculum

By providing a stand-alone project for the new pupils to work on, the initial confusion of starting in the middle of something, and the associated anxiety which this may cause, is removed. Also, the project does not require the pupils to move around the classroom, or to use a wide range of new equipment and therefore provides a calmer, and possibly less confusing, introduction to the new environment. Additionally, for pupils who have varying levels of experience of the kind of work carried out in Design and Technology, this task will provide a focused and achievable introduction to the subject.

By setting a cultural context for the project, the pupils are provided with an opportunity to work in a context which is familiar to them. This may make it easier for them to think of initial design ideas. It will also allow the pupils to express their cultural identity and tell the teacher something about themselves and their life. As previously stated, in the case of refugee children, working on the project may also help them to come to terms with their present circumstances.

In practical terms, the scale of the project should mean that the pupil will require less individual help, following the initial introduction to the project. This is of benefit for both the teacher and the pupil: for the teacher, because it will mean they can divide their time equally between all the pupils in the class, and for the pupil because it means they will not waste a lot of time waiting to be shown how to do the next task, becoming increasingly frustrated as they do so. Clearly, in some cases the pupil may be insecure about their own ability and will need lots of encouragement, but this is no different from other pupils in the class who have been in the school for a longer time.

Acquisition of essential skills

By providing a clearly defined task for the pupils it is possible to encourage the development of specific types of skills. These are designing skills, graphical skills and modelling skills, all of which are essential requirements for successful work in Design and Technology.

Throughout the project it will be necessary for the teacher to monitor the range of skills which the pupil is using and to provide guidance about how to progress, in order to maximize the learning potential of the project. In some cases this will involve the teaching of a specific skill, which will allow the pupils to move on to the next stage of the development of their ideas.

In discussing their designs with the teacher and other pupils, it is hoped that pupils will acquire some basic subject-specific vocabulary. It is also hoped that they will be able to use this vocabulary to start producing some simple annotation on their design ideas, based on the suggestions given at the outset of the project. This is very important in terms of the development of their design ability because, in the case of pupils designing in their own language, almost all design graphics are annotated allowing them to express more information about the designs and, as a result, to identify areas for further improvement and development.

Assessment of the pupil's ability

An additional expected benefit of the pupil completing an entire project is that it should allow the teacher to make an assessment of the pupil's overall designing and making ability. This is very important in terms of assisting the pupil to progress at an appropriate rate in future work.

Conclusion

The initial situation which inspired the development of a new teaching resource was the arrival of EAL pupils at an early stage of their learning of English, into the Design and Technology classroom. The problems which were identified were:

- the limited language skills of the pupils
- the fact that the pupils often arrive in the middle of a project
- the fact that pupils could be located in any of the material specialist areas
- the pupils' varying levels of previous experience in design and technology
- the fact that, in the case of refugee pupils, the Design and Technology classroom may be an intimidating environment, with the proliferation of equipment and the requirement for pupils to move around during a lesson.

I feel that the project which has been developed has the potential to overcome most of the above problems as follows:

- the use of graphics to both explain and carry out the task helps to overcome language difficulties

- the stand-alone nature of the project allows it to be started at any point in the school year and last for varying lengths of time
- the resource is compact in size and can be easily stored in each material specialist room, and it will contain all the materials and equipment which the pupils require to complete the project
- the complexity of the project and the skills required can vary according to a pupil's abilities. The project also allows the pupils to develop new skills which will be of great value in their later work in Design and Technology.
- the project can be carried out without having to move around the classroom, or use a wide range of equipment.

However, one problem which may arise from the use of this learning resource is that the pupil will feel even more isolated in the classroom than they would with their language limitations alone. They may feel that, rather than being 'special' because they are allowed to do different work, they are simply 'different' and not really part of the mainstream, as they had expected. The fact that they are working independently may also reduce the amount of social contact they have with other pupils in the class and, as a result, the language development which could have occurred.

Overall, however, I feel that the potential benefits of this project outweigh the potential problems and that it will provide not only a very valuable learning experience for the pupil but also a more manageable situation for the teacher.

References and other useful sources

Cross, A. (1986) 'Towards an understanding of the intrinsic values of design education', in A. Cross, and R. McCormick (eds) *Technology in Schools*, Milton Keynes: The Open University.

Kahin, M.H. (1997) *Educating Somali Children in Britain*, Stoke-on-Trent: Trentham Books.

Matthews, J. (1993) *I Come from Somalia*, London: Aladdin Books Ltd.

Meadows, S. (1993) *The Child as Thinker*, London: Routledge.

Meizak, S. and Warner, R. (1992) *Integrating Refugee Children into Schools*, London: The Minority Rights Group.

Murray, J. (1994) 'The relationship between 'modelling' and designing and making with food as a material in design and technology', in F. Banks (ed.) *Teaching Technology*, London: Open University Press.

Rutter, J. (1994) *Refugee Children in the Classroom*, Stoke-on-Trent: Trentham Books.

Rutter, J. (1991) *Refugees: We Left Because We Had To*, London: The Refugee Council.

Shirley, K. (1989) *Land of the Emirates*, Dubai: Motivate Publishing.

Warner, R. (ed.) (1991) *Voices from Kurdistan*, London: The Minority Rights Group.

Wilkes, S. (1994) *One Day we had to Run!*, London: Evans Brothers Ltd.

24 Industrial practices in Design and Technology

This chapter is made up of two articles previously published separately. The first describes two projects for pupils in lower secondary school, to introduce them to manufacturing methods found in industry.

The second article in the chapter looks at the relationship between the designing and making processes followed in Design and Technology, and working practices in industry and commerce. It gives suggestions of how working practices can be translated into classroom practice at Key Stage 4 in all the material areas. It then focuses on the textile industry, but the example given could be adapted to other areas.

Modelling industrial production methods in lower secondary school Design and Technology projects

Marshall Hughes

Introduction

Despite the fact that almost every manufactured product we use today has been mass-produced, in many schools the most common making experience for our students is that of individual production. There are, of course, sound educational reasons for this. Students personally engage in and experience a wide range of design and practical skills and they are wholly responsible for what they produce. However, by concentrating solely on this type of manufacturing method I believe we are missing out on an important opportunity to expose our students to a wider variety of production methods. Table 24.1 shows a chart of the projects/topics undertaken by Key Stage 3 pupils at my school, along with the type of production which each project involves.

Group production methods we witnessed on industrial visits to local factories and businesses are a vital facet of the Design and Technology curriculum, but by modelling industrial production methods in school-based projects our students can experience the techniques first-hand. This article will illustrate and explain two such units of study: one a Year 8 mass production project and the other a Year 9 batch production exercise.

Table 24.1 Key Stage 3 projects

Year	Project/Topic	Production
7	Electronics	Individual
	CAD Marble Maze	Individual
	Mechanisms: Levers	Individual
	Control: Air-con systems	Single sex 2/3
	Structures: Bridge testing	Mixed pairs
	IDEA: Pencil case evaluation	Mixed groups of 4/5
	CAD Key-tag	Individual
	Graphics	Individual
8	Ergonomics: Sports trophy	Individual
	Control: Alarm systems	Single sex 2/3
	Graphics	Individual
	Electronics: Switching	Individual
	Soma cube	Individual
	Mechanisms: Linkages	Individual
	Band-powered buggy	**Mass production**
	IDEA: Toy evaluation	Individual
9	Graphics: Logo design	Individual
	Machining: Logo stamp	Individual
	Mechanisms: Cams and cranks	Individual
	Electronics: Capacitance	Individual
	3D puzzle	**Batch production**
	Control: Robotics	Single sex 2/3
	IDEA: Consumer goods	Mixed groups of 4/5
	Graphics	Individual
	Product design: Mirrors	Individual

Mass produced band powered buggy (Year 8)

The project is introduced with a short video extract of Charlie Chaplin in the classic movie *Modern Times*. Chaplin works on a factory production line with hilarious but disastrous results and, using this as a stimulus for discussion, the pupils quickly grasp the fundamental principles of the division of labour, moving the work to the worker, interdependence and parallel production lines. A sample vehicle is then displayed and the individual tasks required to produce it are discussed. At this point, depending on the time available and the emphasis required, the production lines can either be established by the students themselves, or the stages can be provided in the form of the worksheet 'Parallel Production Lines for Buggy Manufacture' (Figure 24.1).

Students then negotiate and sign up for the jobs on offer with extra workers being assigned the roles of runners, supervisors or quality controllers. The use of prepared jigs and fixtures is explained and their vital role, in ensuring that repetitive work is done quickly and accurately, is heavily stressed. Finally, the jobs are demonstrated, the optimum lay-out of the room is agreed upon and the class is now primed to go into buggy production. Experience has shown that a class of 20 students can make 20 finished and fully operational buggies in under one hour. This compares with about a four-week timescale using individual production for the same task. A graphical element can be added at this point if 'bodywork' in the form of card nets are made, decorated and fitted to the chassis with double-sided tape. This allows for extension work into areas such as airflow, resistance and drag. The practical aspect of the project concludes with the testing of the vehicles and, again, there are opportunities for extension work into stored energy, wheel-spin, friction, tyres and lubrication. It is also possible to achieve an efficiency rating for the buggy, by dividing the distance travelled by the number of turns of the rubber band. This can be calculated manually or by using a spreadsheet if an element of IT is included.

Batch produced 3D puzzle (Year 9)

The second project involves making a 3D wooden puzzle. The students are split into production units of four or five, based loosely on friendship groupings in the hope that this will promote team cooperation. Each group has to make a 'batch' of four or five puzzles. The starting point is a consideration of the differences between individual, batch and mass production, and the work on buggies from the previous year proves useful here. Again, the use of jigs to ensure accuracy and speed is heavily stressed. Working in groups, the students then plan out their order of production. The second stage is to translate this chronological sequence into four or five 'parallel production' lines for each member of the group, to show specifically what he or she will do. Finally, a dedicated work area for each group is set up and production begins. We have found that the groups can produce their quota of puzzles in one double lesson and, once again, this is much faster than if the same work were undertaken using individual production.

Conclusion

As with most design and technology projects, the final stage of both these units is to produce an evaluation. This time, however, it is the production method which is evaluated, not the artefacts which are produced, as these should be fairly standardized products. A study of student evaluations shows that as a result of their first-hand experience, all are able to identify at least some strengths and weaknesses of the system. The more perceptive students have, in the past, suggested some very sophisticated solutions to the inevitable problems of worker boredom, such as re-training, job rotation and team production (of a type used by Volvo and other major manufacturers). They were also able to identify the organizational faults which sometimes caused smooth production to be disrupted. Secondly, enjoyment of the work was

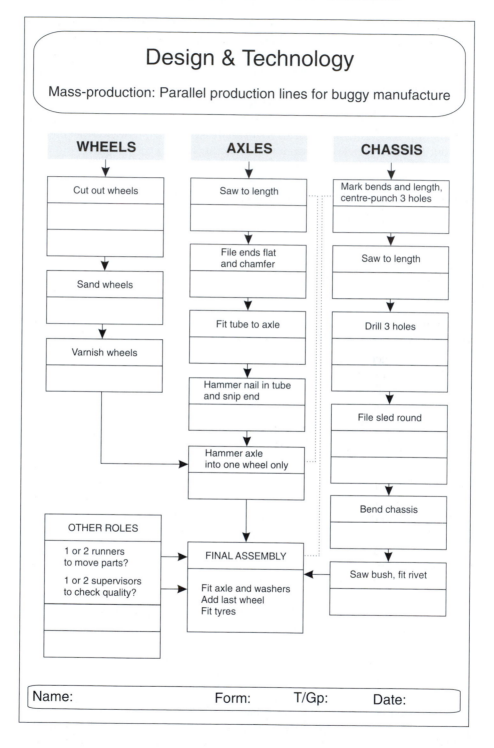

Figure 24.1 Parallel production lines for buggy manufacture

abundantly apparent and undoubtedly a key factor in the high levels of motivation exhibited by the students. Finally, because of the methods involved and the use of effective jigs, every student was able to take home an accurate, working, quality product. The value of this should never be underestimated when producing design and technology outcomes.

Our experiences with these popular projects suggest that the approach is a worthwhile and meaningful adjunct to our regular industrial visits. The variety of teaching and learning styles which they inject into the Design and Technology curriculum is also felt to be highly beneficial.

Industrial practices, systems and control at Key Stage 4

Lesley Cresswell

In Design and Technology we follow a design and manufacturing process that is based in an industrial model. At Key Stage 4 the National Curriculum document refers to these activities as 'industrial practices'.

In industry these designing and manufacturing processes enable manufacturers to make high-quality, cost-effective products at a profit. Many industrial design practices and manufacturing systems make use of Computer Aided Design and Computer Aided Manufacture (CAD/CAM) and Information and Communications Technology (ICT). These have revolutionized the way industry works, enabling companies to communicate information quickly and to design and manufacture on a global scale.

Thus it is that these practices are part of the requirements of the National Curriculum for Design and Technology; they are also practices used by UK industry to achieve the successful manufacture of innovative products that provide valuable exports. Industrial practices used in this way enable and encourage creativity.

In education, we need to use them in the same way, as *processes* that enable students to design and make innovative products. We also need to provide a curriculum that is relevant and forward looking. Using up-to-date industrial practices will enable us to do this, as long as we use them as *processes* for encouraging creativity, innovation and enjoyment of design and technology. Bringing industrial practices into the classroom will also give students:

- a wider understanding of the importance of industry and what it has to offer
- an understanding of how ICT has revolutionized industry, enabling manufacturing on a global scale
- the opportunity for improved motivation and higher levels of achievement
- an understanding of the need for change.

A further reason for including industrial and commercial practices in Design and Technology is to enable an understanding of the need for change and how to manage it. In the future a job will not be for life. We will all have to be adaptable. The future for our students is life-long learning if they are to stay in the job market. Design and

Technology is one of the few subjects in the curriculum that will enable students to learn to be flexible and develop an understanding of change.

Designers and technologists are well placed to manage change because design and technology training encourages new thinking and new ideas.

So what is the way forward?

If our subject area is to expand we need to keep up with new ideas and new technology. We need to encourage familiar design and making skills but we also need to emphasize the importance of new ideas, creativity and innovation. We need to find a balance between 'design' and 'technology'. Recently there has been an emphasis on 'technology' and on 'manufacturing' aspects in design and technology, which may have stilted imaginative thinking, but if we balance the technological side with creative aspects, our subject can move forward with confidence. Incorporating industrial practices that include 'designing' and 'manufacturing' and creativity will enable this.

In order to manage constant change and in order to keep our subject at the leading edge of the curriculum we need to have access to up-to-date materials, ICT and the internet. Access to new materials and technology must be easy and new information needs to be relevant. We also need to enable the easy integration of industrial and commercial practices into design and technology work.

There are a number of questions related to design and technology that need to be answered. Design and manufacturing practices can involve designing and making for one-off, batch or high volume. Why do we need to know about this? Are we simply enabling students to have an informed choice or a greater understanding of the importance of designing for manufacture? Should we be encouraging more designers when we already produce many brilliant designers that our industry fails to employ? If we encourage an interest in manufacturing as well as design will we enable students interested in product design to become more employable? These are issues that also face higher education. There is no doubt that industry needs innovative designers but ones who also have an understanding of designing cost-effective commercial products. Industry needs technologists who can source materials, have an understanding of them and develop products to a price point. Industry doesn't need designers, it needs design technologists. This is one reason why design and technology is important. Check out higher education courses relating to design or technology – the content of many of these courses is now much more closely related to the Design and Technology curriculum.

Industrial and commercial practices commonly used in designing and manufacturing and how these can be translated into classroom practice in different focus material areas

Industrial and commercial practices are process-based activities that enable manufacturers to make cost-effective products at a profit. Industrial practices include manufacturing *and* designing activities, used to ensure the production of high-quality products for specific market groups.

The industrial practices used by manufacturers depend on the type of products they make, the scale of production and the target market group. Many industrial practices are common to a range of manufacturing sectors, where the influence of style and 'values' issues on design is increasing; in a global manufacturing environment successful products cannot compete on cost alone, but need the 'added value' that quality of design can bring. Design and Technology encourages an understanding of quality of design and manufacture.

Translating industrial practices into classroom activities

The left-hand column of Table 24.2 (pages 284–5) shows commonly used industrial and commercial practices. The examples in the right-hand columns show how some of these industrial practices can be translated into classroom activities for different focus material areas.

A unit of work for Key Stage 4 textiles technology

Table 24.3 (pages 286-9) shows a typical Key Stage 4 textiles project. It is written to demonstrate how a variety of industrial practices can easily be integrated into textiles work. It is not possible in the space of this article to include details of every possible activity related to industrial practices.

The unit of work includes:

- learning objectives
- possible teaching activities
- opportunities for building an understanding of industrial practices
- homework ideas and further activities.

References

Cresswell, L. (1998) *Understanding Industrial Practices in Textiles Technology*, Zig Zag, PO Box 24113, London SW18 5WT.

QCA (1998) Draft documents 'Design and Technology – an Exemplar Scheme of Work for Key Stages 1–2' and 'Design and Technology Scheme of Work – Teachers' Guide'.

Table 24.2 Summary of commonly used industrial and commercial practices and how they can be translated into classroom activities for different focus materials areas

Industrial and commercial practices	Examples	
Research and development Investigating and analysing: • market research • product analysis • researching British and international standards legal requirements • researching scientific and technical information • investigating safety requirements and identifying risks • considering values issues (aesthetic, cultural economic, environmental, ethical, political, social, technical) • costing products • developing design specifications	**Resistant materials** Use market research to establish the profile of the target market group, identifying the buying behaviour, age group, lifestyle and brand loyalty of potential customers. **Graphic products** Use a shop report to analyse product types, new ideas and technologies and the competition from other manufacturers.	**Textiles** Monitor the life cycle of a textile product from cradle to grave, to assess its effect on people or the environment. Investigate the raw materials, the design, manufacture, distribution, use and disposal of the product. **Food** Investigate food products already on the market. Use disassembly activities to identify ingredients, taste characteristics, manufacturing processes and value for money. Use the results of the investigation to draw up design specification for a new food product.
Designing for manufacture • Developing ideas. • Modelling and prototyping. • Testing before production. • Designing for different levels of production. • Designing for ease of manufacture, maintenance and product life. • Designing for quality and safety. • Designing for cost-effective manufacture. • Developing manufacturing specifications.	**Food** Generate and model ideas for a variety of food products using a knowledge of materials, texture, composition and flavour. **Graphic products** Use 2D and 3D modelling techniques, including CAD software to prototype products and test before manufacture.	**Systems and control** Design and use test procedures to check the quality and safety of design, so the system meets needs of the user and the environment. **Textiles** Produce a manufacturing specification, to ensure that the product is manufactured as the designer intends. Provide information about styling and construction details, dimensions, materials and components.
Production planning • Producing a production plan. • Identifying and planning materials, components and equipment. • Identifying the method of assembly and the stages of manufacture. • Planning and safety requirements. • Planning time and cost constraints.	**Textiles** Draw up a production plan which includes specifications, details of materials and components, a costing sheet, lay plan, cutting instructions and the work order. **Resistant materials** Use ICT to help plan the ordering of materials and components, so they arrive just in time for production.	**Food** Produce a detailed time plan to set deadlines for the different stages of manufacture. **Systems and control** Use a systems approach to find the most appropriate components and assembly process. Identify critical control points where quality can be checked.

Product manufacture

- Using the most appropriate method of production.
- Product assembly.
- Using finishing processes.

Quality

- Using quality assurance and control.
- Testing and monitoring production.
- Testing against British and international standards.
- Testing against specifications.

Health and safety

- Following legal requirements and standards.
- Using risk assessment and safe working practices.

Systems control

- A systems approach to design and manufacture.
- Control systems.
- Quality systems.
- Manufacturing systems.
- Computer systems.
- ICT systems.
- Marketing systems.

Graphic products

Identify how the method of production could be simplified so the product meets budget requirements.

Systems and control

Use ICT appropriately for controlling and manufacturing components and systems.

Resistant materials

Use a quality assurance system to ensure that products meet the required specifications.

Food

Use qualitative testing against specified quality standards to monitor the quality of food products.

Products

Research the legal requirements related to safety standards in the workplace, for the consumer and for the environment.

Textiles

Investigate BSI and EU standards relating to textile manufacture, use and disposal.

Resistant materials

Plan a project using a systems approach, to improve planning, to enable the use of feedback and to monitor quality.

Graphic products

Investigate the use of control systems in high volume manufacturing.

Compare high volume printing methods with hand block printing.

Resistant Materials

Explore a range of materials, components and processes to improve the method of production.

Textiles

Use finishing processes to ensure that the product is fault-free and matches the manufacturing specification.

Graphic products

Use CAD systems to customize and control colour quality to enable the manufacture of identical products.

Systems and control

Use quality assurance tests to ensure that product specifications and tolerance levels are met.

Systems and control

Research industry-standard hazard analysis and risk assessment techniques. Explain where hazards are likely to occur in food processing.

Analyse the potential risk of that hazard.

Resistant materials

Demonstrate care, precision and attention to detail in the use of tools, equipment and processes, showing awareness of safety in the workshop and beyond.

Food

Research the use of computer systems in high volume manufacturing. Explain how a computer system can help in the design and manufacture of products.

Textiles

Explore how ICT enables feedback of product sales information to a garment manufacturer. Use a block diagram to explain this process.

Table 24.3 This shows a typical Key Stage 4 textiles project. It demonstrates how a variety of industrial practices can easily be integrated into textiles work

Unit Title: Stylish Textiles

About the unit

Through this unit students develop design and manufacturing skills by analysing, disassembling and evaluating commercial textiles products. They learn that the design of many textiles depends on image, style or fashion as well as on using appropriate materials and processes.

Learning objectives	Possible teaching activities	Opportunities for building an understanding of industrial practices	Homework ideas and further activities
Develop design and manufacturing understanding and skills by analysing and evaluating commercial textile products.	**Design-and-make assignment** ▪ Students are to design a simple decorative textile accessory for a chosen interior, using the influence of a design style or a theme. ▪ Identify the learning purposes of the DMA, analyse the task, set out the assessment criteria and help students plan a step-by-step approach to the project. **IDEA: Style analysis** In pairs choose an interior (could be living room, bedroom, restaurant etc.) from magazines or catalogues and draw up a chart to explain the style of the chosen room, explaining: ▪ type of interior ▪ types of patterns (checks, spots, floral etc.) ▪ colour schemes (warm, cool, bright etc.) ▪ mood of the room (modern, traditional, country etc.). Students could add sketches for colour and pattern/style information.	▪ Analysis of existing products (by hand or eye) is a process used by industrial designers to identify well-designed products and to gather information. It is an opportunity to discuss the design features of existing products and to use technical terminology. ▪ The evaluation of products encourages the recognition of product. ▪ Highlighting topics such as image or lifestyle helps to raise awareness of the marketing of a range of manufactured products and the values issues that go with it.	**Homework** Market research – collect information about style and colour trends for interior accessories. Students can record information in a chart similar to the one used in class. **Further activities** Many manufacturers use image and branding to promote the sale of products. Explain how consumers are encouraged to buy products because of their image. Identify a particular product and evaluate its relationship with a way of life or lifestyle.

Understand how market research and disassembly are used to inspire design ideas.

Recognize that social, moral, cultural, artistic or technological issues influence the development of style in textiles.

Use a moodboard to communicate ideas about design, colour, themes, trends and styling.

Focused practical task:

Market research analysis.

Choose one textile accessory from the market research and explain why it is suitable/not suitable for the chosen interior.

Students could think about:

- aesthetic appeal
- fitness for purpose
- maintenance/ aftercare.

Explain what may have influenced the style/ colour of the textile.

IDEA: Investigating fabrics

In pairs students examine a range of different printed or decorative fabrics and record the pattern style, pattern repeat, fabric properties and possible end-use. Comparisons could be made with the textiles seen in market research, with students writing a simple design specification for one of the textiles that they have evaluated.

- Textile designers regularly analyse fabrics, style and colour trends – they need to be up-to-date. They also disassemble fabrics to get ideas about pattern and properties, which they can use as starting points for designing.

- This links to the use of contextual studies to inspire design work – using art, design and cultural influences.

Moodboards are used widely by designers in the textiles industry to develop ideas and to present them to clients. Students can easily model this practice to help develop their own ideas. The use of themes to develop moods or 'stories' about textiles.

Homework

Students work on moodboards for the chosen interior, using individual themes and the influences of style/ colour trends from research.

Further activities

Students could report on the following: Textiles designers often use the influence of other cultures to develop their ideas. Do we exploit or promote these cultures by making use of their traditional design styles?

Collect pictures of textile products and explain how they have been influenced by other cultures.

Develop and use detailed design specifications when designing textile products.

Use design specifications to generate design ideas.

DMA
Design specification

Each student draws up a design specification for their textile accessory using research infor- mation and moodboards to help them.

Generating ideas

Students generate design ideas that are guided by the design specification. They can base colour schemes on their moodboards. Encourage students to think about:

- colourways, repeats and scale
- developing coordinated fabrics for accessories
- fitness-for-purpose.

- Design specifications are developed through research information and used to generate and evaluate design ideas.

- The homework asks students to develop design ideas and suggests working to a limited colour palate – an industrial practice.

- The video enables students to understand the use of CAD and ICT in industry. If computers are available students can use CAD to develop design ideas and colourways.

Homework

Students develop ideas and colourways for their accessory. You could limit the number of colours to be used in the design – often fabric designs have a maximum of three or four colours.

Further activities

Students can explain the benefits to the textiles industry of using CAD and ICT e.g.

- How CAD is used to develop and adapt designs and colourways etc.
- How designers use ICT to work with clients
- The impact of CAD/ ICT on the develop- ment of prototype textiles products.

FPT: Using CAD

Students watch video 'Talent and Technology' about the use of CAD in the textiles industry. Discuss the impact that computers have on design, modelling and prototyping and how ICT enables designers and clients to 'talk' to each other.

Test and evaluate design ideas against the design specification.

Understand the difference between quality of design and manufacture.

DMA: Star diagrams

Students use star diagrams to evaluate their design ideas against the specification, justifying the chosen design.

FPT: Experimenting with techniques

Students can experiment with techniques to test the decoration of the accessory, using block printing, tie-dye, batik, fabric-painting, appliqué, embroidery etc, depending on students' prior knowledge and teacher expertise.

- Opportunities here for students to explore techniques – industrial designers have to be artistic and have an excellent technical knowledge so that they understand the limitations and possibilities of what they are designing.

- The concept of practising textile techniques – practice makes perfect – can provide the opportunity to discuss the idea of quality of design and manufacture.

Homework

Students can mount samples, write up and evaluate the appropriateness of their experimental techniques for decorating their accessory.

Further activities

Students could investigate manufacturing issues, such as the water pollution caused by dyeing and finishing fabrics.

Produce and use a detailed production plan which identifies the stages of manufacture, the materials, components and equipment required to make a textiles product.

Provide quality checks and feedback to help solve problems.

DMA: Production planning

The production plan includes a manufacturing specification for the accessory, with detailed drawings, design details, dimensions, seam allowances, tolerance, materials and costs, fastenings and finishing details.

- Production planning is a key industrial practice. The manufacturing specification provides clear and detailed instructions about the product's styling, materials and construction.

- Students can use a systems approach – a flow diagram with feedback loops to show how and where quality checks are made to monitor quality.

Homework

Produce a flow diagram to show where and how quality can be checked when making the accessory.

Further activities

Use a computer to produce a work order, giving the assembly processes, equipment required process time and tolerances.

Understand that a textile's quality of manufacture can be judged by the appropriate use of suitable materials, how it meets manufacturing requirements and its fitness for purpose.

DMA: Practical work

Practical work to produce decorative elements for the accessory.

- Designs could be output from a computer and printed onto freezer paper, then ironed onto a fabric base e.g. for sampling a product as in the video 'Talent and Technology'.

Practical work to produce the accessory.

- Students use the production plan to monitor quality and the time available.

- Students use computer-aided equipment where available to produce accurate/repeatable machine work.

- Textiles CDM/CAM equipment is relatively inexpensive and provides opportunities for computer control.

- The information in the production plan will help students to monitor the quality of work, making checks at each stage of production.

Homework

As required.

Further activities

Students can write a checklist to explain what changes would be needed if the accessory was to be made in quantity.

DMA: Presentation of work and evaluation

- Students display and discuss their work.
- Individual evaluation of achievements.
- Exam Board assessment sheet provided for student/ teacher evaluation of success.

- Presenting ideas and finished work is an industrial practice to be encouraged. A display and/or oral session can improve design and evaluation skills and can be motivating for students.

Homework

As required.

25 Design and Technology in the community

Frank Banks

Design and Technology teaching cannot be separated from the world outside school, as it is all about that world. This chapter considers how work can be planned to make effective use of the local environment.

Introduction

Design and Technology, as a subject in school, often deals with topics directly relevant to pupils' lives. It frequently draws on the needs of pupils, and the needs of others, to provide starting points for design-and-make assignments. Evaluation of finished products by a prospective client (real or simulated) is also important. In so many ways, designing and making must take account of the context in which the product is used, and should draw on the products and applications of technology designed by others to help to influence the work of pupils. How then can the work in school be related to the technological activity that goes on in many different contexts outside the classroom? It is the intention of this chapter to suggest some ways in which pupils can use the 'made world' outside school to inform their thinking, and to cover some of the organizational issues that such use will pose for the teacher. I will be considering:

- using the local environment
- places to visit on organized trips
- people who can relate school work to life outside school.

Using the local environment

The local environment of the school can be a very valuable resource which can be exploited without the organizational problems which inevitably surround formal visits requiring transport. The school environment may be used as a source of ideas or information, or as a place where designing and making can occur.

Designing and making for a local project: some examples

The school grounds can provide a suitable place to consider different aspects of environmental design. Without leaving the school property, the pupils can investigate such topics as flow of people around the school, separation of traffic and pedestrians, provision of outdoor seating and litter-bins, layout of interior and exterior spaces (such as the school foyer) and provision of items for decoration such as garden and other open-space accessories.

At St James' High School, Exeter, some Year 10 pupils manufactured garden tubs as a production line simulation. These were costed, produced and sold by the pupils to members of the school and to local tradespeople. Group work was possible in this project and the pupils split the tasks by forming a marketing group and a production group. With guidance from staff, the pupils handled problems of supplies, manufacture and quality assurance. In this particular project, the pupils followed a design strongly influenced by a member of staff in order to move quickly to learning about matters of production. So successful was their enterprise that one order from the manager of a local garden centre amounted to 25 tubs, and he asked for a discount!

A similar enterprise project was undertaken by Builth Wells High School in Wales. The school was short of outdoor seating, and a design of a wood-and-metal garden bench was drawn up by a group of pupils who were working on a scheme called PREP (Powys Rural Enterprise Project). This scheme was integrated into the school's personal and social development (PSE) programme alongside other 'businesses', such as a car valeting service and pet food retailing concern.

In a similar enterprise project, some pupils at a school in Exeter produced jigs to speed production of their benches and to reduce waste of materials. They built a prototype bench and canvassed opinion from potential customers before collecting orders and going into production. Building on this success, the school has since established a reputation for taking on projects related to the local community. These are often used to extend the normal curriculum provision. For example, over recent years some groups of sixth-form pupils, who are not formally involved in post-16 Design and Technology courses, have continued to enhance their studies by working on Design and Technology projects for one lesson per week. Topics as diverse as picnic tables for a local primary school, a laboratory table for a pupil in a wheelchair and signs for local churches have been explored and manufactured by these older pupils.

Gathering information locally

As well as providing opportunities for realistic project work, as described above, looking at technology in the locality can give pupils ideas and insights to use in their work in school. For example, it is often difficult for pupils to produce 'initial ideas' when beginning a project. Looking at magazines and other library work for possible inspiration can readily be supplemented by homework assignments where they are asked to consider the solutions produced by others. This can be small-scale, such as gathering examples of packaging from home, or a wider consideration of local amenities and municipal artefacts.

In the examples considered above, the pupils looked at how existing garden furniture was designed and put together, in order to inform their own ideas. They also looked at how such everyday objects were used. For example, common street furniture such as one finds in any city centre provides many illustrations of how benches, garden accessories and display boards can be made both robust and attractive for that particular urban setting. The extent to which they *are* in fact robust and attractive, however, is open to class debate!

Similarly the consideration of a whole 'environment' could be used to illustrate the linking together of design issues, textiles, resistant materials and structures. For example, a local park or adventure playground provides a context to consider such issues as choice of materials, water-proofing of textiles, use of pulleys, A-frame structures and stability. It may be appropriate to extend this analysis to a consideration of suggested improvements. The pupils will not be short of new ideas, but cost, local planning restrictions and safety regulations would restrict the possibility of making a full-scale artefact. However, planners usually consult on the addition or improvement to local amenities and that may provide the link to a real-life situation.

It is not only in designing that the locality can provide illustrative examples of solutions. A topic such as 'structures' can become rather abstract and 'dry' unless it is related to real objects. A school-based bridge-building exercise in art-straws is useful in reinforcing ideas such as forces in tension and compression. Testing of straws for buckling loads relative to their length, and analysis of the comparative strengths of paper corrugations and cylinders, would be a necessary preliminary task, but it is important to relate the work done in school to real bridges. Pupils in all parts of the country are able to look at different bridge structures and bring those observations to bear in school. No one is too far from pedestrian, road and rail bridges which could be used by pupils as part of a home-based activity to look at the construction and use of beams, arches, suspension cables and frameworks.

Taking advantage of chance circumstances – serendipity!

The suggestions I have outlined are all activities which can be planned and built into a scheme of work in an organized way. However, it would be a shame if detailed planning was so tight and the need to 'get through the project' so pressing that teachers were unable to take advantage of those unexpected events which may occur in or near to the school and which pose real technological problems.

For example, a project for Year 9 pupils called 'Safe and sound' was a regular part of one school's scheme of work and usually focused on the construction of different burglar alarms to teach simple switching circuits. During one presentation of the project, poor signs for some roadworks had caused a problem for traffic near to the school. The 'Safe and sound' electronics project was then altered to look at ways in which road signs and street lighting could be turned on automatically when it became dark. The problem of poor road signs and the designs of new local street lighting was thoroughly investigated by the pupils at weekends or on their way home from school. In school, various automatic light switches were constructed using system electronic boards and some pupils went on to build the simple switching device on to a printed circuit board. The same teaching points were covered – use of systems; potential divider; transistor as a switch; and manufacture of printed circuit boards – but the real life context re-vitalized what had become a rather dull and routine series of lessons.

Organized visits in school time

A well-organized class visit offers a considerable opportunity to provide a shared experience which can instil motivation, give specialist knowledge of a particular context and illustrate a number of possible solutions.

Although the organization can be formidable, there is a considerable benefit to pupils if visits which bring out specific aspects of economic awareness or illustrate some particular use of technology are integrated into a project. I will focus on two sorts of visits:

1   those to local businesses which emphasize economic and social issues
2   those to museums of science and technology which might emphasize social, cultural and environmental factors.

In both cases there is a need to comply with the local arrangements for school trips and to prepare pupils in order that they gain the maximum benefit from their time out of school.

Guidelines for trips

Teachers who are planning a visit in school time need to check that they follow carefully the guidelines which operate within the school. These guidelines will cover both formal requirements such as acquiring insurance and parental approval, and informal expectations such as leaving work for colleagues supervising pupils who will not be on the trip. Here is a checklist of possible requirements:

- Contact the education officer of the museum or personnel manager of the business site to book or get approval for the visit.
- Gain permission from headteacher and governors (usually a school form-based approval system).
- Send an information letter to parents, also informing them of a contact name and number.
- Collect 'consent' forms from parents including any special medical information.
- Organize group insurance cover (usually done on the school approval form).
- Book the minibus or other transport arrangements.
- Organize pupil absence from other timetabled lessons.
- Leave work for any classes missed due to visit.
- Leave details of visit with headteacher and the 'contact' member of staff (time of visit, list of names of all pupils and any medical information).
- Check, duplicate and collate any materials needed during visit.
- Ensure each pupil knows who they are responsible to on the day.
- Explain, before the visit day, the timetable for the visit, how long each part will take, when they will take lunch and the time for departure.

With such organizational hurdles to overcome, it is clearly essential that the pupils be well prepared to gain the maximum benefit from the visit. This means that the pupils need to be clear about how the visit will contribute to their work and what they will need to do after the visit to exploit what they have discovered. Many museums will loan artefacts to act as a prior stimulus or form part of a follow-up activity.

Visits to museums of science and industry

Many museums have a specialist focus, but they still cover issues which will apply to a number of projects. For example, Snibston Discovery Park, Leicester, has general exhibits connected with the industrial revolution, but is also able to reflect the knit-wear and footwear for which Leicestershire was famous. That particular venue, therefore, is especially suitable to illustrate the development of textiles and fashion, including how clothes and shoes are designed and manufactured, how the clothing industry has affected the county's economy and landscape, and how advertising has been used to promote new products.

Once you have managed to transport the pupils to the museum, there is a natural tendency to allow them to wander around the whole of it in order to get 'value for money'. This is misguided, as often a museum will have too many exhibits for pupils to take in properly on one visit. Time is better spent focused on the particular aspect highlighted by the project in hand. For example, the teachers' pack from Snibston gives the following advice:

> From your pre-visit you will have chosen a small number of objects on which to concentrate. These objects should be discussed with the students before the visit. It would be helpful to place these objects within a historical and social context. In the galleries there is a whole range of activities which students can take part in, including drama, role play, observational sketching, recording by tape or picture and discussing how different objects may work. In the past, worksheets have proved to be of limited use in helping achieve a better under-standing of objects. Worksheets encourage students to concentrate only on the word/date that goes in a box rather than on the specimens and why they are important.
>
> (Snibston Discovery Park)

Visits to an industrial or commercial site

Some industrial visits, particularly those involving hot metal, chemicals or heavy machinery, are inappropriate for school visits due to the difficulty of ensuring the safety of pupils. However, many light industries are able and willing to accommo-date school parties, and some companies, such as chocolate manufacturers, routinely open their doors to visitors and members of the public anyway. In such companies the use of mechanisms, control systems and the application of food technology is well illustrated. However, everyday commercial sites, such as a shopping mall, provide a safe and interesting environment in which to investigate the impact of business criteria on the manufacture of products.

In Southmoor School, Sunderland, Year 10 pupils investigated the type of food service which was appropriate for the food hall at the Metro Centre in Gateshead. They did survey work to find out customer opinions of a range of preferences for different types of service and facilities and linked those choices to the age and gender of the respondents. Such information is very valuable if the pupils are required to present a marketing strategy for their products. A visit to the local fast food outlet, for example, although concentrating on only one type of food outlet, could open up the project to look at some wider concerns. For example:

- What is an appropriate fast food?
- What packaging designs would be attractive to the perceived customers?
- How could the food and drink be packaged to carry in a car without upset?
- What strategies should the local fast food chain adopt to take advantage of local factors, such as its site (for example, opening times in relation to the local cinemas) and regional expectations (for example, including some variations to the menu)?

A large supermarket, a garden centre or a tourist site such as a butterfly farm all provide opportunities to link the context for designing and making to the values held by the participants in the enterprise: customers, shop-floor workers and technicians such as food technologists, buyers or entomologists! For example, the manufacture of supermarket three-dimensional display stands might lead to a consideration of sales techniques for displaying food or other products in order to make them attractive to the buyer:

- Are all goods 'well displayed'?
- How and where would you display and promote unusual foods such as exotic fruits or continental cheeses?
- What are the ethics of placing sweets at child height near to check-out tills?

A wooden souvenir 'commissioned' by the butterfly farm offers opportunities to talk about using these valuable resources for such purposes and the desirability or otherwise of keeping animals in captivity. These issues are separate from the more commercial concerns suggested by these real contexts, but no less worthy of being addressed.

People who can relate school work to life outside school

As I have illustrated, taking pupils *en bloc* to investigate the context for their designing and making gives a realistic context for them to consider and generally raises motivation for the task. An alternative is to arrange for individuals, such as a representative of a specific industry or a member of a particular client group, to come into school. Pupils could also go out and work on an individual basis in a business context. It is to the use of 'people outside the classroom' that I now turn.

Using adults other than teachers

Visitors to the school can be used in a number of ways to enhance work done in Design and Technology lessons. They might:

- provide a particular expertise or background knowledge to assist with designing and making
- give insight into the special needs of potential users
- act as evaluators of particular solutions and artefacts.

Business partnership schemes exist in different parts of the country to raise awareness of the role of commerce and industry. People such as product development managers may be willing to come and talk about their role and responsibility within a company. Sometimes a business will come in as a small team to work with pupils on games and simulations which illustrate how people co-operate together in 'the world of work'. A project with a business and industry context might be enhanced by a visit from such industry representatives. Contact with industry can be through Education Business Partnerships (EBPs), Training and Enterprise Councils (TECs) – or the Chamber of Commerce. Parents and governors may be able to assist either directly or by using their own contacts. Such contacts are invaluable in so many ways:

- providing background data and support materials
- briefing groups and individuals involved in a specific project
- acting as an observer of activities and debriefing the group.

It follows that all adults need to be fully informed about what is required of them and given the necessary feedback to illustrate that their involvement was worthwhile.

The Engineering Council runs a scheme called 'Neighbourhood Engineers'. Here a local engineer will link with a Design and Technology faculty to offer practical support to the teachers, usually on a specific project which highlights the particular industry in which the engineer works. This support may be in equipment and resources, but more often it is personal classroom assistance with project work. In their day-to-day contact with the pupils, the engineer is able to illustrate his or her approach to technological problems.

In Northfield School, Billingham, for example, a neighbourhood engineer assisted the teacher with providing a 'real' industrial problem concerning the movement of materials around a chemical works. The engineer produced a video to illustrate the problem (as a visit was considered inappropriate for safety reasons) and visited the school regularly to work with the Year 10 pupils on their control technology projects. Hennessy and McCormick (1994) have described such links between pupils and experts as a 'cognitive apprenticeship', and believe that such exposure to people who practise technology enables pupils to understand better how to transfer problem-solving strategies from one context to another. In this way, the role model is much deeper than simply asking someone to come into school to talk about their job.

The visitor need not have a particular 'technological' expertise. At Bradford CTC, a local librarian was invited to explain the different types of children's books available which use 'paper technology' to keep young people interested. This was part of a project entitled 'Children's books' where pupils were asked to produce a graphic backdrop and plastic story character for young children to act out a story that was read to them.

Often Design and Technology projects are targeted at a specific audience such as a nursery, the elderly or those with a physical disability. It gives a sense of purpose and a better learning experience to pupils if the intended audience for their work can be introduced to the pupils. For example, a meal targeted at those with specific dietary requirements could be introduced by the dietician from the local health authority or by people who have those needs themselves. What foods do they like? What food types do they have to avoid? Similarly a partially sighted person could come and talk about day-to-day problems, such as filling cups with hot water. The clients could be asked to set the context and also return to perform 'user trips', either at the final evaluation or at an earlier consolidation stage of the project.

Using work placements

The Education (Work Experience) Act was passed as long ago as 1973. By the end of the 1980s, 91 per cent of schools arranged work experience for pupils. This experience usually takes place either in Years 9 and 10 (sometimes at the very end of Year 11) and is often for two weeks following either internal or external examinations. In this way, disruption to the curriculum is minimized. However, the experience provides an excellent source for GCSE coursework and its link with project work in Design and Technology is most beneficial.

Before attending the placement a pupil should make a visit to prepare themselves properly. This should cover such issues as health and safety but could also be used as an opportunity to investigate possible needs and opportunities for a project conducted either on the placement or afterwards back in school, based upon the work experience. For example, the pupil could interview a member of the firm about what they do and the constraints on their operation. During the placement they might work-shadow an employee, taking advantage of the opportunity to be shown sophisticated manufacturing processes such as CAD/CAM and see how it relates to the equipment in school. Opportunities might also exist to look at the way the workplace is organized to facilitate flow of materials, and the company office is set up to process the flow of information. With a sympathetic placement supervisor, properly briefed by the pupil's Design and Technology teacher, a considerable amount of useful work could be done.

One needs, however, to be realistic. In many schools, all the pupils in a year group will be on placement at the same time and not all can have their placement tailored to a design and technology bias as there are simply not enough places available. Neither would such a narrow focus be desirable for all pupils. By building up a relationship with specific firms over the years, however, it is possible to make some of the experience 'routine' with both parties knowing what to expect. A pupil placement workbook can be used to provide a common structure and reduce the chance of the placement passing without some targeted learning taking place.

Conclusion

Since the introduction of the National Curriculum, significantly more pupils are studying Design and Technology in Britain. One of the arguments for the introduction of the subject has been that it will raise the awareness of pupils about the way technology impinges on their lives. To fulfil the aim of making pupils aware of the influences of technology, and of their responsibilities as citizens in a democratic society which exploits it, it is essential that the technology studied in school is linked explicitly with the way it is used in the world outside the classroom or workshop. Technology cannot exist independently of the clients who will use its products, the solutions which already exist and the values which are used to judge whether a particular outcome is acceptable. By bringing people into school to work with pupils, and by taking pupils outside to consider and evaluate technology around us, many of these issues may be addressed.

References

Discovery Park, Snibston (undated) *Educational Visits Information Pack*, Snibston, Leicestershire.

Hennessy, S. and McCormick, R. (1994) 'The general problem-solving process in technology education: myth or reality?', in F. Banks (ed.) *Teaching Technology*, London: Routledge.

Index